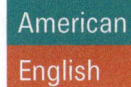

Personal Best

B2 Upper Intermediate

Student's Book and Workbook combined edition **B**

Series Editor
Jim Scrivener

Student's Book Author
Luiz Otávio Barros

Workbook Authors
Elizabeth Walters and Kate Woodford

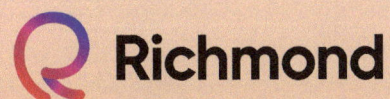

STUDENT'S BOOK CONTENTS

	LANGUAGE			SKILLS	
	GRAMMAR	PRONUNCIATION	VOCABULARY		
7 Lifelong learning 7A Unique college programs p58 7B Successful learning p60 7C If I remember correctly … p62 7D It's never too late to learn! p64	• relative clauses; reduced and comment clauses • present and future real conditions	• comment clauses • sentence stress in conditional sentences	• collocations with *attend*, *get*, *make*, and *submit* • ability • mind and memory	**LISTENING** • identifying sequence • reduced forms	**WRITING** • writing a set of guidelines • linkers to add ideas **PERSONAL BEST** • a blog post on something you've learned or would like to learn
8 The changing media 8A TV in the 21st Century p66 8B Digital media for you p68 8C Binge-watching p70 8D Ads to drive you crazy p72	• using linkers (2) • -*ing* forms and infinitives	• emphatic stress • *to*	• the media • expressions with *at*, *for*, *in*, and *on*	**READING** • inferring meaning using related words • generalizing	**SPEAKING** • expressing annoyance and indifference • clarifying and reacting **PERSONAL BEST** • talking about annoying things on TV
7 and 8 REVIEW and PRACTICE	p74				
9 The power of design 9A Steps to a better life p76 9B Good or bad design? p78 9C Extreme designs p80 9D Accessible spaces p82	• position of adverbs • passives and causative *have*	• syllable stress with adverbs of degree • stress in passive and causative *have* sentences	• collocations with *have* and *take* • colors • dimensions and weight	**LISTENING** • understanding key points • silent *h*	**WRITING** • writing a magazine article • articles *a*, *an*, *the*, and zero (–) **PERSONAL BEST** • an article about improving your city or neighborhood
10 The business world 10A Careers on the rise p84 10B Starting your own business p86 10C Job interview tips p88 10D Two job offers p90	• quantifiers • comparison	• *(a) few* and *(a) little* • sentence stress with *the* … *the* comparisons	• trends and business • word pairs: *sooner or later*, *ups and downs*, *side by side*	**READING** • understanding text development • complex negative sentences	**SPEAKING** • discussing pros and cons • being supportive **PERSONAL BEST** • talking about things that upset you and offering support
9 and 10 REVIEW and PRACTICE	p92				
11 Fact and fiction 11A It can't have been real! p94 11B Fake news p96 11C The science of sleep p98 11D I first met Julia … p100	• present and past modals of deduction • reported speech patterns	• reduction of past modals • /t/ and /d/	• science • opposite adjectives • sleep	**LISTENING** • identifying conclusions • the "flap" in American English	**WRITING** • writing a personal recommendation • order of adjectives **PERSONAL BEST** • a recommendation using adjectives of opinion and fact
12 New discoveries 12A Must-have apps p102 12B A robot revolution? p104 12C Changes and regrets p106 12D Fads and trends p108	• present and future unreal conditions • past unreal conditions	• consonant-vowel linking • stress in conditional sentences	• phrasal verbs (2) • collocations with *come*, *do*, *go*, and *make*	**READING** • predicting • adverbs and intended meaning	**SPEAKING** • talking about future trends • keeping a conversation going **PERSONAL BEST** • having an extended conversation about fads and trends
11 and 12 REVIEW and PRACTICE	p110				

Grammar practice p124   Vocabulary practice p145   Communication practice p161   Phrasal verbs p174   Irregular verbs p175

Language App with unit-by-unit grammar and vocabulary games

WORKBOOK CONTENTS

		LANGUAGE			SKILLS	
		GRAMMAR	PRONUNCIATION	VOCABULARY		
7 Lifelong learning 7A p38 7B p39 7C p40 7D p41		• relative clauses; reduced and comment clauses • present and future real conditions	• comment clauses • sentence stress in conditional sentences	• collocations with *attend, get, make,* and *submit* • ability • mind and memory	LISTENING • identifying sequence	WRITING • writing a set of guidelines
7 REVIEW and PRACTICE		p42				
8 The changing media 8A p44 8B p45 8C p46 8D p47		• using linkers (2) • *-ing* forms and infinitives	• emphatic stress • *to*	• the media • expressions with *at, for, in,* and *on*	READING • inferring meaning using related words	SPEAKING • expressing annoyance and indifference
8 REVIEW and PRACTICE		p48				
9 The power of design 9A p50 9B p51 9C p52 9D p53		• position of adverbs • passives and causative *have*	• syllable stress with adverbs of degree • stress in passive and causative *have* sentences	• collocations with *have* and *take* • colors • dimensions and weight	LISTENING • understanding key points	WRITING • writing a magazine article
9 REVIEW and PRACTICE		p54				
10 The business world 10A p56 10B p57 10C p58 10D p59		• quantifiers • comparison	• *(a) few* and *(a) little* • sentence stress with *the … the* comparisons	• trends and business • word pairs: *sooner or later, ups and downs, side by side*	READING • understanding text development	SPEAKING • discussing pros and cons
10 REVIEW and PRACTICE		p60				
11 Fact and fiction 11A p62 11B p63 11C p64 11D p65		• present and past modals of deduction • reported speech patterns	• reduction of past modals • /t/ and /d/	• science • opposite adjectives • sleep	LISTENING • identifying conclusions	WRITING • writing a personal recommendation
11 REVIEW and PRACTICE		p66				
12 New discoveries 12A p68 12B p69 12C p70 12D p71		• present and future unreal conditions • past unreal conditions	• consonant-vowel linking • stress in conditional sentences	• phrasal verbs (2) • collocations with *come, do, go,* and *make*	READING • predicting	SPEAKING • talking about future trends
12 REVIEW and PRACTICE		p72				

Writing practice p77

UNIT 7
Lifelong learning

LANGUAGE relative clauses ■ collocations with *attend*, *get*, *make*, and *submit*

7A Unique college programs

1 In pairs, discuss the statements below about college programs. Do you agree?
1 You won't get ahead in life if you don't go to college.
2 It makes a big difference exactly which college you go to.
3 At college, it's better to study online than to attend classes.
4 No one should need to submit a college application. The transition from high school should be automatic.

Go to Vocabulary practice: collocations with *attend*, *get*, *make*, and *submit*, page 145

2 A Read the text. In pairs, say which program you like the best and explain why.
B Do the underlined sentences in the text mean the same as sentences 1–4 below?
1 In Surf Science and Technology, students only learn how to make a surfboard.
2 Comic Art appeals to a specific group of potential students.
3 Comic Art only teaches students how to express themselves artistically.
4 Ethical Hacking students will learn how hackers gain access to information illegally.

Undergraduate programs you didn't know existed!

Struggling to choose a career? Not interested in traditional options like engineering, education, or business administration? I have good news! If you have a passion or a hobby, there's a chance you can get a degree in that subject, which means you can make the most of your hobby or interest, doing something you love! Here's a list of our favorite unusual-but-cool programs.

Surf Science and Technology:
Cornwall College, UK

If you're into surfing, this two-year program is just what you need. It covers the history of surfing, explores the psychology of being a successful surfer, and investigates people's attitudes to fitness. [1]There are both lectures and practical modules focusing on surfboard building, so, yes, you'll need to attend the classes. This program won't teach you how to surf, though!

Comic Art:
Minneapolis College of Art and Design, U.S.

[2]Anyone interested in comics should take a closer look at this innovative program. Graduates may even find the job of their dreams in the comic industry or on TV. [3]The program includes courses focusing on both the history of comic art and artistic expression. As you learn about storytelling techniques, you'll also learn how to use colors and lines to get people's attention – and keep them interested.

Ethical Hacking:
University of Abertay Dundee, UK

This four-year program teaches you everything about computer hacking! [4]Students enrolling in the program will study the techniques hackers use to obtain illegal information. The course covers areas such as breaking into web servers, stealing information, and remotely controlling someone's computer. The aim is to show students how illegal computer attacks are carried out, and how to prevent them.

relative clauses ■ collocations with *attend*, *get*, *make*, and *submit*   **LANGUAGE**   **7A**

3 Read the text again and complete the tasks below. Then read the Grammar box.
1 Rephrase the underlined sentences using *that* or *who*.
2 Underline the *which* clause in the text. Does it refer only to the word immediately before *which* or to a complete idea?

> **Grammar** — relative clauses: reduced and comment clauses
>
> **Defining relative clauses – reduced clauses:**
> Students (who are) **living at home** sometimes have a long commute to school.
> I got an e-mail **containing further information** about the program.
> Anyone (who is) **caught cheating** will be suspended immediately.
>
> **Non-defining relative clauses – comment clauses:**
> The test was easy, **which explains why so many students passed.**
> The program was too hard, **which is why I quit.**
>
> **Look!** Students **attending** (= Students who attend) classes should arrive on time!

Go to Grammar practice: relative clauses; reduced and comment clauses, page 124

4 A ▶ 7.3 **Pronunciation: comment clauses** Listen to the conversations. Insert a comma when you hear a pause in B's responses. After *which*, does the intonation go up or down?
1 A So you're getting a degree in surfing?
  B I am! And it's a serious program which most people don't really expect.
2 A How's college?
  B Great! I love creating comics. And I'm good at it which shows I picked the right program.
3 A I can't believe I'm graduating next month!
  B And you've gotten lots of job offers which means the market needs "ethical hackers."

B ▶ 7.3 Listen again and repeat. Then practice the conversations in pairs. Replace the underlined words with your own ideas.

5 A Find the relative clauses in sentences 1–6 below. Then rephrase them using reduced clauses.

SCHOOL RULES from around the world

1 At one school in the U.S., students who skip classes aren't punished.
2 A Canadian school banned hard balls because of a parent who was hit by a ball.
3 Many students who attend high school in Japan have to wear uniforms.
4 In Sweden, students who are aged 10–15 can't use their phones in class.
5 A school in the UK has created a policy that bans students from having best friends.
6 There's a rule in some schools in Australia and the UK that states that students' papers should be graded using green ink.

B In pairs, give your own opinion of each rule, using comment clauses.

(… which is a good/terrible idea because …) (… which means that …) (… which makes a lot of/no sense because …)
(… which explains why …) (… which makes me wonder if …)

At one school in the U.S., students skipping classes aren't punished, which is a terrible idea because …

Go to Communication practice: Student A page 161, Student B page 167

6 Think of two high school/college/workplace rules that you don't agree with. Discuss your ideas in groups.

(Students attending …) (Employees arriving …) (Anyone caught …) (People absent from …)

Personal Best Write five rules for a school or work poster.

7 SKILLS   LISTENING   identifying sequence ■ reduced forms ■ ability

7B Successful learning

1 A Read the comments. In pairs, decide if any of these sentences are true for you.

I struggle to read magazine articles in English without using a dictionary, but I try to sometimes.

I keep looking up the difference between will and going to, but I can't quite manage to understand it!

I'm pretty good at listening. I watch movies in English, and I understand a lot of what is said.

B In pairs, summarize your top three tips for learning English.

Go to Vocabulary practice: ability, page 146

2 A ▶ 7.5 Watch or listen to the first part of *Talking Zone*. What is a Polyglot edutainer? How does Cameron reach his students?

B Check (✓) the language learning tips that are mentioned.

a Listen to songs so you can learn new words. ☐
b Watch TV programs like soap operas to help you learn. ☐
c Don't worry about making errors when you speak. ☐
d Follow the news and watch movies with subtitles. ☐
e Find a pen pal you can write to every week. ☐
f Keep practicing! ☐
g Be sure to study grammar also. ☐

Skill   identifying sequence

When someone gives you tips or advice, they often follow a sequence, and are in the form of commands. These are some ways to identify the steps you should follow.
- When two activities are mentioned together, think about which one logically comes first: *Once you've saved some money, you can buy a new car.* (First you save some money, then you buy a car.)
- Listen for expressions that tell you what to do first: *Don't wait until level 5 before you try to understand movies.* (You can try to understand movies before level 5.)
- Remember previous advice and pay attention to intonation: *Finally, don't give up!*

3 ▶ 7.5 Read the Skill box. Then watch or listen again and complete the sentences with *before* or *after*.

1 Cameron thinks you should make friends in your new language _____ you become fluent.
2 He says you should correct your mistakes _____ you try to speak the language.
3 Cameron studied foreign languages _____ he turned twenty, but was more successful _____ that age.

identifying sequence ■ reduced forms ■ ability **LISTENING** SKILLS **7B**

4 In pairs, think of three excuses people sometimes use for not learning a language.

5 ▶ 7.6 Watch or listen to the second part of the show. Are any of your ideas from exercise 4 mentioned?

6 ▶ 7.6 Watch or listen again. Complete the notes with one or two words in each blank.

> **As a kid:** short attention span – Cameron couldn't [1]_____ .
> **Babies:** [2]_____ languages easily, but adults can learn, too!
> **Adults:** very good at learning [3]_____ .
> **Difficulty:** could be easy or difficult – depends on your [4]_____ language.
> **Important:** adults can learn if they're [5]_____ .
> **Common excuse from** [6]_____ : "I don't have that kind of brain!"
> **Important slogan:** Make it [7]_____ !

Listening builder | **reduced forms**

In natural spoken English, words like *to, for, as, do/does, was/were* and *can* may be hard to understand because they are usually pronounced as a "schwa" /ə/.

I had **to** /tə/ change my mindset.
It's too late **for** /fər/ me!
We do that **as** /əz/ adults, too.

Does /dəz/ he speak another language?
It **was** /wəz/ totally addictive.
You **can** /kən/ correct your mistakes later.

7 A ▶ 7.7 Read the Listening builder. Then listen and complete each sentence from the show with two words. Which words that you filled in have reduced forms?

1 People come up with a lot of reasons not _____ a language.
2 If a baby _____ it, why can't I?
3 There are languages that are trickier to learn _____ .
4 As _____ we're motivated, we do that as adults, too.
5 Thank you, Cameron, and thank you _____ .

B Practice saying each sentence.

8 In pairs, rank skills a–d from 1 (easy to learn) to 4 (hard to learn). Explain the reasons for your ranking with real examples.

a swimming

b speaking in public

c drawing or painting

d dancing

Personal Best Describe something you found difficult to learn. Include some tips.

7 LANGUAGE

present and future real conditions ■ mind and memory

7C If I remember correctly …

1 A Look at the pictures for 10 seconds. Close your book and make a list of everything you remember. In pairs, compare your lists.

B In pairs, discuss the questions. Which of you has the best memory?

1 How many pictures were you able to recall? What do you think made them memorable?
2 How did you try to remember the pictures?
3 In general, do you find it easy to learn things by heart?

Go to Vocabulary practice: mind and memory, page 146

2 Read the text. Which suggestions do you follow? Did any of the information surprise you? Discuss in pairs.

3 simple ways to improve your memory

Your brain is constantly changing. Every day it can grow new cells, form new connections, and help you remember things more easily – provided you give it a little help. Here are three examples of daily habits that can boost your memory.

1 Students occasionally stay awake before a big test, but it's better to get a good night's sleep. Your brain receives lots of information when you're awake, and it uses the time you're asleep to process this information. Unless you get enough sleep, your mind might go blank the next day.

2 Listening to music before you start studying is a good way to help you recall new facts – as long as the music is relaxing and provided it's not too loud! But once you start work, turn the music off. Research has shown that any kind of background noise can be distracting.

3 "Nuts are good for your memory! Avoid sweets!" Does this sound familiar? As it turns out, it's not only what you eat that affects your memory – it's also what you drink! Our brains are over 70% water, so keep in mind that dehydration can interfere with both attention and memory. Drink lots of water throughout the day, even if you're not particularly thirsty.

3 A Statements 1–4 below are all false. In pairs, <u>underline</u> the evidence in the text.

1 A lack of sleep won't interfere with your memory.
2 Any kind of music can help you remember information.
3 Music can boost your memory, and volume isn't important.
4 You should only drink water when you feel like it.

B Look at the sentences you <u>underlined</u>. Which words below can replace *as long as*? Then read the Grammar box.

a provided   b unless   c even if

present and future real conditions ■ mind and memory   LANGUAGE 7C

Grammar: present and future real conditions

Zero and first conditionals:
If/When I **study** every day, I **do** better on tests.
If you **want** to pass this exam, you **'ll need** to study hard.

Future time clauses:
I**'ll finish** my paper as soon as I **get** home.
I **tend** to forget new words until I **see** them again.

Alternatives to if:
As long as you **review** your notes, you**'ll remember** what you've learned.
Provided (that) you **study**, I**'m** sure you'll pass.
Unless you **practice** every day, you **won't learn** to play an instrument.
Even if your memory **is** good, you still **need** to take notes.

Go to Grammar practice: present and future real conditions, page 125

4 A ▶ 7.11 **Pronunciation:** sentence stress in conditional sentences Listen to the sentences. Which are the two stressed words in each underlined phrase?
1 Oh, all right, you can borrow it, as long as <u>you promise to be careful</u>!
2 I'll be there at about 10, provided <u>the bus is on time</u>.
3 Unless <u>you tell her a story</u>, she won't go to sleep.
4 You should exercise every day, even if <u>it's only for ten minutes</u>.

B ▶ 7.11 Listen again and repeat. Then, in pairs, think of a question that would produce each sentence as a response.

5 A Read the text and choose the correct options.

Five tips to help you remember new vocabulary
Which ones would work best for you?

1. Before you can use a new word confidently, you need to see it again and again. *Unless* / *As long as* you have a really good memory, constant review is essential.
2. Repeating words out loud is a simple but powerful way to help you remember vocabulary – *even if* / *provided that* you know what the words mean, of course!
3. Try to "play" with the new vocabulary. For example, to learn the expression "keep an open mind," imagine your brain and an open window, *even if* / *as long as* it feels a bit strange!
4. When you learn a new word or expression, close your eyes and try to visualize it, *even if* / *as long as* it's an abstract concept such as "love" or "peace."
5. You can remember new words more easily *unless* / *as long as* you learn them with words they go with. For example, instead of simply learning "boost," try to memorize "boost your memory."

B ▶ 7.12 Listen to a teacher and student discussing the tips in exercise 5A and check your answers. In pairs, say which tip you like the best.

Go to Communication practice: Both students, page 172

6 In groups, share your suggestions for getting ready for exams. Use the ideas below to help you, and use present real conditions in your suggestions.

The day before the exam	The day of the exam	During the actual exam
How many hours of review? Breaks? Alone? Background music? Bedtime?	Last-minute review? What kind of food? Any physical exercise? Tea or coffee?	Relaxation techniques? Easy questions first? Memory problems? Timing?

On the day before the exam, I spend as much time studying as I can, even if I have to go to bed at 2:00 a.m.!

Personal Best Using alternatives to *if*, complete this sentence in four different ways: *I will become fluent in English ...*

7 SKILLS WRITING writing a set of guidelines ■ linkers to add ideas

7D It's never too late to learn!

1 A Look at the categories below. What would you like to learn in the next two years? Add two ideas to each category.

Sport
"I'd like to become a better tennis player."

Music
"I've always wanted to play the guitar."

Art
"I'd love to draw better than a five-year-old."

Technology
"I want to design phone apps and sell them."

B In pairs, compare your answers. Which goals sound the easiest? Which sound the most difficult?

2 A Read Ann's blog post, ignoring the blanks. Then match headings a–d below with tips 1–4 in the text.
- a Work hard
- b Choose something you care about
- c Establish concrete goals
- d Get a good teacher

B Which tip seems most useful?

Learning a new skill

Login

BLOG   ABOUT   PROFILE

There are a lot of reasons why you might want to learn a new skill. Maybe you're trying to get a promotion. Perhaps you want to keep your mind active. Or you might just be looking for a new challenge. No matter what you want to learn and why, these four tips will help you.

1
Even if you want to learn three sports, pick one you're truly passionate about. If you choose a sport you're not really interested in, the chances are you won't be very good at it! (a) _____ , you'll find it hard to keep yourself motivated. Trust me – I've quit soccer practice three times!

2
It's easier to accomplish goals that are realistic. When I learned Portuguese, instead of saying, "I want to learn Portuguese," I told myself, "I want to be able to communicate in everyday situations when I go to Brazil." (b) _____ , I gave myself a deadline ("in six months"), which helped.

3
You can learn a new skill on your own, but it's easier when you have someone guide you. For example, you can create a professional-looking website by watching online tutorials, but a teacher helped me speed up the process. (c) _____ , he or she will give you feedback, which is a good thing.

4
Research shows that talent has less to do with your genes and more with your attitude. For example, I'm taking art lessons, and I'm not naturally good at drawing or painting. (d) _____ , I'm making good progress, and people seem to like my work. My secret? Two hours of practice every day.

Lastly, here's my most important piece of advice for you: keep in mind that making mistakes is a normal part of the learning process. As an adult, you're good at lots of different things, and it's difficult to be a beginner again. (e) _____ , we all need to learn to start over and get things wrong before we get them right. Good luck!

Posted by Ann   Share   Like 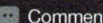 Comment

writing a set of guidelines ■ linkers to add ideas **WRITING** **SKILLS** **7D**

3 Think of something you've learned to do well. Make a list of three strategies that helped you. Then discuss them in pairs. Were any of your ideas mentioned in the blog post?

> **Skill** writing a set of guidelines
>
> Guidelines or tips that give advice on how to do something should be easy to follow, friendly, and interesting.
> - Organize your tips into short paragraphs.
> - Give each tip a title summarizing the advice.
> - Make sure each tip includes the reason why it's important.
> - Include examples or personal experiences to help you make your point.
> - "Speak" to the reader directly, using "you" and "your."

4 Read the Skill box. Then read tips 1–4 in Ann's blog post again and underline ...
  1 the reason behind each of Ann's four tips.
  2 Ann's personal experience.

5 Choose the correct option for three additional points for the Skill box. Check your answers in Ann's blog post to help you.

> - Write a ^{1}short / detailed introduction explaining the purpose of your post.
> - Write ^{2}one / two tip(s) per paragraph. You ^{3}can / shouldn't number the paragraphs.
> - Decide where to put the most important tip. You ^{4}can / can't include it in the conclusion.

> **Text builder** linkers to add ideas
>
> We use the linkers *besides*, *in addition*, and *moreover* to connect similar ideas:
> Practice helps you play better. **Besides**, it can boost your confidence.
> I'm fluent in Spanish. **In addition**, I speak very good German.
> It's a good idea to watch YouTube tutorials. **Moreover**, reading on the subject is useful, too.
>
> **Look!** When the words in **bold** in the sentences above connect two independent clauses, always start a new sentence:
> I'm a skilled drummer. **In addition**, I can play the guitar quite well.
> NOT ~~I'm a skilled drummer, in addition, I can play the guitar quite well.~~

6 Read the Text builder. Choose the correct linkers for blanks a–e in the blog post.
  a *Besides / Although*
  b *Moreover / Though*
  c *In addition / Despite*
  d *Besides / However*
  e *In addition / However*

7 Write two sentences for each item 1–4 below. Connect them using a linker in the Text builder.
  1 Health: yoga / good / health – can boost / memory
     Yoga is good for your health. Besides, it can boost your memory.
  2 Hobbies: good idea / watch YouTube videos – try / follow experts / social media
  3 Singing: important / warm up / voice when you sing – don't forget / drink / plenty / water
  4 Language learning: no "right" age / learn / foreign language – no "right" method

8 A PREPARE Choose something you've learned or would like to learn to do well. Decide on three important tips.
  B PRACTICE Use the Skill box to help you write a blog post. Add ideas using linkers.
  C PERSONAL BEST Exchange posts with a partner. Rank the tips in order of importance. Would you change the order of any of them?

Personal Best Can you learn a new skill completely on your own? Write a paragraph answering this question.

UNIT 8

The changing media

LANGUAGE using linkers (2) ■ the media

8A TV in the 21st Century

1 Read the responses from a survey. In pairs, say which ones are true for you.
   a "I prefer to get my news from independent sources, which I think are less biased."
   b "There are so many good shows on TV that I don't know which ones to follow!"
   c "I love to watch the evening news, especially when there's breaking news."
   d "I rarely watch regular TV. I prefer to stream shows and watch them when I feel like it."

   Go to Vocabulary practice: the media, page 147

2 Read the text and fill in the blank in the first line with "In some ways" or "No, not at all."

Is this the end of TV as we know it?

"_____," says media expert Jane Midler, who has just released the results of a survey she conducted recently.

The role of television in our lives has changed a lot. Viewing habits in the U.S. are very different from ten years ago, and we can expect even more changes in the near future.

1 Fewer shows in the future

<u>¹In 2010, media companies produced about 200 original TV shows, whereas seven years later this number had more than doubled.</u> <u>²While variety is a good idea, most of the people I have interviewed about this trend say there is now too much to choose from</u>, and this creates a problem for TV networks. <u>³Since there are too many shows for too few viewers, audiences tend to be small</u>, which means fewer ads and less money. As a result, the number of shows will probably drop in the near future.

2 More subscription services

I have interviewed nearly 100 people between the ages of 16–22, and most of them have grown up watching less TV than their parents. So, <u>⁴unlike older adults, it seems that teens and young adults are abandoning television</u>. When they want to watch a show, they simply go online and watch it on their phone or computer – anywhere, any time. <u>⁵Due to this desire for flexibility, services like Netflix will undoubtedly remain popular for many years to come.</u>

3 The death of the evening news as we know it

My survey has also revealed that fewer people seem to trust the evening news. Words like "fair," "objective," and "accurate" rarely came up in their opinions, and it is not hard to understand why. <u>⁶Viewers have access to hundreds of sites and online channels where they can compare different perspectives and form their own opinions. Therefore, they have become more critical.</u> Unless the evening news reinvents itself, networks will continue to lose viewers.

3 Match sentences a–d in exercise 1 with sections 1–3 of the text. There is one extra sentence.

4 Look at the <u>underlined</u> sentences 1–6 in the text. What kind of idea does each one express: contrast/comparison or reason? Then read the Grammar box.

using linkers (2) ■ the media   LANGUAGE   **8A**

📖 Grammar — using linkers (2)

Expressing a contrast or comparison:
Only 50% of teens say they watch TV, **whereas/while** the rest use streaming services.
While/Whereas every home had a TV in the 90s, today some homes don't have one.
Unlike the younger generation, some adults still prefer to read print newspapers.

Expressing a reason:
Since/As technology has changed so quickly, the press has had to adapt.
Due to/Because of/As a result of advances in technology, e-books are easier to read than before.
I rarely watch the news. **Therefore/As a result**, I don't know what's going on in the world.

Go to Grammar practice: using linkers (2), page 126

5 A ▶ 8.3 **Pronunciation:** emphatic stress Listen to the sentences. Notice how the underlined words are stressed to emphasize a contrast or a reason.

1 I watch *The Simpsons* regularly, <u>unlike</u> most of my friends.
2 I can stream my favorite films. <u>As a result</u>, I've been going to the movies less often.
3 I like to watch subtitled movies, <u>whereas</u> my brother prefers the dubbed versions.
4 Reading is a unique experience, and, <u>therefore</u>, movies based on books are never very good.

B ▶ 8.3 Listen again and repeat. Then choose a statement that is true for you and discuss it in pairs.

6 ▶ 8.4 Choose the correct options to complete the text. Listen and check.

How **virtual reality** might change the movie industry

¹*Because of / As* rising costs and recent improvements in home entertainment technology, movie attendance has declined over the past few years. However, the movie industry has been quick to respond, and now audiences can enjoy advanced 3D projections, complete with surround sound.
But ²*since / whereas* movie tickets are still expensive, studios are now trying to change people's experiences of going to the movies. And this is where 360-degree virtual reality comes in. Soon moviegoers will be wearing special glasses that, ³*whereas / unlike* 3D glasses, will make them feel as if they are "surrounded" by the movie. ⁴*Due to / Therefore*, audiences will feel closer to the action and more connected with the characters. ⁵*As / While* none of this is guaranteed to bring viewers back, it seems like a step in the right direction.

7 Rewrite each person's reason for not going to the movies anymore in two different ways. Use the words in parentheses.

1 "Movie theaters are too expensive, and this is why I prefer to watch movies at home." (since / as a result)
2 "Movies from the 1990s were great. Today's movies are silly." (unlike / whereas)
3 "I don't go to movie theaters anymore because people always talk during the movie." (as a result / since)

Go to Communication practice: Student A page 161, Student B page 167

8 Choose a picture and think about the questions below. Then, in pairs, answer the questions using linkers to express contrast/comparison or give reasons.

a   b   c   d

1 How often do you/your friends/your family use this piece of technology?
2 In general, is it more/less popular than it used to be? Why?
3 What do you think will happen in the next ten years or so? Why?

Most of my friends still have laptops. They're still very popular since they've become much lighter and easier to carry. I don't think many people will have them in 10 years as tablets have become more popular, too.

Personal Best Choose a different piece of technology and answer the questions in exercise 8.

8 SKILLS

READING inferring meaning using related words ■ generalizing

8B Digital media for you

1 Look at the pictures on page 69 showing people using various kinds of social media. Which opinion best represents you? Why?

2 Look at the title. What is the purpose of the text? Choose from a–c. Read the introduction and check.
   a to describe the results of a survey
   b to help readers deal with a problem
   c to report a news event that has happened

3 Check (✓) the sentence (1 or 2) that best summarizes each person's main point. Then match it with his/her advice a or b.

Larry
1 ☐ Social media platforms don't give us the opportunity to see things in different ways.
2 ☐ We allow social media to spy on us.

a We should be willing to consider ideas we may disagree with.
b We should spend less time on social media.

Sue
1 ☐ Serious news sources are disappearing.
2 ☐ Today, it's hard to distinguish real news from fake news.

a We should read or watch the news critically.
b We should never depend on online sources.

Skill inferring meaning using related words

When you are trying to infer the meaning of unknown vocabulary, look for related words. These are often:
- in the same sentence as the unknown vocabulary item.
- synonyms or near-synonyms to the vocabulary item.
- the same part of speech as the vocabulary item (e.g., both are adjectives).

4 A Read the Skill box and the example below. Then underline a synonym (or a word with a similar meaning) for each word in **bold** in the text.

*Digital news platforms make it easier than ever to find information about almost any topic on **virtually** any device.*

B Complete the sentence below with the correct option.

Related words, such as synonyms or the same part of speech, can be found *before / after / either before or after* the word they refer to.

Text builder generalizing

We can use the expressions in **bold** below to make generalizations:
Generally speaking, news sources in my country are trustworthy.
On the whole, I consider myself tolerant of other people's opinions.
As a rule, I don't read or watch the news in English.
For the most part, I get my news from Facebook and Twitter.

5 Read the Text builder. Complete each sentence from the text with the appropriate expression.
1 Are we getting a balanced perspective? Apparently, _____ , no.
2 _____ , people prefer to watch or read things they agree with.
3 _____ , though, it's easy to be deceived by misleading, one-sided, or fake stories.
4 _____ , unknown sites may not be trustworthy.

6 1 Which sentences in exercise 5 do you agree with? Has the text made you change any of your opinions?
   2 In pairs, modify the sentences in the Text builder so they are true for you.

FACTS or "FACTS"?

Digital news platforms make it easier than ever to find information about almost any topic on **virtually** any device. But are we getting a balanced perspective? Apparently, for the most part, no. Social media experts Larry Jones and Sue Herrera explain why this is so and what we can do about it.

Unbelievable! I've got to share this.

That's it! I'm not following this site anymore.

I just love my Facebook friends!

LARRY JONES

Research has shown that, generally speaking, people prefer to watch or read things they agree with. As a result, algorithms – the secret codes that power social media platforms – tend to show us what *they* think we want to read or watch, based on who we interact with, what we've read in the past, and the sites we visit. This means that the version of the world we find every day in our own personal newsfeed has been pre-selected to confirm our opinions and **reinforce** our beliefs. In a sense, it's as if we're all **trapped** inside social media's walls, stuck in our own bubbles. So it's no surprise that we're sometimes tempted to block people whose tastes and opinions are different from ours. However, we actually should do the exact opposite: actively follow people who don't necessarily share our point of view, and try to see things from *their* **perspective**. Not only is this a good exercise in empathy, it will also get algorithms "confused" and stop media platforms from flooding our newsfeed with ideas and opinions that are identical to ours.

SUE HERRERA

In the newsfeed on your phone, most stories look believable – whether or not they come from a "serious" source. True, some fake news sites are so bad they're easy to spot: missing references, no authors' names, spelling and grammar mistakes. As a rule, though, it's easy to be deceived by misleading, one-sided, or fake stories, which are sometimes read and watched even more widely than real stories. So here's what you should do so you don't get **fooled**.

First, if you're reading or watching the news on an unknown site, check out other articles and videos the site has posted. On the whole, unknown sites may not be **trustworthy**, and you may need to look for a more reliable source so you can compare different news outlets that report the same piece of news. Second, when you're reading an article, be sure to read past the headline and also go **beyond** the opening paragraph, which are usually designed to sound convincing and may mislead you. Last but not least, please remember: If a news story sounds **phony**, don't share it because sharing fake news generally makes it go higher up in search-result pages. This, ironically, will make even more people read or watch it!

8 LANGUAGE -ing forms and infinitives ■ expressions with *at*, *for*, *in*, and *on*

8C Binge-watching

1 Think about how we use technology or the media today. Complete the sentence in three different ways.
I don't think it's healthy to …
I don't think it's healthy to play video games for more than two hours.

2 A Look at the picture and read the entry from an online encyclopedia, ignoring the blanks. How often do you binge-watch?

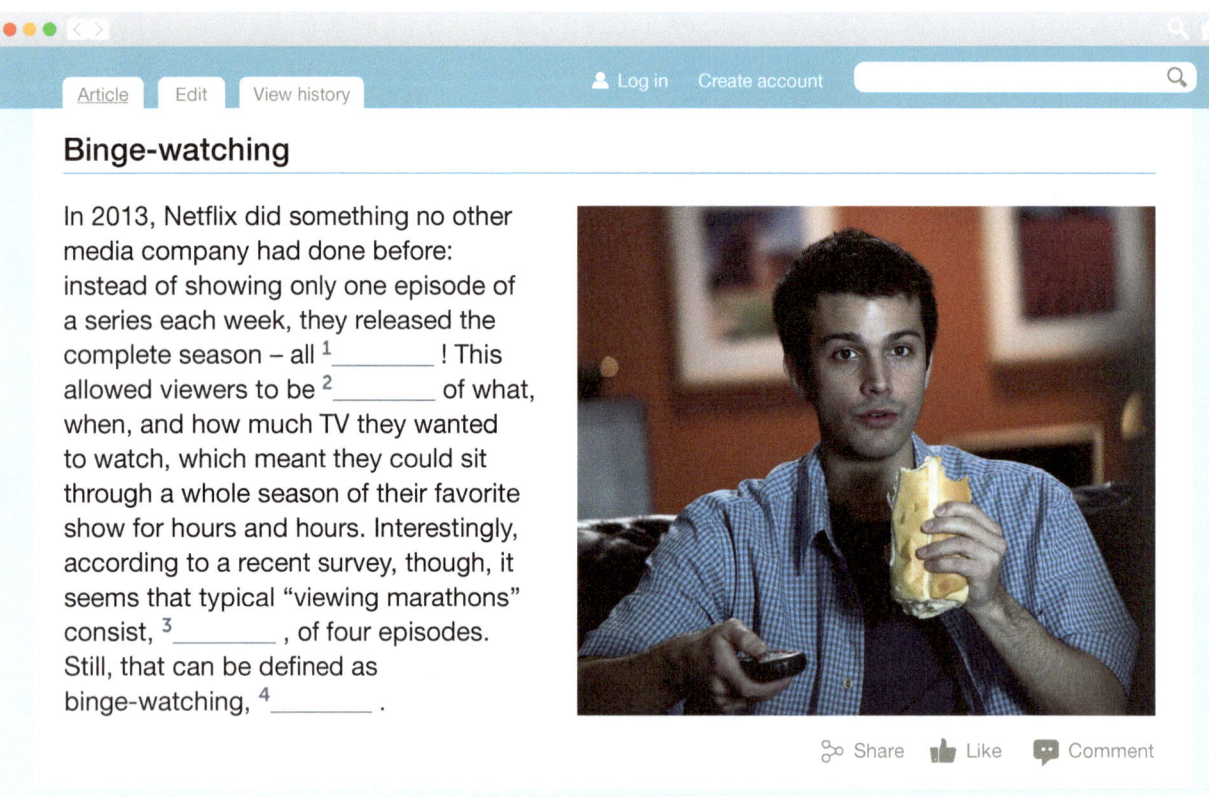

Binge-watching

In 2013, Netflix did something no other media company had done before: instead of showing only one episode of a series each week, they released the complete season – all ¹_____ ! This allowed viewers to be ²_____ of what, when, and how much TV they wanted to watch, which meant they could sit through a whole season of their favorite show for hours and hours. Interestingly, according to a recent survey, though, it seems that typical "viewing marathons" consist, ³_____ , of four episodes. Still, that can be defined as binge-watching, ⁴_____ .

B Complete the text in exercise 2A with the expressions in the box.

> for sure   at once   in control   on average

Go to Vocabulary practice: expressions with *at*, *for*, *in*, and *on*, page 148

3 A ▶ 8.7 Listen to Anna and Fred talking about binge-watching. Who likes/dislikes it? Who changes his/her mind in the end?

B ▶ 8.7 Listen again and complete each sentence with one or two words.
1 I'm going to stay home _____ some rest if it's OK.
2 When I finish an episode, I can't help _____ the next one.
3 _____ for a new episode is fun, too. It makes me look forward to it even more.
4 I'm sick and tired of _____ spoilers.

4 Look at exercise 3B again. Match sentences 1–4 with rules a–d. Then read the Grammar box.
Use the:
a *-ing* form if a verb is the subject of a sentence.   _____
b *-ing* form after an expression with a negative meaning.   _____
c infinitive to give a reason.   _____
d *-ing* form after a preposition.   _____

-ing forms and infinitives ■ expressions with *at*, *for*, *in*, and *on*

LANGUAGE 8C

Grammar: -ing forms and infinitives

-ing forms
1 after prepositions and certain verbs:
I'm not **into playing** computer games, but I **enjoy streaming** movies.
2 as the subject of a sentence:
Watching horror movies is fun.
3 in expressions with a negative meaning:
There's **no point**/It's **no use trying** to stop.
I **have trouble staying** away from social media.

Infinitives
1 after certain verbs:
I **decided to go** to the movies.
2 after adjectives:
It's **impossible** not **to cry** during this movie.
3 to give a reason:
I went home early **to catch** my favorite show.

Infinitive vs. base form:
I **encouraged** her **to take** a look at the news.
I **made** him **put** the phone down.

Look! *Stop* has a different meaning when it is followed by an infinitive rather than by an *-ing* form:
I **stopped** for a second **to check** my messages. (I stopped what I was doing to check them.)
I **stopped watching** TV, and now I'm a lot happier. (I don't watch TV anymore.)

Go to Grammar practice: *-ing* forms and infinitives, page 127

5 A ▶ 8.9 **Pronunciation:** *to* Listen to the sentences. Notice the unstressed pronunciation of *to*.

1 No, it's no use trying to convince her.
2 Well, I can't help feeling that you're lying to me.
3 Yes, I'd love to spend a week there.
4 Well, I only stopped by to say "hi."

B ▶ 8.9 Listen again and repeat.

6 A Complete the sentences in *italics* with the correct form of the verbs in the box. Add *not* if necessary.

answer   eat (x2)   pick up   save   spend   try

My three favorite obsessions
by Jake Sullivan

» **Binge-texting:** On average, I send and receive about 100 text messages per day. No matter where I am, if I get a new message, *I can't help ¹_____ the phone so I can read it.* When I'm with friends and family, *I try my best ²_____ text messages, though.*

» **Binge-eating:** ³_____ *a slice of cake every once in a while is normal,* I know, but I eat at least three slices of banana cake every day. *My mother tries to encourage me ⁴_____ healthier food,* but *it's no use ⁵_____ to convince me* to cut down on sugar. Life's too short!

» **Binge-shopping:** *I've always found it hard ⁶_____ money,* but it feels as if I might be getting worse! *I can't stop ⁷_____ money on things I don't need,* especially new pens. Yes, pens of all kinds! Thank goodness I've never ended up in debt.

B Rephrase the sentences in *italics* from exercise 6A with the words below. In pairs, say which of Jake's habits are true for you.

1 It's hard not
2 I avoid
3 It's normal
4 My mother tries to make
5 There's no point
6 I have trouble
7 I keep

Go to Communication practice: Student A page 161, Student B page 167

7 What are *your* three favorite addictive habits? Share your ideas with your partner.

> I try my best not to … , but I can't help …
> I find it hard not to …
> I've always had trouble …
> I know it's no use trying to …
> I should definitely stop …

Personal Best Write four sentences saying what your parents encouraged you to do/made you do as a child.

71

8 SKILLS SPEAKING expressing annoyance and indifference ■ clarifying and reacting

8D Ads to drive you crazy

1 Discuss the questions in pairs.

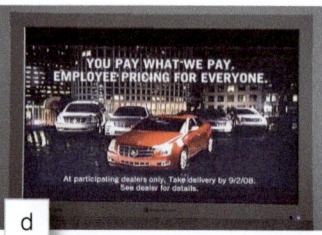

a b c d

e f g h

1 What ads do you like/hate on TV or online?
2 What are "infomercials"? Do you ever buy anything after watching them?

2 ▶ 8.10 Watch or listen to the first part of *Talking Zone*. Ben and Abigail are talking about an exercise machine Ben saw on an infomercial. Check (✔) the arguments that they make.

Infomercials …

1 make products sound affordable. ☐
2 use psychology to convince us. ☐
3 work better with younger audiences. ☐
4 have good arguments. ☐
5 can be funny. ☐

3 ▶ 8.10 Complete sentences 1–4 with the expressions in the box. Watch or listen again and check.

> however hard I try   whatever it takes   whatever way you look at it   whenever I watch

1 "Call now, and we'll double the offer!" They'll do _____ to convince you!
2 They're manipulating you. _____ , that's what it's all about.
3 It's just that _____ an infomercial, something strange happens.
4 It's almost as if I've been hypnotized. _____ , I can't help it.

Conversation builder — expressing annoyance and indifference

Expressing annoyance:
I end up buying **whatever** (product) they advertise.
However effective these ads may be, they're sometimes dishonest.
These ads follow me **wherever** I go.
Whenever an infomercial comes on, I mute the TV.

Expressing indifference (or dismissing what someone says):
People say I should spend my money more wisely.
Well, **whatever**.

Words with *-ever* include *whatever* (= any thing), *however* (= any way), *wherever* (= any place) and *whenever* (= any time).

expressing annoyance and indifference ■ clarifying and reacting   SPEAKING   SKILLS   8D

4 A Read the Conversation builder. Rank a–d from 1 (least annoying) to 4 (most annoying).
- a an <u>infomercial</u> about the latest cleaning product ☐
- b a musical <u>jingle</u> for a TV advert ☐
- c a <u>pop-up</u> ad from your favorite shoe company ☐
- d a <u>trailer</u> at the beginning of a film ☐

B Share your opinions with your partner.

I can't stand jingles. However hard I try to forget them, they keep playing in my head!

5 ▶ 8.11 Watch or listen to the second part of the show. Choose the main point.
- a Regular TV is becoming less and less popular.
- b Ads may work even if you're not paying attention.
- c Repetitive ads are annoying.

6 ▶ 8.11 Watch or listen again and number sentences a–f in the order you hear them.
- a ☐ So, what's the point of running a TV ad if most viewers might not even notice it?
- b ☐ I see what you mean, in theory, but I'm not sure that happens.
- c ☐ You see, here's what I don't get. How do they ever sell any products?
- d ☐ I think it's all about creating familiarity. It's kind of subliminal.
- e ☐ It's hard to tell, but I think ads might work even if you don't remember seeing them.
- f ☐ Yeah, that makes sense. It's the same principle as a song that keeps replaying in your head.

🔧 **Skill   clarifying and reacting**

When you discuss something concrete, you may need to clarify what you say and react to what others say.
- You can express doubt about something: *What's the point of answering? Jamie never listens. Here's what I don't get…*
- You can offer an explanation, even if you're not sure: *It's hard to tell why Bill hasn't called, but maybe it's because he's been sick.*
- You can acknowledge a point/what someone has said: *Yeah, that makes sense. Let's invite a few more people over. I see what you mean in theory, but…*

7 Read the Skill box. Look at the sentences in exercise 6 again. In pairs, decide which expressions Ben and Abigail use to clarify and react. <u>Underline</u> them and identify the function of each one.

8 ▶ 8.12 In pairs, order sentences a–f to make a conversation. Listen and check.
- a ☐ Good question. I think it's all about making your product known, no matter how.
- b ☐ Neither do I. Here's what I don't get. What's the point of trying to get people to buy something by annoying them?
- c ☐ 1 I often find flyers on my windshield or in my mailbox. It really gets on my nerves.
- d ☐ Flyers? They drive me crazy, too. And I never want or need whatever they're advertising.
- e ☐ I think most people do. But flyers are cheap, if two or three customers call, maybe that's better than nothing.
- f ☐ Yeah, that makes sense, but don't people throw those flyers away as soon as they see them? I know I do.

Go to Communication practice: Student A page 162, Student B page 168

9 A PREPARE Think of three really annoying things you see on TV (an ad, a show, the news, etc.) Choose one and prepare a conversation about it.

B PRACTICE In pairs, practice the conversation. Take turns clarifying how you feel and reacting to your partner's comments.

C PERSONAL BEST Choose another idea and practice a similar conversation. Can you improve the way you clarify and react?

Personal Best Write a paragraph about an annoying problem in your neighborhood.

7 and 8 REVIEW and PRACTICE

Grammar

1 Choose the correct options to complete the sentences.

1 The most famous broadcaster in the UK is the BBC, _____ is funded by the public.
   a which
   b who
   c that

2 My sister likes going out _____ , I prefer staying in.
   a unlike
   b as
   c while

3 I spent a long time preparing for the interview _____ myself a good chance of getting the job.
   a by giving
   b to give
   c while giving

4 _____ the snow, most trains will be running late.
   a Because
   b Since
   c Due to

5 That man _____ the street was my first music teacher!
   a crossing
   b who crosses
   c crossed

6 I don't take my phone out in the evening because I'm afraid of _____ it.
   a lose
   b losing
   c to lose

7 I got the highest grades, _____ made me very proud.
   a as
   b which
   c that

8 We stopped _____ the car with gas because we had almost run out.
   a filling
   b by filling
   c to fill

2 Complete the sentences with the correct forms of the verbs in parentheses.

1 I'm very tired today, so I _____ (go) to bed as soon as I _____ (finish) my homework.

2 _____ (live) in Spain is more fun than _____ (live) in the UK.

3 As long as you _____ (not call) me after 9 p.m. tonight, I _____ (answer) the phone.

4 It's no use _____ (ask) me to change my mind because I've decided _____ (quit).

5 If there _____ (not be) any buses running tomorrow, I _____ (have to) walk to work.

6 We _____ (have) our classes outside every Friday unless it _____ (not be) warm enough.

3 Choose the correct options to complete the text.

Two experts give their predictions about the classrooms of the future.

Expert 1: ¹*Whereas / Since* many professions have been replaced by machines in recent years, teachers should generally feel safe ²*therefore / due to* the nature of their work. ³*Unlike / Whereas* factory workers or store cashiers, teachers require skills ⁴*who / that* machines do not currently have. ⁵*While / As* robots can perform many physical and logical tasks, they are not able to do things ⁶*require / that require* emotional intelligence. ⁷*Unless / If* a robot is invented that can do these things, teaching ⁸*continues / will continue* to be done by humans. And ⁹*even if / provided* a robot is invented with these qualities, people would rather be taught by a human than by a machine.

Expert 2: In just ten years, machines ¹⁰*will be / are* a lot more intelligent than they are today, ¹¹*that / which* should really worry teachers. These new machines will listen to the voices of learners and read their faces. ¹²*Therefore, / Since* they will be able to adapt their teaching methods to each individual student. ¹³*As soon / As soon as* these machines ¹⁴*are / will be* available in schools, teachers will simply become classroom assistants in charge of discipline and responsible for setting up equipment. ¹⁵*Learning / To learn* will take place in an environment managed by robots.

Vocabulary

1 Circle the word or expression that is different. Explain why.

1 can't seem   fail   can't manage   succeed
2 host   tabloid   press   headlines
3 learn by heart   cross your mind   recall   remind
4 report   application   proposal   conference
5 viewer   tabloid   broadcast   television
6 every day   once in a while   at once   on a regular basis

REVIEW and PRACTICE 7 and 8

2 Match the words and expressions in the box with definitions 1–8.

> keep an open mind   memorable   get ahead
> get hold of   keep something in mind
> make the most out of   can't quite manage
> change your mind

1. easy to remember _____
2. just unable _____
3. have a new, different opinion to before _____
4. become successful in life or in a career _____
5. wait before making a judgment _____
6. successfully contact _____
7. use to the greatest advantage _____
8. remember and think about something _____

3 Choose the correct options to complete the sentences.

1. That was awful! I had studied hard, but when the exam started, *I kept an open mind / my mind went blank*.
2. My friend knows a website where you can *stream / host* live soccer games for free!
3. It's funny that we've become such good friends because at *once / first*, we didn't get along.
4. I don't trust any news channels because they're all *biased / objective*.
5. Yesterday you said "Yes," but today you're saying "No." I wish you would *make up your / keep an open* mind!
6. I've come to pick up some medicine *for the sake of / on behalf of* my mother.
7. If you want to *make the most out of / get hold of* your time in college, you should live with other students.
8. Could you *recall / remind* me to call my brother today? It's his birthday.

4 Complete the text with the words in the box.

> struggling   matters   at   hard   across
> of   breaking news   in

One of the most significant recent trends in media has been the decrease in newspaper sales. Until quite recently, many newspapers were pretty successful ¹_____ getting their message ²_____ to their readers, but today they are ³_____ to survive. Several national newspapers are finding it ⁴_____ to sell enough copies and are ⁵_____ debt, while some have closed down completely. One of the reasons for this is the rise in the number of online news sites, which are capable ⁶_____ delivering ⁷_____ much more quickly. To make ⁸_____ worse for the newspaper industry, people are less willing to pay for their news and are increasingly turning to free news sites online.

Personal Best

Lesson 7A
Describe four recent events. Use a relative clause to comment on each one.

Lesson 8A
Write four sentences about a well-known media organization in your country.

Lesson 7A
Name two things you can do with these verbs: *attend, make, get, submit*.

Lesson 8A
Write three sentences about current news stories using these linkers: *due to, whereas, unlike*.

Lesson 7B
Describe something you struggle to do, have a talent for, have succeeded at, and are very bad at.

Lesson 8B
Describe how you use the Internet, using four different generalizing expressions.

Lesson 7C
Name four possible future events or situations. Describe the consequences of each.

Lesson 8C
Name five expressions which use these prepositions: *for, on, at, in*.

Lesson 7C
Write two sentences containing the word *memory* and two containing the word *mind*.

Lesson 8C
Write four sentences about your classmates: two with *-ing* forms, and two with infinitives.

Lesson 7D
Write three pairs of sentences. Begin each second sentence with *besides, in addition*, and *moreover*.

Lesson 8D
Describe four situations in your life using these words: *whatever, whenever, however, wherever*.

75

UNIT 9
The power of design

LANGUAGE — position of adverbs ■ collocations with *have* and *take*

9A Steps to a better life

1 Imagine a happy day in your life. Where are you? Who are you with? Why are you there? What are you doing? Now tell your partner.

2 Match quotes a–c with sentences 1–3. Which is your favorite quote?

a "A table, a chair, a bowl of fruit, and a violin; what else does a man need to be happy?" (Albert Einstein)

b "If you don't like something, change it. If you can't change it, change your attitude." (Maya Angelou)

c "Be happy for no reason, just like a child." (Deepak Chopra)

1 To be happy, you should **have an open mind** and **take responsibility for** your life.

2 If you want to be happy, don't **take things too seriously**.

3 If you're **having trouble** being happy, **take pleasure in** the small things.

Go to Vocabulary practice: collocations with *have* and *take*, page 149

3 Read the text. Which sentence (1–3) from exercise 2 best summarizes it?

Happiness by design

How many times have you seen this meme on social media this past month? Probably more than once or twice, right? People sometimes dislike their colleges, their jobs, or their lifestyles, but feel that if they just live one day at a time, something will magically change. But you don't need to live on autopilot – you can live by design! The key is to establish clear goals and create a plan to achieve them. Here are three "musts" to take into account when setting goals.

1 They must be personally important to you. You probably won't do everything necessary to achieve a goal unless it's something that you're really passionate about.

   WRONG: *Learning how to play the piano might be fun. I guess I could give it a try.*
   RIGHT: *I truly love the sound of the piano, and I'd really like to learn how to play it well.*

2 They must be something you can visualize. Otherwise, your brain will have trouble getting the message.

   WRONG: *I want to have my own business.*
   RIGHT: *I'd like to create a start-up and sell clothes online.*

3 They must be specific and measurable. Ideally, you should give yourself a deadline. If you don't, you won't feel your goal is urgent.

   WRONG: *I need to lose some weight.*
   RIGHT: *I want to lose seven pounds by April.*

One last important point: people often forget that goals must be realistic. You won't go from couch potato to marathon runner in a week. Or become fluent in a foreign language in six months, even if you live abroad. So you should take care not to set goals that you can't realistically achieve.

I HATE MONDAYS

position of adverbs ■ collocations with *have* and *take* | **LANGUAGE 9A**

4 Find the underlined adverbs in the text in exercise 3. Check (✓) the correct option(s) below. Then read the Grammar box.

Adverbs can go _____ of a sentence.
a at the beginning ☐   b in the middle ☐   c at the end ☐

> **Grammar** position of adverbs
>
> **Beginning of a sentence:**
> *Fortunately*, I have a stress-free life. (comment)
>
> **Middle of a sentence:**
> He has an **extremely** positive outlook on life. (degree)
> She **quickly** adopted a healthier lifestyle. (manner)
> I've **often** thought about changing my diet. (frequency)
>
> **End of a sentence:**
> I'd like to learn to play the guitar **well**. (manner)
>
> **Look!** We cannot place an adverb between the verb and its object:
> She **quickly** adopted a healthier lifestyle. NOT ~~She adopted quickly a healthier lifestyle.~~

Go to Grammar practice: position of adverbs, page 128

5 A ▶ 9.4 **Pronunciation:** syllable stress with adverbs of degree Listen to the sentences. Mark the stressed syllable in the underlined words.
1 I thought Stephen King's novel *It* was surprisingly good.
2 My nephew's birthday party was terribly boring.
3 It's unusually cold for this time of year.
4 My grandfather is remarkably active for a 90-year-old man.
5 Kelly Clarkson is a truly talented artist. She sings amazingly well.

B ▶ 9.4 Listen, check, and repeat. Then, in pairs, choose two sentences and change the details to make the sentences true for you.

6 A Insert the adverbs in parentheses into the correct places in the sentences or phrases in *italics*.

> **Five simple steps to a happier you**
>
> ❶ **Keep learning new things.** *Learning affects your well-being in lots of positive ways.* (not surprisingly) It exposes you to new ideas and encourages curiosity.
>
> ❷ **Stop saying, "I'll do it later – maybe next month."** *Procrastinating tends to have a negative impact on your well-being.* (extremely)
>
> ❸ **Do things for others.** *Helping other people makes us happier and healthier.* (usually) *It's not all about money.* (obviously) We can also offer others our time, ideas, and energy.
>
> ❹ **Take care of your body.** *Your body and your mind are connected, so being active is important.* (physically) *It can change your life.* (easily)
>
> ❺ **Be comfortable with who you are.** *Nobody's perfect, but we forget that!* (often) *If you accept yourself,* (truly) *you'll be a lot happier.* (probably)

B In pairs, discuss the tips above and decide which ones you like best.

Go to Communication practice: Student A page 162, Student B page 168

7 How can you plan for a happier life? Choose two of the ideas below and tell your partner how each one will make you happier. Use some of the adverbs in the box.

| fortunately   easily   extremely   obviously   personally   realistically   truly |

| spending quality time with your family | making a lot of money | learning when to say "no" | having a stress-free lifestyle |

Obviously, my job's very important to me, but I think I could spend more quality time with my family.

Personal Best Write a paragraph about your plan for a happier life in exercise 7.

77

9 SKILLS

LISTENING understanding key points ■ silent *h* ■ colors

Talking Zone

9B Good or bad design?

1 A Discuss the questions in pairs.

 a
 b
c

1 Which chair looks the nicest?
2 Which one looks the most comfortable?
3 Which one would look better in a different color?
4 Which one would you never consider buying?

B Match descriptions 1–3 with pictures a–c.

1 a brownish-green 1950s style armchair
2 a dark green rocking chair with a wooden frame
3 a light green armless designer chair

Go to Vocabulary practice: colors, page 150

Skill understanding key points

When listening, it's important to understand the speaker's key points and differentiate them from supporting details and examples. Speakers often:
- repeat a key point more than once, using different words.
- explain it using an example or comparison.
- stress certain key words for emphasis.

2  9.6 Read the Skill box. Then watch or listen to the first part of *Talking Zone*. Check (✓) the key point Ava makes about good design.

a Use is more important than style. ☐
b Use is less important than style. ☐
c Use is as important as style. ☐

Ava

3 A ▶ 9.6 Ava repeats her key point several times during the program. Can you remember the missing words? Watch or listen again and check.

1 A lot of people still seem to think that _____ is always second to function.
2 Design and function are like a pair of _____ – you can't have one without the other!
3 The look and _____ of a product should work together.
4 Tupperware might not be _____ for the way it looks, but I think it's a fantastic example of good design.
5 And that's what good design is all about. Creating something that is both _____ and efficient.

B Look at the sentences in exercise 3A. Which sentences:
- offer a comparison ____
- provide an example ____
- make the same point with different words ____ ____

4 In pairs, look at exercise 2 again. Discuss which statement best matches your own opinion.

understanding key points ■ silent *h* ■ colors **LISTENING** SKILLS **9B**

5 ▶ 9.7 Watch or listen to the second part of the show. Check (✓) the picture that Ava describes as an example of bad design.

Modern London Underground map

Sydney Opera House

6 ▶ 9.7 Watch or listen again. Choose the correct options.
1 Early London underground maps were *more / less* accurate than today's maps.
2 Harry Beck made his version of the map more *detailed / practical*.
3 The Sydney Opera House has poor *acoustics / visibility* so it's hard to *hear / see* well.
4 The Guangzhou Opera House in China is a *good / bad* example of design and function working together.

> **Listening builder**   silent *h*
>
> When the letter *h* isn't pronounced, speech can be harder to understand. It is almost always silent in pronouns or auxiliaries after a consonant: ask h̶i̶m̶, tell h̶e̶r̶, must h̶a̶v̶e̶. In fast speech, it is sometimes silent:
> • in pronouns that start a sentence: H̶e̶ didn't call.
> • when the main verb is *have*, even after a vowel: She h̶a̶s̶ a new car.
> • in content words, especially after consonants: I was h̶u̶n̶g̶r̶y̶.
> However, it is never silent when a word is emphasized: I said I wanted <u>hot</u> coffee, not <u>iced</u> coffee.
> When in doubt, always pronounce the letter *h*, especially when speaking slowly.

7 A ▶ 9.8 Read the Listening builder. Then listen to the sentences from the video. Cross out the letter *h* when you don't hear it pronounced.
1 Today I'm with Ava Janssen to talk about **h**er brilliantly written book.
2 They were messy and much, much **h**arder to read.
3 **H**e straightened the lines and put the stations equal distances apart.
4 Most metro stations **h**ave symmetrical, color-coded maps.
5 It's the Sydney Opera **H**ouse.
6 I cannot recommend the book **h**ighly enough.

B In pairs, practice saying each sentence.

8 In pairs, discuss two objects or places that each match one of the categories below. Can you support your opinion with examples or analogies?
a It's both beautiful and practical.
b It's beautiful, but not practical.
c It's practical, but not beautiful.
d It's neither beautiful nor practical.

Personal Best Describe something in your home where function and design work well together.

79

9 LANGUAGE
passives and causative *have* ■ dimensions and weight

9C Extreme designs

1 A Look at the house in the picture. Do you think it's a piece of art or a real house? Read the text and check.

Unconventional design: this week's top picks

If you like unconventional architecture, you will love House NA, a 914-square-foot home made almost entirely of glass! That's 85 square meters.

Located in the Koenji neighborhood in Tokyo, this three-story house is unlike anything you've ever seen. Instead of walls or doors, there are large floor-to-ceiling windows, which means that just about everything can be seen from the outside!

House NA was designed as a modern version of an adult treehouse, where all the different "rooms" are connected to each other. I'd love to have a house like this designed specially for me and my family.

This house is so special it's been featured in dozens of specialized magazines since it was built in 2011. It's definitely worth checking out, though the owners probably won't let you in!

B How big is your home in square feet? Multiply the length by the width to find out. Describe it to your partner.

Go to Vocabulary practice: dimensions and weight, page 151

2 A ▶ 9.11 Listen to a couple talking about House NA. Who thinks it would make a good office?
the woman ☐   the man ☐   both ☐   neither ☐

B ▶ 9.11 Listen again and complete the sentences.
1 They _____ a famous Japanese architect _____ it.
2 It looks as if it _____ _____ simply as a concept. You know, like modern art.
3 This glass building really makes us think about how a house should _____ _____.
4 I'm guessing they probably _____ blinds _____ up or something.
5 Save money? You mean because the lights would _____ _____ _____ during the day?

3 Match sentences 1–5 from exercise 2B with patterns a–c. Are patterns a and b active or passive? Then read the Grammar box.

a *be* + past participle
b *have* + object + past participle
c *have* + object + base form

passives and causative *have* ■ dimensions and weight   **LANGUAGE 9C**

Grammar: passives and causative *have*

Passives:
The building **was designed** by a very famous architect.
When we got to the airport, all the flights **had been canceled**.
The new expressway **will have been finished** by 2025.
More houses **should be built**.

Causative *have*:
They **had** me **write down** every word they said. (active)
We **had** our house **designed** by a well-known architect. (passive)
It's important to **have** your eyes **tested** from time to time. (passive)

Go to Grammar practice: passives and causative *have*, page 129

4 A ▶ 9.13 **Pronunciation:** stress in passive and causative *have* sentences Listen to the sentences. Which of the underlined words is stressed?

1 My phone <u>was stolen</u> last month.
2 I've <u>been interviewed</u> for lots of jobs this year.
3 My hair's too long. I should probably <u>have it cut</u>.
4 I think I should have <u>been given</u> a pay raise.

B ▶ 9.13 Listen again and repeat. Then, in pairs, tell your partner if any of the sentences are true for you.

5 Rewrite the underlined phrases using the passive or causative *have*.

What's the most practical innovation of the last 25 years?

1 I think people installing home surveillance cameras is really practical. I like to <u>protect my home</u> from burglars, 24/7.

2 I love postal tracking. I sent a package yesterday, and they let me know exactly what time <u>they had delivered it</u>. How great is that?

3 I love the fact that, before you choose a hotel, you can go online and find out whether <u>other guests have recommended it</u>.

4 Definitely bitcoin. I wonder, though, if by 2030, <u>people will replace it</u> with other payment methods.

5 Online shopping. I like <u>other people delivering stuff to my door</u>!

6 Here's something that <u>they should have invented</u> by now: a device that automatically throws balls for dogs to catch.

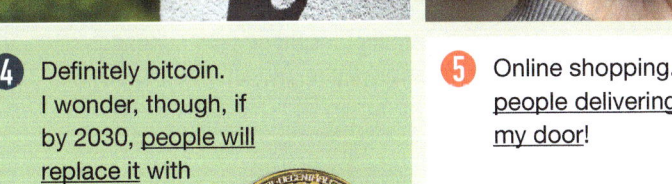

Go to Communication practice: Student A page 162, Student B page 168

6 In pairs, think of three more innovations and describe them, using passives or causative *have*. Say what makes them practical.

Personal Best Write sentences about things you're going to have done in the next month, e.g. *I'm going to have my hair cut.*

9 SKILLS WRITING writing a magazine article ■ articles: *a*, *an*, *the*, zero (–)

9D Accessible spaces

1 A Look at the three pairs of pictures below. Then, in pairs, identify two advantages of picture a over picture b.

1

2

3

B Read the article. Which of your ideas were mentioned?

Universal design

Our city is one of the state's most important tourist destinations, and it's easy to understand why: We have the best parks, museums, and restaurants in the region. The proposed shopping area next to (a) <u>Luna Park</u> will be open seven days (b) <u>a week</u> when it opens in 2022. But, unlike most of the tourist attractions we have now, it should be designed to be accessible.

1 _____?
(c) <u>The new streets and buildings</u> that are planned should meet the needs of all users, including people who may have a physical or learning disability. They should also be practical. Here are a few simple examples:
- Wheelchair-friendly entrances with no steps, which are also safer for (d) <u>the visually-impaired.</u>
- Larger restroom stalls, which provide easier access for wheelchairs.
- Clear signs that use well-known symbols to help people who can't read.

2 _____?
Firstly, making "universal" design decisions means fewer expensive changes in the future. Secondly, these decisions can benefit both people who are physically disabled and those who are not. For example, entrances that don't have steps and larger restroom stalls are more practical for those with suitcases or strollers. User-friendly signs can also be more easily understood by (e) <u>people</u> who don't understand English very well.

3 _____?
Our government has recently passed a law on universal access, and now we have a chance to test its success. Sign this online petition now to remind our leaders that all new buildings and streets must be accessible to everyone.
As a society, we have (f) <u>a moral obligation</u> to everyone who lives here. People need to be able to access and use public spaces and buildings safely and comfortably.

2 Match headings a–c with blanks 1–3 in the article in exercise 1B.
 a What are the benefits?
 b What can *you* do to help?
 c What do we need to do?

9D writing a magazine article ▪ articles: *a, an, the*, zero (–) WRITING SKILLS

 Skill writing a magazine article

To write an effective magazine or newspaper article, it is important to catch and hold the reader's attention.
- Give your article an interesting title.
- Avoid talking about yourself. You are writing for the general public.
- Introduce the topic in an opening paragraph that readers can relate to.
- Develop your ideas in two or three paragraphs. You can use headings to keep the reader interested.
- Summarize your ideas in the last paragraph. Don't add any new information.

3 Read the Skill box. What is the purpose of each paragraph in the article in exercise 1B?

4 In pairs, make a list of four ways to make your city or neighborhood more accessible to those with disabilities.

5 Look at the headings in the article again. In pairs, summarize the answer to each question.

Text builder articles: *a, an, the*, zero (–)

- Use the indefinite article (*a/an*):
1 to talk about something/someone for the first time: ***A*** *new plan is needed.*
2 in expressions of frequency: *This entrance is used several times **a** day.*
- Use the definite article (*the*):
3 before a collective group: *He's collecting money for **the** homeless.*
4 when something has already been mentioned, or is specific: *I really like **the** car across the street.*
- Don't use an article (–):
5 before uncountable and plural nouns in general: (–) *Street signs should be easy to read.*
6 with most proper nouns and cities: (–) *Fifth Avenue is in* (–) *New York*.

6 Read the Text builder. Then match <u>underlined</u> examples a–f in the article with rules 1–6.

7 A Fill in the blanks in the text below with *a/an, the*, or zero (–).

Four ways to make your city a better place now

1 Support culture. _____ great way to support your community is through _____ art because _____ artists and _____ writers can tell _____ story of a city better than anyone else.

2 Bike to work. Commuting can be _____ frustrating experience. Taking _____ public transportation helps to reduce _____ traffic – and your carbon footprint!

3 Volunteer. We know you're busy, but any time you can spare could make _____ huge difference to _____ city you live in.

4 And last but not least, show _____ friendly face. You should treat _____ other people the way you would like to be treated.

B In pairs, rank the ideas in exercise 7A in order of importance for your city. Add two new suggestions.

8 A PREPARE Think of how you want to improve your city or neighborhood, e.g., a stronger community or a better environment and three ways to achieve it.

B PRACTICE Write your article, using the Skill box to help you develop your ideas. Pay attention to the use of definite and indefinite articles.

C PERSONAL BEST Exchange articles with a partner. How many similar ideas did you have?

Personal Best How accessible is your house or apartment? Write a paragraph answering this question.

UNIT 10 The business world

LANGUAGE quantifiers ■ trends and business

10A Careers on the rise

1 A Look at the pictures and read the information about U.S. job trends. Are the numbers increasing or falling?

a Health care professionals
2010: 14 million   2020: 18 million

b Mail carriers
2010: 315,000   2020: 280,000

c Elementary school teachers
2010: 1.5 million   2020: 1.7 million

B In pairs, discuss the information in exercise 1A. Can you think of a reason for each trend? Are the job trends the same in your country?

Go to Vocabulary practice: trends and business, page 152

2 Read the text. Which job would you most/least like to have?

Are these professions for you?

Jobs in some traditional professions are decreasing, while in new fields they're increasing! Whether you're launching your career for the first time or setting up a new business, here are a few options you might like to consider.

1 Video game developers
Have you ever considered a career in game development? If so, you'll probably have little trouble finding a well-paid job. Game designers are in high demand, and the reason is your phone. Mobile technology has created a need for new games, and experts expect to see a major increase in the gaming industry over the next decade.

2 User-experience designers
Would you like to study people's reactions when they use a new product or system, and find ways to improve it based on their feedback? There are few qualified professionals available, so demand is high and growing steadily. Average salaries have nearly doubled in the past decade. Expect quite a few exciting opportunities in the coming years.

3 Health and wellness educators
These days, most people work under a great deal of stress. As a result, an increasing number of companies are hiring health and wellness educators to look after their employees' physical and mental well-being. These specialists offer individual advice and guidance, which usually increases productivity for the company.

---

3 A Are the sentences true (T) or false (F)? Read the text again and <u>underline</u> the four sentences that contain the relevant information.

1 Game developers usually earn high salaries. _____
2 It's relatively easy to find good user-experience designers. _____
3 The job market for user-experience designers is likely to increase. _____
4 Most employees have stressful jobs. _____

B Find the expressions of quantity in the sentences you <u>underlined</u>. Which ones describe large quantities? Which ones describe small ones? Then read the Grammar box.

quantifiers ■ trends and business   **LANGUAGE**   **10A**

Grammar: quantifiers

Large quantities
1 countable:
   I sent my résumé to **quite a few** companies.
   A large number of professions are growing.
2 uncountable:
   A great deal of/A lot of time is needed to apply for jobs.
   He has **a fair amount of** experience in web design.

Small quantities
1 countable:
   I have **a few** business contacts in Japan.
   There are **few/not many** good candidates for this position.
2 uncountable:
   I can invest **a little** money in your company.
   There's **little/not much** information on the website.

Look! We use **both/neither** when referring to two people or things, and **all/none** for more than two people or things:
   Both my parents work. **Neither** (of them) is very happy.
   All my friends are unemployed. **None** (of them) have found work.

Go to Grammar practice: quantifiers, page 130

4 A ▶10.4 **Pronunciation:** *(a) few* and *(a) little* Listen to the conversations. Notice how *a few*, *few*, *a little*, and *little* are pronounced.

1 **Ann** So, how was your first day at work?
   Luke There were quite **a few** friendly faces, but I had very **little** time to socialize.
2 **Bob** So, how was your last day at work?
   Sue Very **few** people came to say good-bye, so I did **a little** work, instead.

B ▶10.4 Listen again and repeat.

5 Read the text and choose the correct options. Can you think of other jobs at risk?

Declining careers: Is your job at risk?

Telemarketers: In the past ten years, job opportunities have fallen by more than 10%, and the reason is simple. ¹*Few / A few* people enjoy receiving sales calls, and as call-blocking technology has improved, ²*a large number of / a fair amount of* companies are now looking for other ways to reach customers.

Bank tellers: ³*Quite a few / A great deal of* tellers will lose their jobs in the next few years, and ⁴*not much / not many* can be done about it. Improvements in mobile banking are to blame, as there's ⁵*little / a little* that can't be done online.

Reporters: Newspapers have lost ⁶*a large number of / a great deal of* money in recent years, and if this trend continues, reporters and other media professionals might lose their jobs. Social media sites, which have changed the way people get their news, are ⁷*all / both* responsible for this.

6 A Rewrite sentences 1–6 below using the words in parentheses.
1 Lots of small stores have gone out of business in my neighborhood. (quite)
2 I had a lot of information about the job market when I finished college. (fair)
3 I don't know many people who raise money for charity. (few)
4 Both my parents are working under a lot of stress right now. (deal)
5 I didn't have much experience when I got my first job. (little)
6 Last year, all my job interviews were unsuccessful. (none)

B Choose two of the sentences and make them true for you, using quantifiers from the Grammar box.

Go to Communication practice: Student A page 162, Student B page 168

7 Look at the trends below. Have the activities increased, decreased, or remained stable?

| dropping out of college | emigrating | using Facebook | watching sports on broadcast TV |

I think quite a few people have dropped out of college in recent years. This is probably because …

Write a paragraph describing one of the trends in exercise 7.

10 SKILLS READING understanding text development ■ complex negative sentences

10B Starting your own business

1 If you wanted to start your own business, which of these ideas would you consider? Give reasons.

- an interior design company
- a café or tea shop
- selling used books
- a computer repair shop
- a health and fitness center
- a marketing business

2 What are the advantages and disadvantages of starting your own business when you're young? In pairs, add an idea to each column below.

Advantages	Disadvantages
(+) You have fewer responsibilities.	(−) You have less time to study.
(+) You can make your parents proud.	(−) It can be hard to raise money.
(+) _____	(−) _____

3 A Read the text, ignoring the blanks. Complete the title with *best* or *worst*.

B In pairs, discuss the text. Which ideas from exercise 2 are mentioned? Which would be true for you?

Skill understanding text development

In a text, sentences are often related to each other. When you recognize the connections, you can understand the text better.
- related words: *Feeling under **pressure**? Here are three strategies to help you deal with job-related **stress**.*
- reference words: *I have two college **degrees**. Neither of **them** has helped me get a job.*
- time and contrast words: ***At first**, I hated my job. **However**, I **soon** got used to it.*

4 Read the Skill box. Fill in blanks 1–5 in the text with a–e below, paying attention to the words in **bold**.

a I **eventually** leased a new car, bought a house, and got my hours down to 50 or 60 hours a week.
b I'm sure that my parents would have **lent** me the $13,000 I needed to start my little shop, but I was committed to doing it myself.
c **In spite of** these **advancements**, the core risks and worries for young entrepreneurs have not changed.
d If I were to risk **it all** now, I'd have a lot to lose.
e **While** I suffered from **both**, I overcame them with blood, sweat, and tears – and time.

Text builder complex negative sentences

Negative sentences are easier to understand if you try to rephrase them:
He had **no one** to trust **but** his parents. = He **only** trusted his parents.
He was **never unsure** of what to do. = He was **always sure** of what to do.
His **lack of** money was a problem. = He **didn't have** any money, and that was a problem.
Worrying **does little to** solve problems. = Worrying **doesn't really** solve problems.

5 Read the Text builder. What do the underlined sentences (a–c) in the text mean?

6 Discuss the questions in pairs.
1 When you choose a career, how important is it to do what you really love? Why?
2 Can you imagine making a decision like the author's? Why/Why not?

Why starting a business at 19 was one of the _____ decisions I ever made

Special to The Globe and Mail Published Tuesday, Sep. 17, 2013   CHRIS GRIFFITHS

I started my first business when I was 19 years old, and that was long before youth entrepreneurship was celebrated the way it is now. I had a retail showroom and a service shop, employees, inventory, bank debt and all the joys and stresses that came with them.

I remember getting a fair bit of attention for starting a business at that age, but it didn't seem like a big deal to me. To me it made perfect sense; after all, I was single, had no dependents and was still living at home. My future seemed like a blank page that allowed me to write my own story.

Being young wasn't helpful when it came to raising capital, I can assure you. (a) Having nothing but a high school education and a well-written business plan did little to calm the nerves of my family's bank.

1_____ Although I was very nervous about getting into debt, a wise man reminded me that $13,000 is a small car payment for most people, and for that amount of risk, you get to try and make a dream come true that could impact the rest of your life.

He was right. The thought of not doing it, and spending the rest of my life wondering "What if?" was riskier than borrowing the money. I sold my rusty Ford and rented a small spot in the center of town. I was officially in business.

Taking the city bus to your own business and scheduling appointments around when you can borrow your parents' car wasn't the glorious start to entrepreneurship I had imagined, but it was a start. In my first year of business, I regularly booked 95-hour work weeks, seldom went out with friends and paid myself only $781 for the entire first year.

Every dollar went back into the business as I needed a strong foundation to build upon. Over time, things started to improve. 2_____ Getting to this point took years, and to be honest, I don't know how I would have done it if it weren't for the advantages of my youth.

You see, I started with the burden of the two most common reasons for business failure: lack of experience and lack of capital. 3_____

I was able to risk all that I had because I didn't have anything. That gets tougher to do later in life. Now I have a marriage, a mortgage and three kids. 4_____ I also don't have the ability to work 95 hours a week or accept $781 as an annual salary. Starting a business later in life requires better planning and more support systems. Sure it's possible, but I definitely benefited from the flexibility that came with starting a business in my youth.

The great thing about starting a small business in my 20s was that I was able to make mistakes on a small scale and learn from them. The more experience I gained, the more the business grew. (b) I was using my youth to my advantage and never really saw it as a disadvantage.

Today I see a lot more support systems for young entrepreneurs and I am pleased to see it become a hot topic and a celebrated achievement. 5_____ (o) They worry about their own lack of experience and lack of ability to raise capital. They worry about taking on such responsibility and risk at a young age.

My advice is always the same: imagine yourself not pursuing your passion; decades from now, will you be looking back on today's opportunity and wondering "What if?"

Chris Griffiths is the Toronto-based director of *fine tune consulting*, a boutique management consulting practice. Over the past 20 years, he has started or acquired and exited seven businesses.

Personal Best   Write a paragraph about someone you know who took a risk.

10 LANGUAGE — comparison ■ word pairs

10C Job interview tips

1 Read the text. Complete blanks 1–4 with a–d below. In pairs, discuss why you shouldn't say a–d in a job interview.

a "I hated my last company."
b "Well, it's on my résumé."
c "I'm really nervous."
d "Things are difficult right now."

Four things you should never say in a job interview

The big day has come. The company has looked through dozens – if not hundreds – of résumés, and one of its managers wants to meet you. So now it's your turn to make an impression! Here are four things you should never ever say!

1 _____ The person interviewing you is aware of that. But even if you're more anxious than you've ever been, please don't say it out loud **over and over**! Companies want to hire people who are confident and who can use self-control.

2 _____ No matter how bad a job was, criticizing a former employer in an interview is one of the worst mistakes you can make. Negativity should be avoided during job interviews, so focus on what you learned while working there.

3 _____ While it's true that the interviewer has this information, he or she needs to listen to you and see if you are as good as your résumé says. How good are your communication and social skills? Can you express yourself clearly? Do you make eye contact? Use the question you're asked as your chance to impress.

4 _____ **Sooner or later**, we all have to face life's **ups and downs**, and most interviewers would be sympathetic to someone who's having a family crisis. But even if you think you may need to take time off, now is not the time to give the impression that your personal life might affect your performance. So, remember: the less you talk about your personal issues, the better.

Do you have an interview coming up? Click here for more advice on how to get your dream job!

2 Match the **bold** expressions in the text above with their definitions 1–3.
1 at some future time _____
2 good and bad experiences _____
3 repeatedly _____

Go to Vocabulary practice: word pairs, page 153

3 A ▶ 10.7 Listen to two friends, Tony and Claire, discussing a job interview. Complete the sentences. Which mistake from the text in exercise 1 did Claire make?

1 For starters, the traffic was slightly _____ _____ usual, so I got there ten minutes late.
2 She was really friendly – by far _____ _____ person ever to interview me.
3 She asked me why I'd left my previous job, and I tried to be _____ _____ _____ possible.
4 But _____ _____ details I gave, _____ _____ she smiled.

B Look at sentences 1–4 in exercise 3A again. Choose the correct option to complete each sentence below.

1 The traffic was *a little* / *a lot* worse than usual.
2 *Some* / *None* of the other interviewers were this friendly.
3 I was *completely* / *mostly* honest.
4 The interview ended *better* / *worse* than it started.

comparison ■ word pairs   **LANGUAGE 10C**

4 Find four sentences expressing comparison in the text in exercise 1. Which one is a superlative sentence? Then read the Grammar box.

> **Grammar   comparison**
>
> **Comparatives:**
> The interview was **far easier than** I'd imagined.
> It's important to listen **more carefully than** usual.
>
> **the ... the:**
> **The less** prepared you are, **the worse** you'll do.
> **The more** questions she asked, **the more** nervous I became.
>
> **Superlatives:**
> That was by far **my worst** interview.
> I was clearly **the least experienced** candidate.
>
> **as ... as:**
> The interview went **as well as** I'd expected.
> The experience wasn't quite **as bad as** I'd thought it would be.
>
> **Look!** After *one of* + a superlative, we use a plural noun:
> He was **one of** the best **candidates** in the group. NOT ~~one of the best candidate~~

Go to Grammar practice: comparison, page 131

5 A ▶ 10.9 **Pronunciation:** sentence stress with *the ... the* comparisons Listen to the sentences. Which words are stressed in each one?

1 The more I study English, the more I like it!
2 The more chocolate I eat, the happier I get!
3 The less I exercise, the more tired I feel!

B ▶ 10.9 Listen again and repeat. Then, in pairs, change the sentences so they are true for you.

6 A Read the text. Complete the sentences with patterns from the Grammar box, using the correct forms of the prompts in parentheses.

New job? Here's your survival guide for the first few weeks.

- **Dress professionally.**
  Research shows that people make a judgment about you almost ¹_____ (soon / they / meet) you. So, to make a good first impression, ²_____ (few / things / important) than dressing professionally.

- **Learn people's names.**
  ³_____ (fast / you / learn / everyone's name / easy) it will be to get along with your coworkers. If you're bad with names, google some memory tricks you can use to help you.

- **Arrive early and leave late.**
  During the first few weeks, make sure you ⁴_____ (arrive / early / leave / late) than most of your coworkers.

- **Listen more than you talk.**
  This can be ⁵_____ (one / hard / skill) to learn, but if you talk too much, you may sound arrogant.

- **Avoid gossip.**
  There may be a lot of gossip at work, but try not to get involved. Repeating gossip is probably ⁶_____ (one / productive / way) to spend your time at work.

B In pairs, discuss the tips in exercise 6A. Which ones are also helpful for college?

Go to Communication practice: Both students, page 1/2

7 In pairs, think of two tips for each topic. Give reasons using comparisons.

Things you should never say or do:
- when talking to a police officer
- on a first date
- when meeting your in-laws for the first time

On a first date, you should never ...
The more you ... , the less you ...

Personal Best   Write three sentences comparing yourself to a family member.

10 SKILLS   SPEAKING   discussing pros and cons ■ being supportive

10D Two job offers

1 A What's most important to you when choosing a job? Take the survey. Rank each factor from 1 (not important) to 5 (very important).

My dream job would have …

1 a boss I respect. ____		4 lots of room for growth. ____
2 coworkers I get along with. ____		5 above-average pay. ____
3 a low level of stress. ____		6 excellent benefits. ____

B In pairs, discuss your answers. How many were the same?

2 ▶ 10.10 Watch or listen to the first part of *Talking Zone*. Write S (Synergy) or FB (Future Bytes) for each sentence.

1 ____ was the second company to approach Ben.
2 ____ has a more relaxed working atmosphere.
3 ____ is closer to his home.
4 ____ pays less.
5 ____ offers room for growth.

3 A ▶ 10.10 Watch or listen again to Ben talking about the two companies. Write P (Pros) or C (Cons) next to each of the things he mentions.

Synergy
____ creativity   ____ hours
____ distance   ____ atmosphere

Future Bytes
____ distance   ____ benefits
____ pay   ____ atmosphere

B How did Ben discuss the two jobs? Complete sentences 1–5 with the words in the box.

> Each one has its pros   I can't make up my mind whether   I'm torn between
> I'm leaning towards   One of the drawbacks of

1 _____ to take it or not.
2 _____ the two jobs.
3 _____ and cons.
4 _____ working there … is that it's really far.
5 _____ Future Bytes.

Conversation builder | discussing pros and cons

We use a variety of phrases to weigh up and consider our options.
I'm torn between working at home and taking an office job.
Each option has its pros and cons.
I can't make up my mind whether to stay with John or break up.
One of the drawbacks of my current job is the pressure.
I'm leaning towards going away for the summer.

4 A Read the Conversation builder. In pairs, ask and answer questions 1–4, using the words in parentheses.

1 I hear you're buying a new car. Congratulations! Have you picked a model? (*I'm leaning … ,*)
2 I'm thinking of renting a house near you. What do you think? (*… pros and cons/One of the drawbacks …*)
3 Any plans for New Year's Eve? (*I can't make up …*)
4 So, have you chosen the baby's name? (*I'm torn …*)

B In pairs, discuss something you haven't made up your mind about yet.

discussing pros and cons ■ being supportive **SPEAKING** SKILLS **10D**

5 ▶ 10.11 Watch or listen to the second part of the show. Why is Ben less enthusiastic about Future Bytes than he was after the first interview? Choose the correct answer.
  a He was misled in the first interview.
  b He didn't do well on the second interview.
  c He got a better offer from another company.

6 ▶ 10.11 Watch or listen again. Are the sentences true (T) or false (F)?
  1 If he does an MBA, Future Bytes will not pay the full tuition fee. ____
  2 Future Bytes has changed its mind about the salary. ____
  3 Ben hasn't given Synergy a final answer yet. ____
  4 Ben made a decision he regrets. ____

> **Skill** being supportive
>
> To be supportive when talking to someone who has a problem, you can:
> - listen carefully, nod, and make eye contact.
> - show sympathy: *I really sympathize.*
> - show the positive side of the problem: *Look on the bright side. The pay is good.*
> - make a suggestion: *You could always call them.*
> - try to cheer the other person up: *Don't let it get you down.*

7 ▶ 10.12 Read the Skill box. Listen to conversations 1–3. Check (✓) the strategies used in each one.

Strategy	1	2	3
show sympathy	☐	☐	☐
show the positive side of a problem	☐	☐	☐
make a suggestion	☐	☐	☐
cheer the other person up	☐	☐	☐

Go to Communication practice: Student A page 163, Student B page 169

8 A PREPARE In pairs, imagine you're upset about something. Prepare a conversation, using one of the ideas below. Think about the pros and cons of the situation, as well as how you feel.

You stained your favorite shirt, and it's difficult to clean.

You can't get tickets for a concert you really wanted to go to.

You haven't heard from a friend for a long time.

You had an accident and damaged your bike.

B PRACTICE Practice the conversation. Take turns explaining why you're upset and being supportive.

C PERSONAL BEST Can you improve the way you show support to each other? Practice again with a new partner. Talk about a different idea.

Personal Best Choose a new situation from exercise 8 and write about the pros and cons of the situation.

9 and 10 REVIEW and PRACTICE

Grammar

1 Cross (**X**) the sentence that is NOT correct.

1. a Unfortunately, my mother slipped on the ice and fell.
   b My mother slipped unfortunately on the ice and fell.
   c My mother slipped on the ice and fell, unfortunately.

2. a Elena has two children, but neither of them go to the school across from their house.
   b Elena has two children, and all of them go to the school across from their house.
   c Elena has two children, and both of them go to the school across from their house.

3. a He has a good memory, extremely.
   b He has an extremely good memory.
   c His memory is extremely good.

4. a A fair amount of people I know work from home.
   b A fair number of people I know work from home.
   c Quite a few people I know work from home.

5. a My boss had me work until 8 p.m. yesterday!
   b I was worked by my boss until 8 p.m. yesterday!
   c I had to work until 8 p.m. yesterday!

6. a The more money you make, the more taxes you should pay.
   b If you earn a lot of money, you should pay a lot of taxes.
   c As much money you make, as much taxes you should pay.

7. a We had our plants watered while we were away.
   b A neighbor watered our plants while we were away.
   c Our plants had watered while we were away.

8. a Lima is by far the biggest city in Peru.
   b Lima is one of the biggest city in South America.
   c Lima is much bigger than all the other cities in Peru.

2 Use the words in parentheses to complete the sentences so they mean the same as the first sentence.

1. Our house is the same size as my cousin's house.
   Our house _____ my cousin's house. (big)
2. I realized a thief had stolen my bag.
   I realized _____ a thief. (stolen)
3. Schools spend a lot of money on books.
   Schools spend _____ on books. (deal)
4. If I go to bed late, I feel tired in the morning.
   The later _____ in the morning. (more)
5. Did you know that Alex has cut Yolanda's hair?
   Did you know that _____ Alex? (had)
6. She doesn't leave the house very often anymore.
   She _____ . (rarely)

3 Choose the correct options to complete the text.

To: _____
From: _____

This is a photo of the house we bought three years ago. As you can imagine, we ¹*immediately started / started immediately* making a lot of changes. Since we bought it, ²*we have / we've had* a ³*great deal / large number* of work done to the house. Before, there was very ⁴*few / little* light downstairs, but that problem ⁵*solved / was solved* by having one of the walls ⁶*took / taken* out. We also ⁷*added / had added* some new windows in the living room. Our friends thought we were really crazy when we bought it, but now ⁸*they say always / they always say* it's ⁹*a / the* most beautiful house they've ever been in! And, actually, my husband and I agree that the work was far ¹⁰*more / most* enjoyable than ¹¹*all / either* of us had expected. We didn't have as ¹²*many / much* arguments ¹³*than / as* we could have had! In my view, the more work you ¹⁴*have done / had done* on a house, the ¹⁵*most / more* pride you take in it.

Vocabulary

1 Circle the word or expression that is different. Explain why.

1. ruby   multi-colored   maroon   teal
2. ounce   gallon   pint   quart
3. mile   inch   foot   ton
4. light green   reddish   lavender   dark blue
5. lengthen   widen   deep   shorten
6. once or twice   side by side   ups and downs   sick and tired

REVIEW and PRACTICE **9** and **10**

2 Complete the text with the words in the box.

seriously   account   peace
over   cons   taking   clue   raise

A lot of my friends in college spend their weekends at the beach or having each other ¹_____ for lunch, whereas I volunteer at the local hospital with three other students. In addition to ²_____ turns looking after patients, we help manage projects to ³_____ money for the hospital. There are pros and ⁴_____ to volunteering, but I take my role very ⁵_____. Working means I have a good understanding of real-life issues, while most of my friends don't have a ⁶_____ about life outside college. I think my experience at the hospital will definitely be taken into ⁷_____ by future employers when I start to apply for jobs after I graduate. But although I enjoy volunteering, I have to admit I enjoy the ⁸_____ and quiet on my days off!

3 Choose the correct options to complete the sentences.

1 I wish our teacher would type his comments because I *have trouble reading / take care not to read* his handwriting.
2 Sara submits her essays late every week, but she always has *nothing to do with it / an excuse*.
3 He's not a very nice person. He takes *pleasure / pride* in other people's bad luck.
4 *Sooner or later / Now and then* I drive to work, but I usually take the bus.
5 Maria is normally home by 6 p.m., so I don't have *a clue / an open mind* why she isn't here yet.
6 At first I could hardly speak a word of English, but *by and large / little by little* I picked it up, and now I'm pretty fluent.
7 Did I tell you I'm *setting up a / going out of* business? If it's successful, I'll be rich!
8 They're planning on *lengthening / widening* the road here so there's more space for cars to pass.

4 Put the words in the box under the correct headings.

teal   increase   fall   turquoise   ounce   foot
drop   go up   violet   rise   ton   go down
grow   decrease   inch   bronze

Positive trends	Colors
_____ _____	_____ _____
_____ _____	_____ _____
Length and weight	**Negative trends**
_____ _____	_____ _____
_____ _____	_____ _____

Personal Best

Lesson 9A Write four sentences using adverbs of comment, degree, manner, and frequency.

Lesson 10A Name two things you have in large quantities and two you have in small quantities.

Lesson 9A Write five sentences about yourself or people you know using collocations with *have* and *take*.

Lesson 10A Describe three current business or economic trends in your country.

Lesson 9B Describe objects you own that are silver, multicolored, reddish, or light blue.

Lesson 10B Write three complex negative sentences about yourself or people you know.

Lesson 9C Name three things you have had done in the past year.

Lesson 10C Describe four things that are very good, very bad, very strange, and very funny, using superlatives.

Lesson 9C Describe the length and weight of four things you own.

Lesson 10C Write four sentences using word pairs.

Lesson 9D Write three sentences about your classroom using a definite article, an indefinite article, and a zero article.

Lesson 10D Describe the good and the bad aspects of a situation you know about.

93

UNIT 11 Fact and fiction

LANGUAGE present and past modals of deduction ■ science

11A It can't have been real!

1 A Look at the headlines of three articles. Then match the words in **bold** with their definitions a–d.

1. Mind-reading experiment **carried out** on live TV!
2. New **data** to be **gathered** in horoscope study
3. Major **breakthrough** in UFO sightings

a development _____
b done _____
c collected _____
d factual information _____

B Which of the three articles would you like to read most? Do you believe in any of these things?

Go to Vocabulary practice: science, page 154

2 A Read the blog post. Which headline in exercise 1A does it refer to?

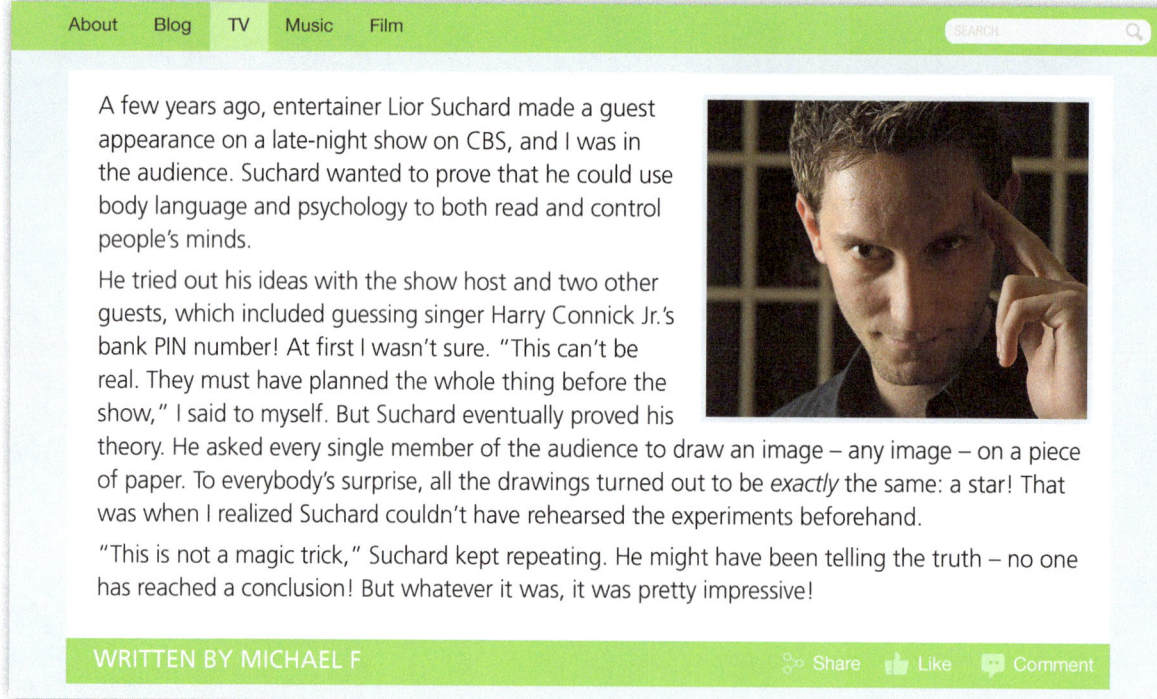

A few years ago, entertainer Lior Suchard made a guest appearance on a late-night show on CBS, and I was in the audience. Suchard wanted to prove that he could use body language and psychology to both read and control people's minds.

He tried out his ideas with the show host and two other guests, which included guessing singer Harry Connick Jr.'s bank PIN number! At first I wasn't sure. "This can't be real. They must have planned the whole thing before the show," I said to myself. But Suchard eventually proved his theory. He asked every single member of the audience to draw an image – any image – on a piece of paper. To everybody's surprise, all the drawings turned out to be *exactly* the same: a star! That was when I realized Suchard couldn't have rehearsed the experiments beforehand.

"This is not a magic trick," Suchard kept repeating. He might have been telling the truth – no one has reached a conclusion! But whatever it was, it was pretty impressive!

WRITTEN BY MICHAEL F

B Choose the correct option to complete the sentence below.

By the end of the show, Michael *thinks he knows / has no idea* how Suchard did his trick.

3 A ▶ 11.4 Listen to a couple watching the show on TV. Who's more skeptical, Mitch or Jane? Do both people agree in the end?

B ▶ 11.4 Who said these sentences, Mitch (M) or Jane (J)? Listen again and check.

1. Oh, come on! <u>They must be pretending</u> they're surprised.
2. Of course not. <u>The man must have known the numbers</u> before the show.
3. <u>He might have known them</u>, but who knows? How can you be so sure?
4. Well, <u>you might be right</u> about ghosts, but "no UFOs"? Come on!
5. No way! <u>That couldn't have been a UFO</u>!

present and past modals of deduction ■ science **LANGUAGE** **11A**

4 A Match meanings a–c with the underlined phrases in sentences 1–5 in exercise 3B.
  a Definitely. I'm sure. ____ ____
  b Definitely not. I don't think it's true. ____
  c Maybe, but I'm not sure. ____ ____

B Which underlined phrases are in the present? Which are in the past? Then read the Grammar box.

Grammar present and past modals of deduction

Something you think is/was true:
You **must be reading** my mind. That's exactly what I think.
What was that noise? You **must have heard** it.

Something you think is/was possibly true:
You **could be** right, I guess. I'll take your advice.
I think I **might have made** a mistake. Sorry!

Something you don't think is/was true:
Are you kidding? This story **can't be** real!
Bad weather? That **must not be** the reason.
It **couldn't have been** Joe you saw. He's on vacation.

5 Read the text in exercise 2A again and find more examples of modals of deduction.

Go to Grammar practice: present and past modals of deduction, page 132

6 A ▶ 11.6 **Pronunciation:** reduction of past modals Listen to the sentences. Notice how *have* is pronounced.
  1 You must **have** seen it – it was right there!
  2 She might **have** forgotten – who knows?
  3 It could **have** been Michael on the phone.
  4 She couldn't **have** left the office yet. It's only 4 p.m.

B ▶ 11.6 Listen again and repeat. In pairs, add a line before each sentence to create a conversation.

7 A Rewrite the two possible underlined responses to 1–5 using modals of deduction.
  1 "What's that bright light in the sky? It doesn't look like an airplane to me!"
    a "Relax! I'm sure it's an airplane."
    b "Weird, isn't it? Maybe it's a UFO or something."
  2 "I just read my horoscope. Tough week ahead!"
    a "You're definitely kidding, right? Who believes in that stuff?"
    b "You mean astrology.com? I'm sure they know what they're talking about."
  3 "I dreamed about my aunt last night, and she called me this morning!"
    a "I'm sure it was a coincidence."
    b "Wow! Maybe she read your mind."
  4 "Who do you think built the pyramids?"
    a "The Egyptians definitely built them. Who else?"
    b "It definitely wasn't anyone on this planet!"
  5 "Homeopathy cured my constant headaches, you know."
    a "Homeopathy? You're definitely not serious!"
    b "I used to suffer from insomnia, and maybe homeopathy cured me, too."

B In pairs, discuss the responses to 1–5 in exercise 7A. Which response, a or b, would you give?

Go to Communication practice: Student A page 163, Student B page 169

8 Look at the three pictures. Who are the people? Where are they? What might have happened in each picture? Use modals of deduction in your answers.

Personal Best Write some sentences explaining what you think happened during the TV show in exercise 2.

11 SKILLS

LISTENING identifying conclusions ■ the "flap" in American English ■ opposite adjectives

11B Fake news

1 In pairs, complete the headlines so they are fake news (= news that isn't true). Use your imagination!

1. Scientists create plant that …
2. A new study reveals that people who …
3. Facebook reveals plans to …
4. The government has announced that …

2 Why is fake news such a big problem these days? In pairs, decide what you think the two most important reasons are.

1. Some journalists are **irresponsible** and don't check their facts.
2. Fake news isn't necessarily **illegal**.
3. **Controversial** news stories attract more clicks.
4. Fake news can sound **believable** sometimes.

Go to Vocabulary practice: opposite adjectives, page 155

3 ▶ 11.8 Watch or listen to the first part of *Talking Zone*. Which ideas from exercise 2 are mentioned? What is Alan's job?

Alan

Skill identifying conclusions

When you listen to informal conversations where lots of ideas are mentioned quickly, it can sometimes be hard to identify the conclusions. It is helpful to listen for:
- a logical order – for example, a problem is usually described before advice is given.
- expressions that show a key point is being repeated: *it's important to point out*, *you should always*, *whereas … now …* , etc.
- words related to the main theme: *fake news*, *propaganda*, *social media*, etc.
- expressions that imply a consequence: *If you don't do x, then y*; *always do x*, etc.

4 ▶ 11.8 Read the Skill box. Then watch or listen again. Number the conclusions below in the order you hear them.

a ☐ Fake news is not a recent phenomenon.
b ☐ It's getting harder and harder to know if a news story is true.
c ☐ You may need to do research in addition to reading the article.
d ☐ There are ways to find out if a news story is fake.
e ☐ Anyone can now create fake news easily.

5 Have you ever accidentally shared fake news stories on social media? How did it happen? Discuss with your partner.

identifying conclusions ■ the "flap" in American English ■ opposite adjectives LISTENING   SKILLS 11B

6 A ▶11.9 Watch or listen to the second part of the show. What story did Alan create?

B What happened to the story? Choose the correct answer.
a Everyone quickly realized that it wasn't true.
b It appeared on a TV news program.
c Alan sent it to various news organizations.

7 ▶11.9 Watch or listen again. Put the sentences in the correct order.
____ He created his website 'fakenewsspotter.com'.
____ He shared it with a fake social media account.
____ The story broke on 'real' TV news.
____ He created a fake picture and news story.
____ The story went viral very quickly.
____ Alan was surprised and tried to deny the story was real.

> **Listening builder** the "flap" in American English
>
> In American English, when the sound /t/ follows a vowel and the next word begins with a vowel, the /t/ can sound like a very light *d* to listeners, or even an *r*. This also occurs when there is a /t/ in the middle of a word, e.g. *better*. This sound is called a "flap."
> *I wish I could help you, **but I** can't.* [bəraɪ]
> *Grab a coat and **put it on**.* [pʊrɪɑn]

8 A ▶11.10 Read the Listening builder. Then listen and (circle) the flap in the underlined part of each sentence from the video.
1 It's gotten <u>a lot of attention</u>!
2 <u>It was about a polar bear</u>, wasn't it?
3 And were you surprised <u>by the reaction at all</u>?
4 So, did you do anything <u>after you saw it on the news</u>?
5 It must have been frustrating <u>that it spread so fast</u>.

B In pairs, practice saying the sentences.

9 In pairs, create a fake news story using one of the photos below. Share your story with another pair. Whose is the funniest? Whose is the most believable?

Personal Best Describe a fake news story you've heard that many people believed.

11 LANGUAGE — reported speech patterns ■ sleep

11C The science of sleep

1 A Match the words in **bold** in the survey with pictures a–d.

Do you have a sleep problem?

Answer each question with a number from 3 (all the time) to 0 (never).

Do you ever:
1. **oversleep**? ____
2. **snore** so loudly it wakes people up? ____
3. wake up often in the middle of the night? ____
4. **doze off** at work/school? ____
5. wake up feeling tired and spend the whole day **yawning**? ____

If you scored more than 10 points, you might have a sleep problem!

B Take the survey in pairs. Who has more trouble sleeping: you or your partner?

Go to Vocabulary practice: sleep, page 156

2 Read the text. Check (✓) the correct answer. Short-sleeping is …

a probably genetic. ☐
b pretty common. ☐
c fully understood by science. ☐

SHORT-SLEEPING: Is it always a problem?

Jimena Sánchez, a 28-year-old teacher, has been living on about four hours of sleep every night for as long as she can remember. Early this year, her husband persuaded her to look for a sleep specialist, and the diagnosis took everyone by surprise.

Dr. John Scorsone, a researcher from the sleep-disorder clinic she attended, assured Jimena she didn't have a sleep problem. After a series of tests, Dr. Scorsone concluded that Jimena was a "short sleeper" – someone who only needs a few hours' sleep each night.

Jimena claims she fits that description: "I go to bed at midnight, wake up at around four, and I never feel tired," she says. Jimena's previous doctors had suggested sleeping pills, but she refused to take them: "I'm glad I said no. Now I know that I'm not sleep-deprived. I just don't need much sleep – that's all."

Dr. Scorsone based his diagnosis on a 2009 study at the University of Utah that discovered a rare gene in a mother and daughter who were able to function well on very little sleep. Since then, other studies have been carried out, but scientists are "only just beginning to understand this phenomenon," Dr. Scorsone claims.

It has been estimated that 1%–3% of the population consists of short-sleepers. For example, former UK Prime Minister Margaret Thatcher supposedly claimed she needed just four hours' sleep a night.

I asked Jimena if she felt short-sleeping was a problem: "No, not at all. It's so peaceful and quiet when I get up. I love it!"

3 A Complete the sentences with the verbs in the box. Then read the text and check.

> assured   claimed   persuaded   refused

1. Jimena's husband _____ her to look for a sleep specialist.
2. Dr. John Scorsone _____ Jimena she didn't have a sleep problem.
3. Jimena's previous doctors had suggested sleeping pills, but she _____ to take them.
4. Margaret Thatcher supposedly _____ she needed just four hours' sleep a night.

reported speech patterns ■ sleep **LANGUAGE 11C**

B Match a–d with sentences 1–4 in exercise 3A. Then read the Grammar box.
a verb + (that) + clause: *He said (that) he was bored.* ____
b verb + object + (that) + clause: *She told me (that) she hadn't been there before.* ____
c verb + infinitive: *My parents agreed to lend me some money.* ____
d verb + object + infinitive: *My doctor advised me to lose some weight.* ____

> **Grammar** reported speech patterns
>
> Direct statements: Reported statements:
> "You need more sleep." → He said (that) I **needed** more sleep.
> "OK, I'll pick up the kids." → She agreed (that) she **'d pick** up the kids./She agreed **to pick up** the kids.
>
> Direct questions: Reported questions:
> "Did you call Tim?" → She asked me if/whether I **had called** Tim.
>
> Direct commands: Reported commands:
> "Apologize to your boss." → She urged me **to apologize** to my boss.

Go to Grammar practice: reported speech patterns, page 133

4 A ▶ 11.14 **Pronunciation:** /t/ and /d/ Listen to the sentences. When are /t/ and /d/ fully pronounced in the underlined phrases?

1 He <u>told me</u> he was selling his car, but I <u>told him</u> I wasn't interested.
2 She <u>urged me</u> to see a doctor, and I <u>promised I</u> would.
3 I <u>asked a</u> simple question, but his explanation <u>confused me</u> even more.
4 My brother <u>asked me</u> to help him, but I <u>said I</u> was busy.

B ▶ 11.14 Listen again and repeat. In pairs, choose two sentences from exercise 4A and create short conversations that include them.

5 ▶ 11.15 Read the conversation and report what Ann and Roy said, using the verbs in parentheses. Listen and check.

Ann You look tired. ¹(tell)
Roy I've been sleep-deprived for weeks. ²(explain)
Ann Oh, is something wrong? ³(ask)
Roy It's just work-related stress. ⁴(assure)
Ann I've been under a lot of stress, too. ⁵(mention)
My boss is a very difficult person. ⁶(say)
Roy Really?
Ann Yes, and I have a secret. ⁷(confess)
Roy What?
Ann I won't tell you. ⁸(refuse)
Roy Why not?
Ann You'll laugh at me! ⁹(think)
Roy I won't laugh! ¹⁰(promise)
Ann I listen to Solfeggio frequencies on YouTube. ¹¹(admit)
You should definitely give them a try. ¹²(encourage)

1 Ann told Roy he looked tired.

Go to Communication practice: Both students, page 173

6 A What strategies have you used to achieve the following?

> quit an unhealthy habit   stick to an exercise program
>
> deal with a difficult person   get over stress at school or work

B Report some of the things your partner told you to the rest of the class.

Gloria told me she was trying to eat less sugar. She explained that ...

Personal Best Write four things people have told you today using reported speech.

99

11 SKILLS WRITING writing a personal recommendation ■ order of adjectives

11D I first met Julia …

1 A When was the last time you recommended the following?

- a restaurant
- a person
- a book
- a movie
- a music track
- a tourist site

B Discuss with your partner and give details.

2 Read the personal recommendation below. What does the writer feel is important in a roommate?

To: Sue Parker
Subject: Julia Bannon

Dear Sue,

1 Julia Bannon has asked me to recommend her as a roommate, and it is with pleasure that I do so. I first met Julia five years ago when I was her geology professor. Last summer, Julia returned to our town for a summer job and lived with me and my family.

2 When she stayed with us, Julia was a cooperative, considerate roommate. She always kept her room neat and clean, helped with the housework, and sometimes even cooked delicious Italian meals for us. Also, Julia is one of the most thoughtful people I have ever met. She was always willing to help, even when we made last-minute requests. Once, my husband and I had to go on an emergency trip, and Julia offered to babysit for us even though she had made other plans.

3 Julia is an easygoing young woman with a great sense of humor. At the same time, she is extremely responsible and hardworking. As a geology major, Julia worked on a number of challenging environmental projects in my classes, and I was impressed by how carefully she gathered and analyzed data before reaching a conclusion. In her personal life, she also avoids reaching quick conclusions and tries to find something in common with everyone she meets. She tries her best to understand people, and, as a result, she has many friends.

4 My experience with Julia Bannon was entirely positive, and I would not hesitate to recommend her as a roommate. Please feel free to contact me at 205-555-3246 with any questions.

Sincerely,
Gloria Winfrey

3 Answer the questions below.
1 How does Gloria know Julia?
2 Does Gloria know Sue, do you think?
3 Is the recommendation written in a formal or informal style?

writing a personal recommendation ■ order of adjectives **WRITING** **SKILLS** **11D**

Skill — writing a personal recommendation

To write an effective personal recommendation, it's important to:
- explain how you know the person: *I first met Julia five years ago.*
- share details about someone's relevant personal qualities: *She was one of the most thoughtful people I have ever met.*
- give specific examples of those qualities: *She offered to babysit for us even though she had made other plans.*
- offer to provide more information: *Please feel free to contact me.*

4 A Read the Skill box. In which paragraph (or paragraphs) does Gloria:
1 say how Sue can get in touch with her? _____
2 say what kind of person Julia is? _____
3 explain how she knows Julia? _____
4 give specific examples of Julia's behavior? _____

B Find at least two examples of points 2 and 4 above in the recommendation in exercise 2.

Text builder — order of adjectives

When we use more than one adjective before a noun, adjectives of opinion come before adjectives of fact:
Julia is an **easygoing young** woman.
She cooked **delicious Italian** meals for us.
Julia worked on a number of **challenging environmental** projects.

Look! Always use a comma between two adjectives of the same kind, e.g., two adjectives of opinion:
Julia was a **cooperative, considerate** roommate.

5 A Read the Text builder. Then read the extracts from some personal recommendations below. Correct the mistakes in the underlined phrases.
1 Mike's a hardworking reliable member of our team, who is famous for his French classic dishes.
2 Christina is a young bright woman who provided excellent customer service when she worked for us.
3 Kevin is a polite friendly person. He has loved animals since he was a young boy, and dreams of becoming a vet.
4 I met Giselle in high school, and we have developed a close meaningful friendship. She has always been great with children, and I can't think of a better person for the job.
5 As an undergraduate motivated student, Pablo wrote dozens of literary interesting essays, and he has achieved a very high level of English.

B Use the adjectives in exercise 5A to talk about people you know.

6 A Match the people in sentences 1–5 of exercise 5A with positions a–e below.
a sales representative _____
b chef in a restaurant _____
c English teacher _____
d dog walker _____
e babysitter _____

B Now match these adjectives with the positions. There is more than one answer.

> caring creative responsible gentle energetic
> outgoing amusing lively supportive trustworthy

7 A **PREPARE** Choose one of the positions in exercise 6A and think of someone you would like to recommend.

B **PRACTICE** Write your recommendation, using the Skill box to help you develop your ideas. Include some examples of adjectives of opinion and fact.

C **PERSONAL BEST** Exchange recommendations with your partner. Is your partner's recommendation convincing?

Personal Best Write a paragraph recommending yourself for one of the positions in exercise 6A.

UNIT 12 New discoveries

LANGUAGE present and future unreal conditions ■ phrasal verbs (2)

12A Must-have apps

1 A Read the descriptions of three apps. Match the phrasal verbs in **bold** with definitions a–c.

Best apps of the decade: our critics' picks

Always forgetting your password? *1Password* remembers all your log-in information for you and lets you **sign in** to different websites with just one password. Definitely worth a try.

Trying to **work out** a way to deal with the junk on your phone? Get *CCleaner* and delete all the files that may be making your phone slow. Highly recommended.

Can't find a pen and paper? *Evernote* helps you **note down** all kinds of things at home, work, and school. It's just like a notepad, so you can even label all your photos. A must-have.

a write down ____   b log in ____   c discover ____

B Are you familiar with these apps? In pairs, tell your partner about your top three apps.

Go to Vocabulary practice: phrasal verbs (2), page 157

2 A Read the social media comments. Do they refer to real or imaginary apps?

1. Wouldn't it be cool if they <u>invented</u> an app that could send some of your battery – wirelessly – to someone whose phone was running out of power?
   💬 5 ♡ 20 ⇄ 9

2. <u>I wish</u> there was an app that would go through my social-media feed and automatically delete all political discussions!
   💬 16 ♡ 40 ⇄ 12

3. <u>If only</u> there were an app that would let me back up my work phone conversations. Now that would be useful for legal reasons.
   💬 9 ♡ 14 ⇄ 3

4. <u>It's about time</u> they came up with an app to help me translate what my cat is trying to say! I mean, surely that's not impossible?
   💬 56 ♡ 73 ⇄ 25

5. To be honest, there are more important apps missing. <u>I'd rather</u> they created an app to hang up the phone whenever I got a call from a telemarketer!
   💬 13 ♡ 8 ⇄ 15

B In pairs, discuss which two apps you think would be the most popular. Why?

3 Read the comments in exercise 2A again and choose the correct options below. Then read the Grammar box.
1. In comment 1, *invented* has a *past / future* meaning.
2. The underlined expressions in 2–5 are used to talk about *real / imaginary* situations.
3. *Wish* and *if only* express the *same / different* ideas.
4. *Would rather* expresses a *preference / warning*.

102

present and future unreal conditions ■ phrasal verbs (2) **LANGUAGE** **12A**

Grammar: present and future unreal conditions

Second conditional:
If they **invented** a robot to clean my house, it **would save** me a lot of time.

wish and **if only**:
I **wish** there **was/were** someone that could help me!
If only my computer **didn't have** a virus.

It's about time:
It's about time they **fixed** the bugs in this app.

would rather:
I'**d rather** my son **didn't spend** so much time online.

Look! We use a past-tense verb to refer to present or future time in most unreal conditional sentences, but we use *would* or *could* to express future time after *wish* or *if only*:
Present: *If only my computer didn't have a virus* (but it does).
Future: *I wish they would invent an app to cook my dinner* (but they haven't yet).

Go to Grammar practice: present and future unreal conditions, page 134

4 A ▶ 12.3 **Pronunciation:** consonant-vowel linking Find two or three examples of consonant-vowel linking in the underlined part of each sentence.

1 <u>I wish I had a little more time</u> to spend with my family and friends.
2 <u>If only I could spend a week away</u> from home. I'm really stressed out.
3 <u>It's about time I went back</u> to the gym and lost a few pounds.
4 <u>I'd rather our English teacher didn't give us</u> so much homework every class!

B ▶ 12.3 Listen again and repeat. Which sentences are true for you?

5 Complete the blanks with the correct form of the verbs in the box.

> be   work   exist   have   invent   say   not waste

What's a product that you wish ¹_____**, but doesn't?**   Log in   Search

A device designed to display how much water is being used during a shower. We ²_____ so much water if we had a device like that. **TomD**

I have very cold feet – literally – and I often tell myself, "If only there ³_____ something I could wear to keep my feet warmer." Erm … electric socks maybe? **Ann87**

It's about time they ⁴_____ a washer-dryer that could also fold clothes. **Madguy**

I wish I ⁵_____ a gadget to erase people's memories – like in the movie *Men in Black*. So if I ever ⁶_____ something I regretted, I'd just have to push a button. **Luk4**

↳ Well, I'd rather they ⁷_____ out a way to block people – but not online! I mean, in real life! **Jennifer22**

6 Rewrite the sentences using the words in parentheses.
1 It's a shame cell-phone batteries die so quickly. (wish / last / longer)
   I wish cell-phone batteries lasted longer.
2 It's a shame "quality" tablets are so expensive. (wish / be / affordable)
3 Why do commercial sites have so many pop-ups? (if only / have / fewer)
4 Why is the weather in my country so cold? (rather / be / warmer)
5 I'm really impatient. (if only / be / patient) I'd like to be calmer. (wish / be)
6 I don't have a fast Internet connection. (about time / get / faster)

Go to Communication practice: Student A page 163, Student B page 169

7 Choose at least two topics to discuss in pairs. Use present and future unreal conditional sentences. What would you change about your …

> personality?   routine?   neighborhood?   home?   career/studies?   country?

Personal Best Add a social media comment to exercise 2A.

12 SKILLS READING predicting ■ adverbs and intended meaning

12B A robot revolution?

1 Look at the pictures on page 105. In pairs, discuss which jobs you think robots can learn to do better than humans.

2 Look at the title of the text. In pairs, discuss how you would answer the question. Then read paragraphs 1 and 2 to check if you were right.

> **Skill | predicting**
>
> **Predicting helps you become actively involved in the reading process and increase your understanding of a text. You can use:**
> - your knowledge of the topic and text type to predict the kind of information that will be presented.
> - the last sentence(s) of a paragraph to predict the content of the next one.
> - linking words and adverbs to help you predict the rest of the sentence.

3 A Read the Skill box. Check (✓) the topics you think the text will discuss.
1. Why robots are taking human jobs ☐
2. The difficulties of teaching robots good manners ☐
3. Whether robots can increase productivity ☐
4. The importance of politeness in general ☐
5. Why it's important for robots to behave like humans ☐

B Read the rest of the text and check.

4 Read the text again. Predict the correct question, a or b, for the blanks in paragraphs 3 and 5. Then <u>underline</u> the answers in paragraphs 4 and 6.

Paragraph 3:
a Why would we want robots to mimic human behavior?
b What if robots become more polite than humans?

Paragraph 5:
a But should they be taught?
b But are they impossible to learn?

> **Text builder | adverbs and intended meaning**
>
> Adverbs can help you understand a writer's intended meaning clearly. Often these are "comment adverbs."
> *Will robots take over the world?* **Fortunately**, *the answer is no.* (I'm glad they won't.)
> **Apparently**, *scientists are working on a new model.* (This is what I've heard.)
> *The XKX model is* **surprisingly** *intelligent.* (I didn't expect it to be.)

5 Read the Text builder. Then look at the <u>underlined</u> adverbs in the text. Are the sentences below true (T) or false (F)?

The writer is:
1. very surprised that robots might be able to learn good manners. _____
2. sure that robots will learn how to say "please" and "thank you" at the right time. _____
3. surprised that some people think this research is a waste of time. _____
4. not sure whether it's possible to teach robots complex social rules. _____
5. happy that robots are not going to take over the world. _____

6 Discuss the questions in pairs.
1. Which jobs will robots never be able to do better then humans?
2. Why do some people want to develop the capabilities of robots?
3. Why are others resistant to this?

"Please" and "thank you": can robots be taught how to be polite?

By Tom Goldberg, Staff Writer | December 28, 2018 11:30am ET

1 Imagine you were at an important meeting, and your cellphone rang. You would probably mute the phone or go outside to pick up the call. Now, imagine the call was answered by a robot. Obviously, without the kind of social awareness that humans possess, it would just automatically answer the call and disrupt the meeting. After all, robots can't learn human etiquette. Or can they?

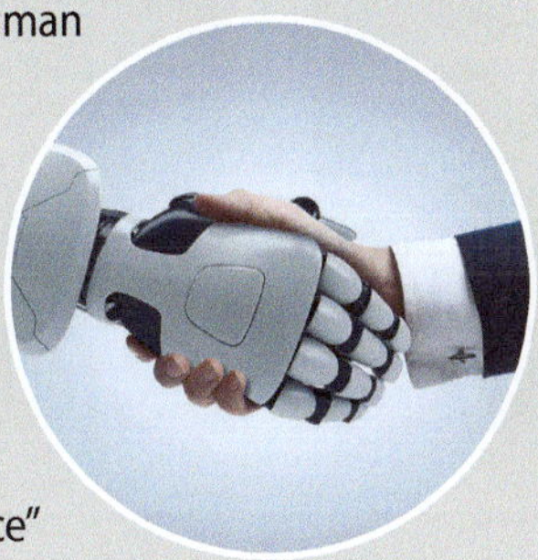

2 [1]Shockingly, in the not-so-distant future they might be able to, thanks to a number of groundbreaking discoveries in the field of artificial intelligence (AI), which studies the "intelligence" of machines.

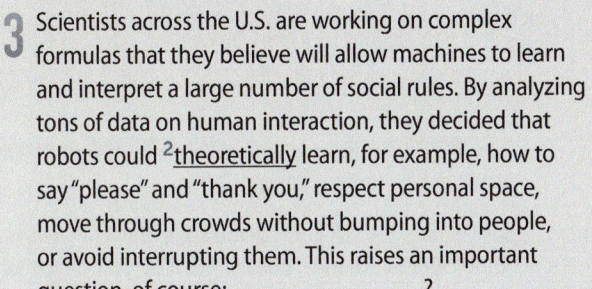

3 Scientists across the U.S. are working on complex formulas that they believe will allow machines to learn and interpret a large number of social rules. By analyzing tons of data on human interaction, they decided that robots could [2]theoretically learn, for example, how to say "please" and "thank you," respect personal space, move through crowds without bumping into people, or avoid interrupting them. This raises an important question, of course: _______________ ?

4 Some people would [3]understandably dismiss these discoveries as a waste of time, but if "machine courtesy" is not relevant now, it might matter in the near future when robots are part of our everyday lives. So if you walked into a coffee shop and you were greeted by an automated barista, at the very least you'd expect it to say "hello," serve you coffee, and thank you at the end. If it yelled at you or dropped your coffee, you'd probably look for another store – and get mad at robots in general. "If robots are rude, people will become even more resistant to artificial intelligence," says Marie Martin, one of the scientists studying the topic.

5 So far, the researchers have managed to create some concepts for this kind of machine learning, but there is still a long road ahead. For robots to learn "good manners" and apply them flexibly, beyond everyday business transactions, they would need to be taught a never-ending list of subtle social rules that humans take decades to pick up on, such as when it's appropriate to interrupt someone and how to have complex interactions with complete strangers. These "rules" are context-sensitive and may also vary from one culture to another. _______________ ?

6 [4]Obviously, it's too soon to tell. Robots might never be able to display human-like behavior – at least not in our lifetimes. But one thing we can be sure of: while robots are busy saying "excuse me" and "thank you," [5]luckily we won't have to worry about them taking over the world!

Personal Best Write a paragraph about one of the questions in exercise 6.

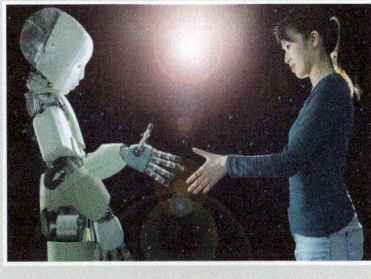

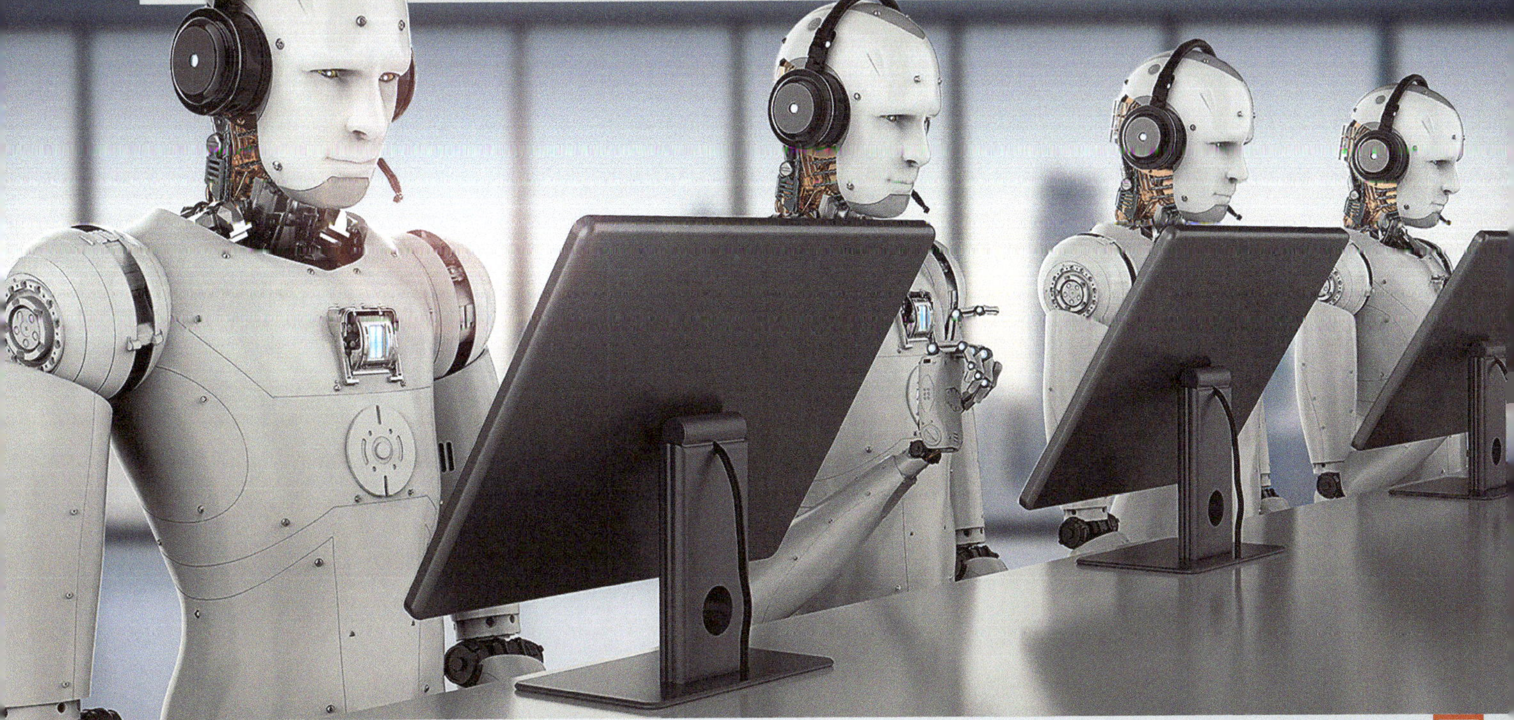

12 LANGUAGE
past unreal conditions ■ collocations with *come*, *do*, *go*, and *make*

12C Changes and regrets

1 Look at the pictures below. What differences are there between the two cars?

2 A Read the text and fill in the blanks with *come*, *do*, *go*, or *make*.

⚡ Going electric

Buying a first car is an exciting event in the lives of many young people. And before long, it may be a fully electric car. That's because in the near future many major cities are planning to ¹_____ away with both gasoline and diesel cars. It could happen fast, some experts say. By the year 2040, 90 percent of cars in the U.S., Canada, and Europe could be electric. And China may have as many as 60 million.

After all, cars replaced horses in a brief 10–15 years. If you had wanted a car in 1910, you might not have been able to afford one. Henry Ford's Model T cost the equivalent of $137,000. However, by 1921, when it had dropped to the equivalent of $35,000, a lot of people decided to ²_____ for it. And even if you still couldn't afford a car, it was easy to ride one of the new electric street cars.

You didn't have to ³_____ much effort at all to enjoy another new form of transportation!

Electric cars are still in the price range of the old Model T, but that may soon change. Lisa Farrow, a 25-year-old writer from Connecticut, bought her first electric car last year and had this to say: "If I'd bought this car sooner, I'd have more money. I wish I hadn't waited." That's because it can go as far as 180 miles on a single charge. "If only someone had told me electric cars were four-times more energy efficient," Lisa added.

Electric cars may be self-powered, too, before too long. Sending a car to pick up your groceries could be a dream that will ⁴_____ true in the very near future!

B In pairs, discuss if you would like to own an electric car. Why/Why not?

Go to Vocabulary practice: collocations with *come*, *do*, *go*, and *make*, page 157

3 ▶ 12.5 Listen to two friends talking about electric cars. Who thinks they are a good idea? Tom, Ann, or both of them?

4 A ▶ 12.5 Choose the correct options to complete the sentences. Listen again and check.
1. I wish I *waited* / *'d waited* a little bit longer before buying my car, too.
2. I might *buy* / *have bought* an electric car last month if I *knew* / *'d known* more about them.
3. If I *bought* / *'d bought* an electric car, I *was* / *'d be* able to save more.
4. If only I *read* / *'d read* this article sooner.

B In pairs, answer the questions about the sentences in exercise 4A. Then read the Grammar box.
1. What tense are the correct verbs in sentences 1 and 4?
2. Which sentence begins in the past, but ends in the present?
3. Which sentences only refer to the past?

past unreal conditions ■ collocations with *come*, *do*, *go*, and *make*

LANGUAGE 12C

📖 Grammar past unreal conditions

Third conditional:
If they **had bought** an electric car sooner, they **would have saved** money.

***wish* and *if only*:**
I **wish** I **hadn't sold** my old motorbike.
If only I **had realized** sooner how much my life **would change**.

Mixed conditional:
If I **had bought** a house in the country last year, life **would be** better today.
If we **didn't have** three cars, we **would have moved** into a smaller place by now.

Go to Grammar practice: past unreal conditions, page 135

5 A ▶ 12.7 **Pronunciation:** stress in conditional sentences Listen to the sentences. Which <u>underlined</u> word in each sentence is stressed?

1. You <u>could have texted</u> me if you'd known you weren't coming.
2. It's a shame you couldn't go to the party. You <u>would have enjoyed</u> it!
3. If I'd gone to the mall last night, I <u>might have seen</u> your brother.
4. If I'd known it was your birthday, I <u>would have bought</u> you a present!

B ▶ 12.7 Listen again and repeat. In pairs, think of a response to each sentence.

6 A ▶ 12.8 Complete the texts with the correct affirmative or negative form of the verbs in the boxes. Listen and check.

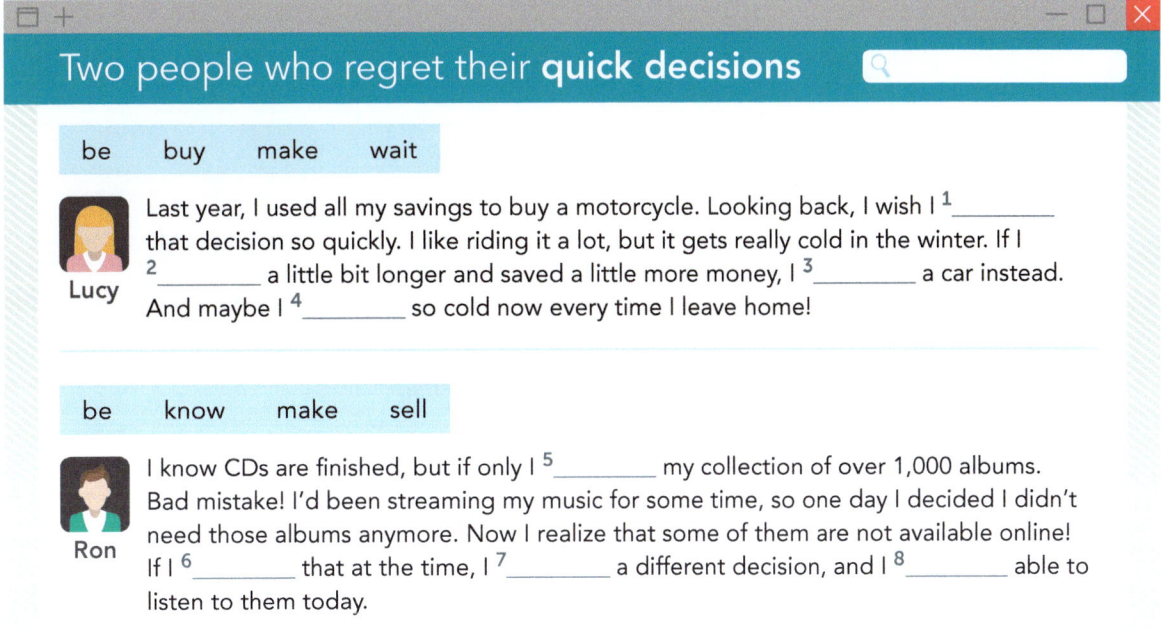

B Have you ever regretted a decision you made too quickly? What would be different now?

Go to Communication practice: Both students, page 173

7 In pairs, choose a topic. Start with *I wish* or *If only* and use third or mixed conditional sentences to explain what happened as a result.

Can you think of …
1. something you wish you hadn't bought/sold?
2. a party you wish you hadn't been to?
3. a city you wish you'd visited sooner?
4. someone you wish you hadn't met?
5. someone you wish you'd met sooner?
6. something you wish you'd said when you had the chance?

Personal Best Write a paragraph about one of the topics in exercise 7.

12 SKILLS SPEAKING talking about future trends ■ keeping a conversation going

12D Fads and trends

1 In pairs, discuss which of these technologies will still exist in 2025. Why do you think they will/won't last?

smartwatch

fitness tracker

smart glasses

2 ▶ 12.9 Watch or listen to the first part of *Talking Zone*. Which items in exercise 1 does Ben think will definitely last?

3 ▶ 12.9 Choose the correct options to complete the excerpts from the conversation. Watch or listen again and check.

Ben	You know, you should probably keep it – the new models are ¹*likely / unlikely* to get bigger as they get even smarter.
Abigail	You think so?
Ben	Oh, yeah. It's totally ²*conceivable / inconceivable* that smartwatches will replace smartphones.
Abigail	That is cool, especially when people are more concerned about health and fitness than ever before.
Ben	And the new models are amazing! There's no going back. All these wearable devices ³*aren't / are* bound to last.
Abigail	Really? I've never seen anyone wearing them.
Ben	Yeah, they're still relatively rare, so whether they'll become more popular or just vanish without a trace ⁴*is anyone's guess / is pretty clear*.

Conversation builder — talking about future trends

We can use a range of structures to talk about future trends and how probable we think they are.
3D printing **is likely to** *last*. (probable)
Robots **are bound to** *become more common*. (very probable)
It's conceivable that *"smart clothes" will become popular*. (possible)
Whether smartphones will last **is anyone's guess**. (not probable)

4 Read the Conversation builder. Which sentence shows that the speaker is not at all sure?

5 Rephrase opinions 1–4 with the words in parentheses. Then, in pairs, say if you agree or disagree.

In the next 10 years …
1 digital downloads will probably disappear. (bound to)
2 we probably won't find intelligent life on other planets. (likely to)
3 flying cars are a real possibility. (conceivable that)
4 who knows if robots will replace teachers. (anyone's guess)

talking about future trends ■ keeping a conversation going **SPEAKING** SKILLS **12D**

6 ▶ 12.10 Watch or listen to the second part of the show. Complete the sentences with one word.
1 Ben finds fidget spinners _____ and compares them to stress balls.
2 Many teachers think fidget spinners are distracting, so they are _____ in many schools.
3 Ben describes the Tamagotchi as an egg-shaped _____ .
4 Abigail had three Tamagotchies, and it was hard to stop them from _____ .
5 Ben used _____ so he would remember to feed his Tamagotchi.

7 ▶ 12.10 Number the sentences from Ben and Abigail's conversation in the order you hear them. Watch or listen again and check.

a ☐ **Abigail** I let the poor things die and moved on to the next fad, <u>whatever it was</u>.
b ☐ **Ben** <u>It's a bit like</u> those stress balls but it's more fun. Give it a try!
c ☐ **Abigail** Speaking of fads, <u>is that one of those</u>, what do you call them, fidget … ?
d ☐ **Ben** I sure did! You had to feed them <u>I don't know how many times</u> a day to keep them alive, right?
e ☐ **Abigail** Yeah, but <u>what exactly</u> do you do with it?
f ☐ **Ben** <u>You mean</u> the virtual pet? <u>The thing that looked like</u> an egg-shaped keychain?
g ☐ **Abigail** <u>That reminds me</u>, did you use to have a Tamagotchi at school?
h ☐ **Ben** Spinners? Pretty cool, huh?
i ☐ **Abigail** That's the one!

🔧 **Skill**   keeping a conversation going

To keep a conversation going, it's important to keep the listener involved. You should:
• smile, nod, and use expressive intonation to show interest.
• introduce a new topic in a general way.
• ask for clarification.
• describe things the listener may be unfamiliar with.
• avoid unnecessary details and be vague, if necessary.

8 Read the Skill box. Then write the <u>underlined</u> phrases in exercise 7 in the correct column(s). Some phrases can go in more than one column.

ask for clarification	describe	introduce a new topic	be vague, if necessary

Go to Communication practice: Both students, page 173

9 A PREPARE In pairs, choose a current fad or trend. Use the ideas in the pictures below. Develop a conversation around it.

smartwatch

smart speaker

eggcutter

instant print camera

B PRACTICE Practice the conversation in pairs, keeping it going for at least one minute.

C PERSONAL BEST Listen to another pair's conversation. How successfully do they keep the conversation going?

Personal Best   Write a paragraph about a fad or trend that you really like.

11 and 12 REVIEW and PRACTICE

Grammar

1 Choose the correct options to complete the sentences.

1 I know a really funny joke, but you might *have to hear / have heard* it before.
2 If I *was / would be* older, I'd be earning a lot more money than I do. It's disgraceful!
3 I can't believe you walk up this hill every day! You must *be / have been* in very good shape.
4 I made a lot of mistakes when I was younger. I wish I *knew / had known* then what I know now.
5 John asked me to *meet / have met* him outside his office. I wonder what he wants.
6 I'd love to stay longer, but I have to go home. If only I *didn't have / wouldn't have* to go to work tomorrow!
7 Yvonne urged me *apply / to apply* for the job.
8 If my parents *hadn't moved / didn't move* to France when I was a child, I wouldn't be fluent in French now.

2 Use the words in parentheses to complete the sentences so they mean the same as the first sentence.

1 I don't think it's possible that Francis lied to me.
   Francis _____ . (couldn't)
2 I wish we had talked about this yesterday.
   It _____ good if _____ about this yesterday. (would)
3 My mother asked, "Did you do your homework?"
   My mother asked me _____ . (whether)
4 His boss said, "You'll have to work on the weekend."
   His boss _____ . (told)
5 You should have apologized to me before now.
   _____ to me. (time)
6 I think you have a lot of money because you have an expensive sports car.
   _____ because you have an expensive sports car. (must)
7 I'm certain they haven't found a cure for diabetes.
   They _____ . (can't)
8 I really don't want him to bother me all the time.
   I _____ . (wish)
9 "I made the chocolates myself."
   She _____ . (explained)
10 You don't live near here, so I can't help you out.
   _____ help you out. (lived)

3 Choose the correct options to complete the job reference.

Anton has been working with us for four years, and during that time, he has been a tremendous asset to the team. In fact, if it ¹*wasn't / isn't* for his hard work, we ²*won't / wouldn't* be in such a strong position today. When he began his role here, I thought he must ³*have worked / work* in a similar position before, but he explained that he ⁴*didn't / hadn't*. He joined us at a very difficult time when everyone was under a lot of pressure, which ⁵*can't / could* have been easy for him, but he didn't seem to have any problems picking up the job. He told us he ⁶*was / will be* just a quick learner! Anton ⁷*must / can* have a natural ability for predicting problems because he has saved us from difficult situations several times. On one occasion, he heard of our plans to restructure our organization, and he politely asked us if we ⁸*considered / had considered* doing things in a different way. At first, we assured him that we ⁹*were / are* experienced enough to know the best course of action, but Anton urged us ¹⁰*to reconsider / reconsidering*. He was able to analyze the situation so effectively that we began to wonder if we ¹¹*might / must* be making a mistake. We took his advice and changed our plans. Looking back, if we ¹²*didn't follow / hadn't followed* his advice, we ¹³*would have / have* had serious problems a few months later. If we ¹⁴*are / were* able to persuade Anton to stay we would, but, frankly, it's about time he ¹⁵*would move / moved* to a bigger company where he can fulfill his potential.

Vocabulary

1 Circle the word or expression that is different. Explain why.

1 take a nap   oversleep   fall asleep   doze off
2 data   prove   gather   analyze
3 note down   sign in   write down   break down
4 geologist   psychology   economics   law
5 decision   experiment   agreement   conclusion
6 unimaginable   unsatisfactory   unacceptable   undesirable

REVIEW and PRACTICE 11 and 12

2 Match the words and expressions in the box with definitions 1–8.

> analyze   irresponsible   do your part
> evidence   uncontroversial   hypothesis
> illegal   go for something

1. against the law
2. unlikely to cause disagreement
3. not properly considering the consequences of your actions
4. look at something in detail
5. a proposed explanation based on limited information
6. try hard to get or achieve something
7. facts or information that show that something is true
8. help to achieve something

3 Choose the correct options to complete the sentences.

1. I was sad when the vacation ended, but all good things *go for / come to* an end.
2. Try not to worry about losing your phone. I'm sure it will *hang up / turn up*.
3. He must be very tired. Did you notice he was *yawning / snoring* throughout dinner?
4. You should have come to the soccer game with us yesterday. Nine goals! It was *unimpressive / unbelievable*!
5. It took a long time to work *out / through* the correct answer.
6. I'm afraid I didn't understand your essay. It really doesn't *make / have* sense.
7. I studied *psychology / psychologist* at college because I'm interested in the human mind.
8. As a visitor, you'll need to sign *in / on* when you arrive.

4 Complete the text with the words in the box.

> controversial   doing   through   came   carried   keep
> sleep-deprived   irresponsible   awake   done

Although scientists have always been interested in sleep, not much research has been ¹_____ out on what happens when someone stays ²_____ for a long time. This is because ³_____ experiments with ⁴_____ people is very ⁵_____ . Due to possible health problems, many scientists believe it is ⁶_____ to ⁷_____ someone awake for long periods. However, the record for the longest time spent staying awake is apparently 11 days! In 1964, Randy Gardner went ⁸_____ this experience, and when the experiment ⁹_____ to an end, he claimed it had not ¹⁰_____ him any harm!

Personal Best

Lesson 11A
Use modal verbs to make three deductions about the people in your classroom.

Lesson 11A
Name four things scientists commonly do.

Lesson 11B
Write six sentences using three pairs of opposite adjectives.

Lesson 11C
Report four things that people have told or asked you recently.

Lesson 11C
Describe your typical sleeping habits using sleep-related vocabulary.

Lesson 11D
Describe five classmates using at least two adjectives for each person.

Lesson 12A
Describe three present and future unreal situations. Explain the consequences of each one.

Lesson 12A
Write six sentences using three phrasal verbs that have more than one meaning.

Lesson 12B
Describe three things that have happened recently and comment on each one with an adverb.

Lesson 12C
Name three important past events and describe the consequences if they had not happened.

Lesson 12C
Name two collocations for *make*, *do*, *go*, and *come* and write a sentence with each one.

Lesson 12D
Describe three trends and predict how these trends could change in the future.

111

GRAMMAR PRACTICE

7A Relative clauses; reduced and comment clauses

 7.2

They're the students **who had the party**.
This is the test **that I'm most worried about**.
Anyone **hoping to learn a language** needs to practice every day.
Anyone **chosen for the play** will be told shortly.
My history professor, **who was excellent,** retired last year.
I think I failed my exam, **which is really a disaster**!

Defining relative clauses

We use a defining relative clause to say which person, thing, or place we are talking about.

He's the person who/that told me about this course.
This is the book that/which I enjoyed so much.
They're the couple whose son was in the news last week.
That's the college where my sister went.

We can omit *who*, *that*, and *which* when the verbs in the main clause and the relative clause have different subjects. We can't omit the relative pronoun when it refers to the subject of the relative clause.

He is the man (who/that) I saw at the library.   *She's the woman who teaches French.*

Reduced relative clauses

We can reduce defining relative clauses that refer to the subject of the sentence. When the original clause is in the simple present, the verb changes to an *-ing* form.

Anyone wanting (= who wants) *to take the exam late needs to speak to me.*
Students waiting (= who are waiting) *to enter the lecture hall should move to the side.*

We can also reduce relative clauses in the passive when they refer to the subject of the sentence. The context determines whether the sentence refers to the present or past.

Assignments submitted (= which <u>were</u> submitted) <u>last month</u> *will be returned in April.*
The actors seen (= who <u>are</u> seen) *on the video you're watching <u>now</u> aren't professionals.*

To make a reduced relative clause negative, we put the word *not* before the verb.

Anyone not waiting (= who's not waiting) *in line, please take a seat.*

Non-defining relative clauses

A non-defining relative clause gives us extra information about something in the main clause. If we omit this clause, the sentence still makes sense. We add a comma before a non-defining clause.

This is my friend Barbara, who was in my math class last year.

A non-defining relative clause in the middle of a sentence is more common in writing.

This course, which is a requirement for psychology majors, is only in the morning.

> **Look!** Notice the difference in meaning between the sentences below.
> *The students who passed the exam received a certificate.* (= only some students passed)
> *The students, who passed the exam, received a certificate.* (= all the students passed)

Comment clauses

We can also use a non-defining relative clause to comment on another clause. Comment clauses are common in conversation.

I failed my biology exam, which my parents weren't too happy about.

1. Link the two sentences with a relative clause. Use commas where necessary.
   1. I'd like to go to a school. I can study surf science there.
      I'd like to go to a school where I can study surf science.
   2. That's the teacher. Her class on ethical hacking was excellent.
      That's the teacher _____.
   3. I can't find my notes. I took them yesterday.
      I can't find my notes _____.
   4. This is my brother's old cell phone. He gave it to me last month.
      This is my brother's old cell phone _____.
   5. In one progressive school, some students skip class. They're not punished.
      In one progressive school, students _____ aren't punished.
   6. The next module is compulsory. It includes creating a comic.
      The next module _____ is compulsory.

2. Rewrite the sentences with reduced relative classes. Check (✓) the sentences that are passive.
   1. Students who cheat on any exam will not graduate.
      Students cheating on any exam will not graduate.
   2. Books that have been borrowed from the library must be returned by tomorrow.
      _____.
   3. Those who want to take the test on Saturday, please come speak to me.
      _____.
   4. Everyone who uses this lab has to be very careful with the equipment.
      _____.
   5. Students who are sent away to school are often homesick.
      _____.
   6. People who don't need foreign languages often don't study them.
      _____.

3. Choose the best comment clauses to complete the sentences.
   1. My children hardly ever put their phones down, *which is really annoying / which is encouraging*.
   2. I'm learning to ski, *which doesn't require any practice at all / which is a lot harder than I thought*.
   3. Students arriving late can't take the exam, *which seems really unfair / which has increased traffic problems*.
   4. They say "practice makes perfect," *which is definitely true / which doesn't apply to playing tennis*.
   5. My neighbor was very noisy, *which isn't why we stayed / which is why we moved*.

◀ Go back to page 59

7C Present and future real conditions

7.10
If I **get up** early, I **do** more during the day.
If you **search** online, you**'ll find** a lot of material.
Until I **try** something, I **won't say** I'm not good at it.
As long as you**'re** motivated, you can learn a new language.
Provided that this room **is** available, we**'ll meet** here next week.
Unless you **learn** to cook, you**'ll spend** a lot of money on food.
Even if you **don't like** the course at first, you might enjoy it later.

Zero and first conditionals

We use the zero conditional to talk about routines or situations that are generally true, including facts. We use the simple present in both the *if* clause and the main clause.

If students take their work seriously, they always do well.
When I listen to my favorite songs, I immediately start to relax.

We use the first conditional to talk about the result of a possible action. We form the *if* clause with *if* + simple present, and we form the main clause with *will* or a modal verb + base form, or an imperative.

They'll be late if they don't leave immediately.
If you come to the party on Saturday, you might meet someone.
If at first you don't succeed, try, try again. (proverb)

We can put either clause first with no change in meaning. However, if we put the main clause first, we don't use a comma between the two clauses.

You'll really like hiking if you give it a try.
If you look for an apartment, you'll find one.

Future time clauses

We use the simple present, not *will* + base form, after words and phrases like *when*, *until*, *before*, *after*, and *as soon as* when we are referring to the future.

I'll give you a call as soon as I get out of class.
She won't talk to him until he apologizes.

Alternatives to *if*

Several other words express conditions and are alternatives to *if*. We use the simple present after them to refer to the future.

As long as and *provided* (*that*) mean the same as *if* and can be followed by an affirmative or negative verb. *Provided* (*that*) is a little more formal than *as long as*.

As long as you know what you want, it's not hard to plan your future.
You'll do well on your finals provided (that) you don't wait until the last minute to study.

We can use *unless* to mean *if* + ... *not*.

Unless you work harder, you won't pass your exam. = *If you don't work harder, you won't pass your exam.*

Even if expresses a contrast and a condition and means *despite the possibility that*.

Even if you find English difficult, you'll definitely improve if you practice.
We can still go out to dinner even if you get home late.

GRAMMAR PRACTICE

1 Check (✓) the sentences that are correct. Correct the incorrect sentences.

1 If you don't understand a word, look at the context. _____
2 If I start my report now, I finish it this afternoon. _____
3 We don't do much work if we study together in the same room. _____
4 Before you will become a serious tennis player, you have to practice a lot. _____
5 If you have some acting lessons, you'll become less self-conscious. _____
6 You won't know if you like skiing until you'll try it. _____

2 Choose the correct options to complete the sentences.

1 You can learn to play an instrument *even if* / *unless* you've never taken lessons before.
2 *As long as* / *Unless* you practice, it's hard to improve your English.
3 The course will begin on Monday, *provided* / *even if* there are enough students.
4 She's planning to get a job *as soon as* / *as long as* she leaves school.
5 I'm sure you'll do very well *unless* / *as long as* you keep working hard.
6 They'll probably want to have a meal *when* / *until* they get here.

3 Rewrite the sentences with *as long as*, *even if*, or *unless*.

1 Provided that I review my notes, I always do well on tests.
_____
2 Despite the possibility that you're not athletic, you can still enjoy learning a sport.
_____
3 If we don't give up social media, we'll never improve our social skills.
_____
4 I'll do my best to help you, provided that you tell me the truth.
_____
5 If I don't make a note of this, I'll forget it.
_____
6 I'm sure you'll have a great time despite the possibility that you don't have much money.
_____

◀ Go back to page 63

GRAMMAR PRACTICE

8A Using linkers (2)

 8.2

Whereas most people sleep late on weekends, I get up early.
Some people like comedy shows, **while** others are really bored.
Unlike many of my friends at school, I'm not interested in technology.
I gave away my TV **as** I never watched it.
Because of the high rent, we've had to close our store.
I'm in much better shape **as a result of** my training program.
This is a very important decision. **Therefore**, we need to think about it carefully.

Expressing a contrast or comparison

We use a clause with *whereas* or *while* to express a contrast or comparison.

Most older people still watch TV, whereas younger people choose YouTube videos.
One of us wants to stay home on weekends, while the other likes to go out.

We can also use *whereas* and *while* to mean *although* or *in spite of the fact that*.

I haven't gone ice-skating in years, whereas I loved it when I was young.
While I don't really like spinach, I eat it sometimes.

We can also use *unlike* to express a comparison.

Unlike all the people I know, I hate shopping.

Look! Be careful not to confuse the two meanings of *while*.
While I was watching TV, my phone rang. (= when)
While I sometimes turn on the TV to relax, I usually read, instead. (= whereas)

Expressing a reason

We use *since* and *as* to express a reason. They mean *because*.

Since I only read e-books, I've thrown out many of my paper books.
I'm going to forget about my friend Dave as he never calls me.

We also use *due to*, *because of*, and *as a result of* to express a reason. They are frequently followed by a noun.

Due to/Because of/As a result of illness, we had to cancel the concert.
We canceled the course due to/because of/as a result of lack of interest.

When *due to* is followed by a clause, we use *due to the fact that*. This is more formal than *because* or *since*.

The library closed due to the fact that it had no money. NOT *due to it had no money.*

We can also express a reason with *therefore* and *as a result*. *Therefore* is a little more formal than *so*.

This show is very popular. Therefore/As a result, other similar shows have been produced. = *This show is very popular, so other similar shows have been produced.*

We start a new sentence with *therefore*. We do not use a comma before it.

The heating system has broken down. Therefore, we have closed the school.
NOT *The heating system has broken down, therefore, we have closed the school.*

Look! Be careful not to confuse the two meanings of *since*. *Since* can be followed by an *-ing* form of a verb only when it means *from the time when*.
Since moving/I moved here, I've made many new friends. (= from the time when)
Since I live in New York, there's always a lot to do. (= because)

---

1 Choose the linker in parentheses which means the same as the linker in the sentence.

1 While (*Whereas / When*) I once wanted to become rich, now I'm not interested in money.
2 Apartments outside the city are cheaper. As a result (*Unlike / Therefore*), many families are moving out.
3 Since (*As / Therefore*) there are so many things to do, I have trouble making a decision.
4 Netflix has been so popular due to (*as a result of / since*) viewers' desire for flexibility.
5 Although (*Unlike / While*) having a dog has many advantages, it's also a lot of work.
6 While (*When / Whereas*) I eat dinner, I sometimes watch the news.

2 Choose the correct options to complete the text.

¹*As / Whereas* moviegoers need to feel they're getting the most for their money, theaters are always looking for new ways to impress them. ²*While / Therefore*, the movie industry is borrowing ideas from the airline industry. Now movie seats may be assigned, ³*since / unlike* just a few years ago. In addition, they may have comfortable foot rests that pop up ⁴*while / whereas* you watch. ⁵*Due to the fact that / As a result of* watching a movie is a much more pleasant experience than it used to be, fewer people are complaining about the cost. They're even buying dinner at the theater ⁶*since / due to* an evening at the movies has become luxury entertainment!

3 Rewrite the sentences with words from the box that mean the same as the underlined words. Use each option once. Add any words you need.

| as a result   as /since   due to   therefore   while |

1 <u>Whereas</u> everyone used to watch programs on TV, now many of us watch them online.
_____
2 Sporting events attract large audiences. <u>Therefore</u>, many TV stations want to broadcast them.
_____
3 <u>Because of</u> new technology, DVDs have become a thing of the past.
_____
4 <u>Due to the fact that</u> there are so many shows, the audience for each one is small.
_____
5 News is always available online, <u>so</u> people don't watch the news on TV so much.
_____

◀ Go back to page 67

8C -ing forms and infinitives

 8.8

Playing computer games can be hard to stop!
I **have trouble concentrating** sometimes!
I **encouraged** my son **to take** a vacation.
I **let** a friend **borrow** my computer.
I **remembered to turn off** my phone before class started.
I **remembered turning off** my phone, but it rang anyway.

We use the -ing form:
- after prepositions and certain verbs, including *avoid, enjoy, feel like, finish, hate, keep, like, love, (don't) mind, miss, prefer, recommend,* and *suggest.*
  We watched six episodes without stopping.   I suggest talking to a lawyer.
- as the subject of a sentence.
  Keeping up with technology is important to me.
- in expressions with a negative meaning, such as *There's no point, It's no use/good, I can't help, I have trouble, I have a hard time,* and *I have a problem.*
  I have trouble saving money.   It's no use talking to him.
- We put *not* before an -ing form to make a negative.
  I love not having to get up early on weekends.

We use the infinitive:
- after certain verbs, including *afford, agree, decide, expect, forget, help, hope, learn, need, offer, plan, promise, refuse, want, would like/love/hate/prefer.*
  I can't afford to buy any more clothes.
- after adjectives.
  It's hard to think about summer when it's so cold.
- to give a reason.
  I called my friend Sally to see if she could help me.
- We put *not* before an infinitive to make a negative.
  I promise not to be so critical of people in the future.

Infinitive vs. base form:
- With some verbs, we use the infinitive after the object. These verbs include *ask, encourage, expect, tell, want,* and *would like.*
  I want you to try to spend less time on the Internet.
- With *make* and *let*, we use the base form after the object. We can also use the base form after *help* + object.
  I made him put his phone away. NOT ~~I made him to put his phone away.~~
  I let her see my photos.   She helped me finish my homework.

We use the -ing form or the infinitive:
- with *begin, continue,* and *start* with no change in meaning.
  I started playing/to play video games when I was very young.
- with *forget, remember, stop,* and *try* with a change in meaning.
  I forgot about inviting everyone to my house. = I forgot that I'd done something.
  I forgot to buy the groceries. = I forgot I needed to do something.
  I remember having a meal here. = I remember that I've done something.
  I remembered to turn off my phone. = I remembered I needed to do something.
  I stopped using social media. = I did not do something any more.
  I stopped to talk to them. = I paused in order to do something.
  I tried not having a TV. = I experimented with something.
  I tried to tell you. = I made an effort to do something.

GRAMMAR PRACTICE

1 Complete the sentences with the correct form of the verbs in parentheses.

1 _____ (eat) a whole bar of chocolate made me realize I was out of control.
2 I always have a hard time _____ (finish) my assignments on time.
3 I really can't afford _____ (go) on vacation.
4 We went to the mall _____ (do) something different for a change.
5 It's really hard not _____ (cry) when I see a sad movie.
6 I expected _____ (be) more surprised when my old boyfriend called.
7 I recognized your face right away and remember _____ (see) you once before.
8 Have you tried _____ (listen) to the radio? That might help you go to sleep.

2 Rewrite the sentences. Correct the mistakes. Some sentences have two mistakes.

1 There's no point spend so much money on shoes.
   _____
2 I'm looking forward to not have so much homework next semester.
   _____
3 I don't mind not have a new phone, but I would like buy a new tablet.
   _____
4 I asked my parents buy me a motorcycle, but they said no.
   _____
5 Don't worry. I won't forget stop to pick up some milk.
   _____
6 I really feel like see the movie, but I don't want go today.
   _____
7 Joe made me to promise go to the doctor about my headaches.
   _____
8 I stopped watch the news on TV a couple of years ago.
   _____

◀ Go back to page 71

GRAMMAR PRACTICE

9A Position of adverbs

 9.3

Luckily, I decided to change my lifestyle.
This book was **amazingly** helpful.
Our teacher **slowly** explained what we had to do.
I've **frequently** considered taking a break from school.
I explained my reasons very **carefully**.

Beginning of a sentence

Comment adverbs (*actually, amazingly, incredibly, luckily, obviously*) give the speaker's opinion and often modify the whole sentence. Therefore, they often go at the beginning of the sentence.

Actually, I'm very unhappy with my apartment right now and want to redesign it.
Amazingly, I got a full scholarship when I was in college.

Middle of a sentence

Comment adverbs can also give the speaker's opinion of an action or state. When they are used like this, they go in the middle of the sentence.

I've stupidly left home without any cash.   *You're obviously artistic.*

Some adverbs of degree (*very, extremely, amazingly, incredibly*) modify adjectives and come before them.

She was amazingly talented. NOT *She was talented amazingly.*

Other adverbs of degree (*a lot, a little, a bit*) modify adjectives or verbs. When they modify adjectives, they come before them, but when they modify verbs, they come after them.

He's a bit talkative. (*a bit* modifies the adjective *talkative*)
She rested a little when she got home. (*a little* modifies the verb *rested*)

Adverbs of manner (*slowly, clearly, carefully, truly*) modify verbs and often go before the verb. We cannot place them between a verb and its object.

She carefully considered her decision. NOT *She considered carefully her decision.*

Adverbs of frequency modify verbs. They go before the main verb, but after the verb *be*.

He's always positive, and he never complains. NOT *he complains never.*

Adverbs of frequency go after an auxiliary verb.

I've often considered changing my lifestyle, but I haven't done anything about it.

Look! Some adverbs (*really, quite*) may be comment adverbs or adverbs of degree. The position of the adverb reflects the meaning.
It's really a fantastic opportunity to study here. (comment adverb)
It's a really great course, and I'm glad I signed up for it. (degree adverb)

End of a sentence

Adverbs of manner (*slowly, clearly, carefully*) may also go at the end of a sentence. Putting adverbs at the end of a sentence gives them more emphasis.

She entered the room suddenly.

An adverb of manner comes after an adverb of degree.

You're not talking very clearly. (degree + manner)

1 Check (✓) the sentences that are correct. Correct the position of the adverbs in the incorrect sentences.
   1 I've considered often changing my job. _____
   2 Incredibly, I got an A on my exam. I never expected it. _____
   3 The thief managed to steal quickly the car. _____
   4 He's shy a bit, and so he sometimes has trouble at work. _____
   5 It was very cold, but we didn't have any gloves. _____
   6 After the phone call, my friends left quickly. _____
   7 He was handsome extremely, but he wasn't a very nice person. _____
   8 I was able to relax a little when the plane landed. _____
   9 They don't know much English, so just pronounce clearly the words. _____
   10 The buses are late in the mornings, so I prefer usually to ride my bike to work. _____

2 Choose the correct options to complete the text.

> ¹*Incredibly / Obviously*, we'd all love to have a beautiful house, but it's ²*really / fortunately* difficult to find a house at a reasonable price. ³*Clearly / Amazingly*, a friend of mine offered to design one for me. I looked over ⁴*the plans carefully / carefully the plans*, and I could ⁵*imagine easily / easily imagine* myself in the house. I was ⁶*actually / extremely* lucky, and I ⁷*often thank / thank often* my friend for her design. It's a great place, and I ⁸*very / truly* love it!

3 Complete the conversations with the adverbs in parentheses in their correct positions.
   1 A Are you excited about going away to college? (very)
     B Well, I feel nervous (a bit), but I'm sure it will be OK.
   2 A You look like someone who's shy, but only at first. (a little)
     B I'd say that's very accurate. (amazingly)
   3 A I'm ready for the exam now. I've prepared for it. (carefully)
     B That's great! You work hard, don't you? (always)
   4 A I admire my uncle. (truly)
     B He's a sensitive person (really), and he's kind. (incredibly)

◀ Go back to page 77

9C Passives and causative *have*

▶ 9.12
The package **was delivered** two days ago.
Our proposal **is being considered** right now.
Before long, all our money **will have been spent**.
Your bike **could be stolen** if you don't lock it up.
The teacher **had us take** our books out.
I might **have my hair cut** this weekend.

Forming the passive

In active sentences, the focus is on the person that does the action. In passive sentences, the focus is on the action itself or on the thing that the action affects. We often use the passive if we don't know, or it's not important, who did the action.

Our office is being painted this week.

We can use *by* in a passive sentence to say who does an action. We often use *by* when the person who does the action is new information.

My sink was fixed by my neighbor. He's a plumber.

We form the passive with a form of the verb *be* + past participle. We can use the passive with most tenses and modal verbs.

	active	passive
simple present	They usually interview people here.	People are usually interviewed here.
simple past	They called him last night.	He was called last night.
present perfect	We've completed the project.	The project has been completed.
present continuous	A doctor is seeing him.	He's being seen by a doctor.
past continuous	She was cleaning the house.	The house was being cleaned.
past perfect	They'd arrested him by the time we arrived.	He'd been arrested by the time we arrived.
modal verbs	You can hire them for $25 a day.	They can be hired for $25 a day.
future perfect	She'll have fixed it by then.	It will have been fixed by then.

We form negatives and questions in the usual way with a form of the verb *be*.

It hasn't been washed.   Has it been washed?

Look! The passive is not usually used in the perfect continuous tenses or with continuous or past modal verbs.
They've been keeping him in the hospital. NOT *He's been being kept in the hospital.*
They might be calling you now. NOT *You might be being called now.*

Causative *have*

A causative sentence may be active or passive. We form an active causative sentence with the verb *have* + object + base form.

They had us wait in line to enter the museum.

We form a passive causative with the verb *have* + object + past participle.

I'm having a swimming pool built. (= I'm having someone build a swimming pool.)

GRAMMAR PRACTICE

1 Rewrite the sentences with the passive.

1 The neighbors give candy to children on Halloween.
___
2 A police officer stopped me on my way home yesterday.
___
3 Eating too much junk food can damage your health.
___
4 Scientists might discover new forms of life by the start of the next century.
___
5 A nurse is examining my brother right now.
___
6 How many students did the college accept this year?
___
7 They won't have finished the new building by next month.
___
8 They were fixing my toilet when you called.
___
9 Someone has stolen my wallet!
___
10 Weather forecasters had warned people about the hurricane.
___

2 Complete the conversations with active or passive causative sentences. Use the verbs in parentheses. Add any words you need.

1 A Your hair's really long!
  B I know! I _____ this Saturday. (cut)
2 A I can't stay with you. Your shower doesn't work.
  B It's OK now. I _____ yesterday. (fix)
3 A What happened? You both look exhausted!
  B The instructor _____ lots of exercises for an hour! (do)
4 A Is this book a gift?
  B Yes. Could I please _____ ? (wrap)
5 A You have a lot of photos of you and your sister!
  B I know! She _____ a lot when we were on vacation. (take)
6 A I can't read very well these days.
  B I think you should _____ (test). Here's the name of my optician.

◀ Go back to page 81

GRAMMAR PRACTICE

10A Quantifiers

 10.3

A lot of people never think about saving money.
There are **quite a few** new ideas these days.
A great deal of patience is needed to succeed.
A few jobs are still available.
Not much money has been spent on our city.
Neither of these professions really appeals to me.

Large quantities

We use *a lot of* and *lots of* in positive statements before countable and uncountable nouns, and *a lot* without a noun.

I think there are lots of different possibilities at that company.
They spend a lot (of money).

An awful lot of means "very many" or "very much" and is used with both countable and uncountable nouns.

There's an awful lot of traffic today!

Quite a few and *a fair/large number of* mean "many." We use these expressions before countable nouns. We add *of* to *quite a few* before pronouns.

We've had quite a few applications in the last week.
A fair/large number of professions didn't exist 50 years ago.

The expressions *a great/good deal of*, *a fair/large amount of/plenty of* also mean "a lot of." We use them with uncountable nouns.

There's a fair amount of information on that topic.

Small quantities

We use *a few* before countable nouns. It means "a small number." We use *a little* before uncountable nouns. It means "a small quantity."

There are a few jobs I'm interested in, but not many.
Can you give me a little help with my résumé?

We use *not many* and *not much* in negative sentences. We use *not many* before countable nouns and *not much* before uncountable nouns.

I haven't had many interviews.   I haven't had much luck finding work.

We also use *few* and *little* (without *a*). They mean "not enough."

Few people have applied. I hope a few will show interest. NOT ~~I hope few will show interest.~~

There's little interest in this course. I hope we see a little enthusiasm. NOT ~~I hope we see little enthusiasm.~~

Both, all, neither, and none

We use *both* (*of*) with countable nouns when we refer to two things.

Both my bosses are very demanding. And both of them make me work late.

We use *all* (*of*) with countable and uncountable nouns to describe the full quantity of something.

All my friends have good jobs. In fact, all of them earn more than I do!

We use *neither* (*of*) with countable nouns and *none* (*of*) with countable or uncountable nouns when the quantity is zero. *Neither* takes a singular verb. *None* takes a singular verb in formal writing, and a plural verb at other times.

Neither of my brothers lives at home. And neither (of them) comes to visit very often.
None of the candidates was suitable.   None of my friends own a car.

1 Choose the correct options to complete the sentences.
   1 I received *little* / *a little* help when I started this job, so I felt quite unhappy.
   2 I think *few* / *a few* people will go on the hike Saturday, and I'm sure someone can give you a ride.
   3 My friends gave me *a fair number* / *a fair amount* of advice, but I didn't take any of it.
   4 Neither of my sisters *is* / *isn't* very helpful at home. I have to do everything!
   5 I have two bosses, and *all* / *both* of them have been giving me a hard time!
   6 I went to the library and found *quite a few* / *a good deal of* information.
   7 *Not much* / *Not many* free hours are needed to volunteer with us.
   8 We have so many choices because there are *quite a few* / *few* good jobs.
   9 *All* / *Few* of us like working here. No one dislikes it.
   10 There are a *great deal of* / *large amount of* things to choose from on this menu.

2 Read the text. Correct the eight mistakes.

A fair amount of young people starting their careers decide to work abroad. Little of them go in order to get away from home, but most go to take advantage of the large deal of opportunities available. I have two brothers, and all of them went to live in New York. They've made a little progress finding an apartment – in fact, none – and are still sleeping on friends' sofas, but not many time has gone by. They have lots stories to tell about their adventures. In fact, neither of them doesn't want to come home anytime soon!

◀ Go back to page 85

10C Comparison

▶ 10.8

She spoke **more quietly than** I'd expected.
The more nervous I was, **the more** I forgot what to say.
The less I worried, **the more relaxed** I felt.
My most successful interview was the first.
He was **just as friendly as** I'd imagined.
It wasn't **quite as bad as** I'd thought it would be.

Comparatives

We use comparative adjectives + *than* to compare two things, people, or places.

With one-syllable adjectives, we add *-er*. With adjectives ending in *-y*, we change the *y* to *i* and add *-er*. For adjectives with more than two syllables, we use *more* or *less*.

Some application forms are easier to complete than others.
I think Jim is more intelligent than Peter.

We also use comparative forms of adverbs. We use *more* or *less* to form most of these.

He talked more excitedly than anyone else.

We can use *a bit*, *a little*, or *slightly* before a comparative to say there is a small difference, and *a lot*, *much*, or *far* to say there is a big difference.

He answered me a bit more rudely than I was expecting.
There are much more qualified candidates than me.

the ... the

We also use the structure *the ... the* to make comparisons. The comparisons may include nouns, adjectives, adverbs, or entire clauses or ideas, too.

The more interviews I have, the more confident I become. (noun, adjective)
The harder I try, the less frustrated I feel. (adverb, adjective)
The more we're prepared, the more we succeed. (clauses/ideas)

Superlatives

We use superlative adjectives to say that something is more or less than all the others in a group. With one-syllable adjectives, we put *the* in front and add *-est*. With two-syllable adjectives ending in *-y*, we change the *y* to *i* and add *-est*. With adjectives of more than two syllables, we use *the most* or *the least*.

The most enjoyable day was the one we spent together.
The least convincing argument was the one you gave!

Some adjectives have irregular comparative and superlative forms.

good – better – best   bad – worse – worst
far – farther/further – farthest/furthest

We can put *by far* before a superlative to make it stronger.

Biology is by far my worst subject.

We use the superlative with the present perfect + *ever* and *one of the* + plural noun.

That was one of the best jobs I've ever had!

as ... as

We use *as ... as* to say that two things are the same and *not (quite) as ... as* to say that two things are different. We can use *just* with *as ... as* to emphasize a similarity.

I was just as angry as he was!   The exam wasn't quite as hard as I expected.

GRAMMAR PRACTICE

1 Complete the second sentences so they mean the same as the first sentences.

1 The second interview wasn't as difficult as the first.
The first interview was _____ the second.
2 The beginning of this movie isn't as good as the end.
The end of this movie is _____ the beginning.
3 Eva behaved more calmly than the other candidates.
Eva behaved _____ of all the candidates.
4 I was really happy, and my sister was happy, too.
My sister was just _____ I was.
5 All the presentations were a lot more interesting than mine.
By far _____ was mine.
6 The hotel was a little larger than we expected.
The hotel wasn't quite _____ we expected.
7 If I don't work many hours, I don't make a lot of money.
The _____ , the _____ money I make.
8 Lauren spoke much more quietly than Katie.
Katie spoke _____ than Lauren.

2 Rewrite the sentences and correct the mistakes. Some sentences have more than one mistake.

1 The lovelyest flowers in the shop were most expensive.
_____
2 More I do my job, more I enjoy it.
_____
3 I have less classes this semester than my friends.
_____
4 It was raining a lot heavily than I thought, so I got pretty wet.
_____
5 The more exciting trip I've taken is when I went to Rome.
_____
6 There are much fast players than me. I'm pretty slow!
_____
7 Matt thinks more creative than the rest of us.
_____
8 Last semester was one of the most happy times I've ever had.
_____

◀ Go back to page 89

GRAMMAR PRACTICE

11A Present and past modals of deduction

▶ 11.5
It **must have** an explanation. It really happened.
It **can't be** true. I don't believe you.
This **might not be** a new discovery. I think I read about it last year.
Rick's in Chicago for the next week. He **must be visiting** his sister there.
You **couldn't have seen** Katie. She didn't go to the party.
Sue is still looking for a job. She **must not have gotten** the other one.

We use modals of deduction to talk about something when we don't know for sure if it's true, or if it was true.

Present modals of deduction

We use *must* + base form when <u>we think something is true</u>, based on logic.

You must be hungry. You haven't eaten anything all day. = I'm sure you're hungry.
He never wears jeans. He must not like them. = I'm sure that he doesn't like them.

We use *can't* or *couldn't* + base form when <u>we are sure that something isn't true</u>.

You can't/couldn't have the right address. The house is empty. = I'm sure you don't have the right address.

We use *might* or *might not* + base form when <u>we think something is true, but we aren't sure</u>.

David isn't at school. He might be sick, or he might not have any classes today. = It's possible that David is sick. It's possible that he doesn't have any classes today.

We also use *may* or *could* + base form when <u>we think something is possible</u>.

This restaurant's very popular, so it may be full.
I'm not sure when her birthday is. It could be next Saturday.

We often use the continuous form of the verb after modals of deduction when we talk about what <u>we think is happening now</u>.

Justin isn't in the living room. He must be watching TV in his bedroom.
Laurie might be getting ready in her room. I know she's going to a party later.

> **Look!** We never use *can* or contract *must not* to say what we think is or is not true. The word *mustn't* has a different meaning and expresses prohibition in British English.
> *Emma looks nervous. She might/could be afraid.* NOT *She can be afraid.*
> *That must not be the reason. It's not convincing.* NOT *That mustn't be the reason.*

Past modals of deduction

We use *must have* + the past participle when <u>we are sure that something was true</u>.

It must have been an alien. It didn't look human! = I'm sure it was an alien.

We use *can't have* or *couldn't have* + the past participle when <u>we are sure something was not true</u>.

The scientists can't/couldn't have found a new form of life. = I'm sure the scientists didn't find a new form of life.

We use *must not have* + the past participle when we <u>think something was probably not true</u>. We never contract *must not have*.

You must not have seen it. NOT *You mustn't have seen it.*

We use *could have, might have, might not have, may have* or *may not have* + the past participle when <u>we think something was possibly true, but we aren't sure</u>.

Adam isn't here yet. He could/might/may have gotten lost.
NOT *He can have gotten lost.*

1 Choose the correct options to complete the conversations.
1 A Bill looks unhappy.
  B He *must not / mustn't* be very comfortable here. He doesn't know anyone.
2 A Why isn't Hillary home yet?
  B I'm not sure. She *might / can't* have decided to work late. She was very busy.
3 A There don't seem to be any buses today.
  B I think the drivers *can / could* be on strike.
4 A I'm afraid this cake doesn't taste very good.
  B Hmm. You *couldn't follow / must not have followed* the recipe exactly.
5 A Why isn't Sarah answering my question?
  B She *may not have heard / may not hear* you. It's noisy in here.
6 A Great news. I got an A in chemistry!
  B You *must / might* have studied really hard. That course was so difficult!
7 A Do you have any history books I could borrow?
  B I *might / can't* have one or two that I could lend you.
8 A Paul has all their albums and goes to every concert.
  B He *could / must* really like them!

2 Rewrite the sentences using modals of deduction.

1 I'm sure Sam ate all the cookies. I'm sure Joe didn't eat them.
___
2 I'm sure that wasn't a magic trick. I'm sure it was real.
___
3 I think I've passed, but I'm not sure. It's possible I've failed.
___
4 Maybe John's sleeping. He's definitely not working.
___
5 I'm not sure that noise is our dog. Maybe it's a burglar!
___
6 It's not possible for you to be 40! I'm sure you're 30!
___
7 I'm sure Kumiko missed her flight. I'm pretty sure she didn't set her alarm.
___
8 I'm sure that they're traveling back today. It's possible that they're back already.
___

◀ Go back to page 95

11C Reported speech patterns

 11.13

I **said that I took it easy** on the weekends.
She **didn't mention that she would be** away.
Phil **didn't admit that he was sleeping** badly.
Rob **asked if I could recommend** a restaurant.
The doctor **asked me when I had started** feeling sick.
Several people **told us to get** our tickets early.
My sister **urged me not to stay** in a job I didn't like.

Reported statements

We use reported speech to say what someone said. We use verbs such as *say*, *tell*, *explain*, *admit*, *mention*, and *report*. In reported speech, we usually change the tense of the verbs.

- simple present ⇒ simple past
  "I live near the school." ⇒ *He said (that) he lived near the school.*
- simple past ⇒ past perfect
  "I failed my exam." ⇒ *She admitted (that) she had failed her exam.*
- present perfect continuous ⇒ past perfect continuous
  "I've been studying art." ⇒ *Sarah explained (that) she'd been studying art.*

Say is followed by (*that*) + a clause. *Tell* is followed by an object + (*that*) + a clause. *Explain*, *admit*, *mention*, and *report* may be followed by *to* + object + (*that*) + a clause.
Jeff said he was coming. NOT ~~Jeff said me he was coming.~~
Sarah told me (that) they might be late. NOT ~~Sarah told (that) they might be late.~~
I explained (to him that) I couldn't go. NOT ~~I explained him (that) I couldn't go.~~

The modal verbs *can*, *will*, and *may* also change in reported speech. The modal verbs *could*, *would*, *might* and *should* don't change in reported speech:
"I can't swim." ⇒ *Mark said (that) he couldn't swim.*
"We could meet you at six." ⇒ *Anna said (that) they could meet us at six.*

The tense usually does not change if the statement expresses something that is still true.
"I want to talk to you after class." ⇒ *Bob said (that) he wants to talk to me after class.*

Reported questions

We report a *Yes/No* question with the following structure: subject + *asked* + (object) + *if/whether* + subject + positive verb form + rest of sentence.
"Do you want your sweater?" ⇒ *She asked (me) if/whether I wanted my sweater.*

We report *wh-* questions with the question word(s) instead of *if/whether*.
"Which class are you in?" ⇒ *He asked (us) which class we were in.*

Look! We often need to change pronouns and words referring to time and place, if the sentence is reported on a different day or in a different place.
"I saw my uncle yesterday." ⇒ *He said he had seen his uncle the day before.*
"I'll wait for you here." ⇒ *He said he'd wait for us there.*

Reported commands

We report a command with the following structure: subject + verb + object + infinitive with (*not*) *to*.
We use verbs such as *tell*, *instruct*, *order*, *remind*, *forbid*, and *urge* to give commands.
"Read as much as possible." ⇒ *Our teacher urged us to read as much as possible.*
"Don't tell anyone." ⇒ *He forbid me to tell anyone./He told me not to tell anyone.*

GRAMMAR PRACTICE

1 Complete the sentences with reported speech.

1 "I'm worried about my test."
   Nancy told me _____ .
2 "Which neighborhood do you live in?"
   The police officer asked us _____ .
3 "Cook the vegetables at a high temperature."
   Jake instructed me _____ .
4 "Take some sun cream on your hike tomorrow."
   My mother reminded me _____ .
5 "I'll be taking part in a sleep study."
   Ben mentioned _____ .
6 "Could you explain the assignment again, please?"
   I asked her _____ .
7 "I haven't been sleeping very well."
   Jane told her doctor _____ .
8 "Many places have a rainy season."
   Mark said _____ .
9 "Don't drive so fast."
   Ellie told me _____ .
10 "Are you going away during the summer?"
   She asked me _____ ?

2 Rewrite the conversation with the verbs in parentheses and reported speech.

Jo My sister's in trouble at school. [1](say)
    Jo said her sister was in trouble at school.
Ed Oh, what happened? [2](ask)
    _____
Jo She's been skipping school a lot. [3](explain)
    _____
Ed Really? Does she have problems at school? [4](ask)
    _____
Jo Yes, some other kids have been mean to her. [5](admit)
    _____
Ed What are your parents doing about it? [6](ask)
    _____
Jo They've told her teachers. [7](answer)
    _____
Ed Will the teachers talk to the other kids? [8](ask)
    _____
Jo Yes, they will. I hope they can stop them from being mean. [9](say)
    _____
Ed Well, don't worry. [10](tell) And talk to your sister as much as possible. [11](urge)
    _____
    _____
Jo Sure. I'm spending tomorrow with her. [12](tell)
    _____

◀ Go back to page 99

GRAMMAR PRACTICE

12A Present and future unreal conditions

> ▶ 12.2
> **If** I **had** a robot to clean my house, **I'd be** very happy.
> I **wish there was** a better solution.
> **If only** the roads **weren't** so busy.
> **It's about time** we **looked** for a bigger apartment.
> **I'd rather** my daughter **spent** more time on her homework.

Second conditional

We use the second conditional to talk about unreal or unlikely conditions in the present or future and their consequences. We form the *if* clause with *if* + simple past, and we form the main clause with *would* + base form.

I'd take a really long vacation if I won the lottery. (unreal; I won't win the lottery)
If we didn't have a TV, we'd read more. (unlikely; we are going to keep our TV)

We can use *might* instead of *would* when the result isn't certain.

If they sold their business, they might be happier.

We can use *could* instead of *would* to talk about an ability in the future.

If I had more money, I could afford more clothes.

With the verb *be*, we often use *were* instead of *was* in more formal speech and writing in the *if* clause with *I*, *he*, *she* and *it*. We always use *were* in the phrase *If I were you …* to give advice.

If John were here, he'd help you.   If I were you, I'd tell your manager.

> **Look!** Don't use *would* in the *if* clause.
> *If it were cooler, I'd go for a run.* NOT *If it would be cooler, I'd go for a run.*

wish and if only

We use *wish* or *if only* to express a desire for a change that is unlikely. We use *wish* or *if only* + simple past to say we want something in the present to be different.

We all wish we were more talented. = we want to be more talented
If only my girlfriend didn't live so far away! = I want my girlfriend to live near me

We can also use *would* after *wish* and *if only* to talk about repeated actions.

I wish he cleaned up/would clean up more often! = I want him to clean up more often.
If only she didn't ask/wouldn't ask so many questions! = I want her not to ask so many questions.

We use *I wish* and *If only* + *would* or *could* to say we want something in the future to be different.

I wish they would improve our public transportation.
If only we could take a vacation next year.

It's (about) time

We use *It's (about) time* + simple past to express a wish for something to happen in the present. *It's about time* is more emphatic than *it's time*.

It's about time you got a new phone. = You really need a new phone.

would rather

We use *would rather* + simple past to say we would prefer somebody to do something, now or in the future. We usually contract *would* in informal speech or writing.

I'd rather he didn't interrupt me all the time. It's annoying!

1 Link the ideas in the two sentences with second conditionals. You may need to change some words.

1 I don't have a good computer. It's not easy to do my work.
If I had a good computer, it would be easier to do my work.
2 We don't have a car. We could do more with one.
___
3 The shower doesn't turn off automatically. We waste so much water.
___
4 I don't wear glasses. That's why I have trouble reading.
___
5 I'm not you. You could invent an app to make decisions for people.
___
6 I don't have an automatic vacuum cleaner. I have to vacuum all the time!
___

2 Choose the correct options to complete the sentences.

1 *I wish I had / If I had* a phone that answered all my calls.
2 If only I *would / could* have a personal shopping assistant!
3 I wish you *might iron / would iron* my clothes for me!
4 *I'd rather you left / It's time you left* a little bit later.
5 If only we *have / had* a stove that cooked our dinner!
6 It's about time we *would get / got* a dishwasher.

3 Complete the conversations. Use the cues in parentheses. Add any words you need.

1 A My car won't start. This is the third time this week! (new car)
  B If only *you could buy a new car*.
2 A I can't understand our biology teacher. He's so confusing. (explain fully)
  B I know. I wish _____ .
3 A I don't have a computer. Can I use yours? (go to library)
  B Well, actually, I'd rather _____ .
4 A There are too many people at this party! (leave)
  B It's about time _____ .
5 A I can't pass my exams. Why not? (study more)
  B If I _____ .
6 A Does your job pay you enough? Mine doesn't. (earn)
  B We all wish _____ .

◀ Go back to page 103

12C Past unreal conditions

 12.6

If I**'d bought** an apartment earlier, **it would have been** a lot cheaper.
I **wish** I**'d called** my brother sooner. Now he's not home.
If only I **hadn't bought** this phone. It broke after two weeks!
If the bus **had come** earlier, I**'d be** home now.
If he **weren't** such a bad driver, he **wouldn't have had** the accident.

Third conditional

We use the third conditional to talk about unreal conditions in the past and their consequences.

If I'd had more money, I would have bought a car. = I didn't have more money, so I didn't buy a car.
If he hadn't been in such a hurry, he wouldn't have forgotten his keys. = He was in a hurry, so he forgot his keys.

We form the *if* clause with *if* + past perfect. We form the main clause with *would have* + past participle. *Had* in the *if* clause is frequently contracted.

If I'd (had) known you were in town, I would have made time to see you.

We use *might/may have* instead of *would have* when the consequences weren't certain.

If I hadn't arrived late for the interview, I might have gotten the job.

We use *could have* instead of *would have* to talk about hypothetical abilities in the past.

If my car hadn't broken down, I could have taken you to the airport yesterday.

wish and *if only*

We use *wish* and *if only* + past perfect to say that we want something in the past to have been different.

I wish I hadn't bought this book. It's awful!
If only she'd been more careful, she wouldn't have fallen.

If only expresses a slightly stronger regret than *wish*.

We wish we'd gotten our plane tickets sooner. Now prices have gone up!
If only we'd gotten our plane tickets sooner. Now they're double the price!

> **Look!** Don't use *would have* after *wish* and *if only*.
> They wish/If only they'd gotten up earlier. NOT ~~They wish/If only they would have gotten up earlier.~~

Mixed conditional

We can use a mixed conditional to describe an unreal condition in the past and a present consequence. We form the *if* clause with *if* + past perfect, and the main clause with *would* + base form.

If Sam and Jane hadn't given up so fast, they'd both have jobs now.
If I'd learned to swim as a child, I'd be a much better swimmer now.

We can also use a mixed conditional to describe an unreal condition in the present and a consequence in the past. We form the *if* clause with *if* + simple past, and the main clause with *would have* + past participle.

If my family was/were rich, I would have gone to different schools.
If Tom wanted a girlfriend, he would have found one by now.

GRAMMAR PRACTICE

1 Write sentences with the third conditional that link the two sentences.

1. I read this article. I found out about this type of car.
   If I hadn't read this article, I wouldn't have found out about this type of car.
2. My parents didn't have a lot of money. They didn't go on vacation every year.
   _____.
3. Lisa didn't enjoy school. She didn't go to college.
   _____.
4. My aunt worked in the theater. She met a fair number of famous actors.
   _____.
5. James didn't get Anna's phone number. He didn't ask her on a date.
   _____.

2 Complete the conversations with the correct form of the verbs in the box.

| get | listen | love | not say | not stay | think |

1. **A** Did you pass your exam?
   B No, I didn't. I wish I _____ out all night the night before!
2. **A** Did you and Al have a good time?
   B No, we had a terrible fight! If only I _____ to you before our trip.
3. **A** It's such a shame you didn't come to the concert.
   B If only I'd known about it! I _____ to come!
4. **A** Why is Rachel annoyed with you?
   B I told her I didn't like her boyfriend. I wish I _____ anything!
5. **A** The traffic's bad! We're not going to get there in time.
   B Yes, I wish we _____ about that before we left.
6. **A** Shelley finally went to the doctor, and now she's in the hospital.
   B If only she'd gone to the doctor earlier, she _____ so sick.

3 Write sentences with mixed conditionals that link the two sentences.

1. I met Joana. I'm married now.
   If I hadn't met Joana, I wouldn't be married now.
2. He studied science in school. He's an engineer now.
   _____
3. We're not rich. We didn't take an expensive vacation.
   _____.
4. I love technology. I bought a new phone last week.
   _____
5. We bought a robot to clean the apartment. We have more free time now.
   _____.

◀ Go back to page 107

VOCABULARY PRACTICE

7A Collocations with *attend*, *get*, *make*, and *submit*

1 ▶ 7.1 Complete the collocations with *attend*, *get*, *make*, and *submit*. Listen and check.
  1 _____ an application, a paper, a proposal, a report
  2 _____ college, classes, a lecture, a conference
  3 _____ a big difference, matters worse, the most out of, a living
  4 _____ something across, ahead, hold of somebody/something, somebody's attention

2 Complete the sentences with collocations from exercise 1.
  1 My grandfather used to _____ by working as a bus driver.
  2 You have to take risks if you want to _____ and succeed in business.
  3 I _____ last night that was so popular I had to stand up! The speaker was great.
  4 Thelma would be a very good politician. She's a very convincing speaker, and she's so good at _____ her message _____ .
  5 There are so many places I'd like to see when I go to Italy next summer. I've decided to rent a car so I can _____ of my stay.
  6 I'm going to _____ to start a school newspaper to the principal. I hope she won't think the budget's too high.
  7 I was already an hour late, and, to _____ , I got stuck in the elevator!
  8 I _____ on the west coast – at UCLA, in fact. That's how I have so many friends in Los Angeles.
  9 I'm not sure where I'll end up going to college, but I'm going to _____ to Harvard.
  10 Maybe Teresa is away. I tried calling her at least five times, but I couldn't _____ her.

◀ Go back to page 58

VOCABULARY PRACTICE

7B Ability

1 ▶ 7.4 Complete the paragraphs with the correct form of the expressions in the boxes, making sure the entire paragraph is logical. Use each expression only once. There may be more than one correct answer. Listen and check.

be capable of   can't seem to   have a talent for   be pretty/reasonably successful at   struggle to/with

Not everyone ¹_____ learning foreign languages. Some people really ²_____ them and ³_____ remember anything they've learned. But, with motivation and practice, even they can ⁴_____ mastering a language. With enough effort, everyone ⁵_____ learning!

find it hard to   succeed at   be pretty good/bad at   fail to   can't quite manage to

Some of us ⁶_____ sports. We ⁷_____ keep up with our teammates and may ⁸_____ win even a single game. But even if we ⁹_____ hit the ball very far or do a high jump, we can all find a sport we're able to ¹⁰_____ . Some don't require strength or endurance at all!

◀ Go back to page 60

7C Mind and memory

1 ▶ 7.8 Which option, a or b, provides the correct interpretation? Listen and check.

1 I tried to remember his name, but **my mind went blank**.
  a I'm glad I didn't have to ask him.
  b In the end, I had to ask him.
2 **Keep in mind** that you won't be allowed in the theater after the performance begins.
  a So please don't be late.
  b But you can arrive late.
3 It never **crossed my mind** that Maria had learned English as a foreign language.
  a She sounds like a native speaker.
  b She's not very fluent.
4 I'm seeing *The Lion King* tomorrow with my nephew. I'm not into musicals, but I'll try to **keep an open mind**.
  a I'm sure I'll hate it.
  b Maybe I'll be pleasantly surprised.
5 At first I thought Jack was unfriendly, but I've **changed my mind**.
  a He's really nice.
  b He's really rude.
6 I can't **make up my mind** which suit I like better.
  a Definitely the blue one.
  b Maybe the blue one.

2 Complete each sentence with the correct form of a verb from exercise 1. You may have to change the tense.
  1 So you're not joining us for dinner? What a shame! But text me if you _____ your mind, OK?
  2 My mind always _____ blank when I'm speaking in public. I don't know why I get so nervous!
  3 I might spend New Year's Eve in London, but I haven't _____ up my mind yet.
  4 If you want to invite Ann for dinner, _____ in mind that she's a vegetarian.

3 ▶ 7.9 For 1–6, complete the second sentence so that it means the same as the first, using the words and expressions in the box. Listen and check.

boost your memory   have a good/bad memory   learn something by heart   memorable   recall   remind

1 I memorize irregular verbs, so I never have to look them up.
  I _____ , and now I never have to look them up.
2 Please don't let me forget to water the plants.
  Please _____ me to water the plants.
3 They say fish oil can improve your memory.
  They say fish oil can _____ .
4 You won't forget this experience.
  This will be a _____ experience.
5 I haven't forgotten my wedding day. I remember it perfectly.
  I can still _____ my wedding day perfectly.
6 I never seem to be able to remember people's names.
  I've always _____ for people's names.

◀ Go back to page 62

VOCABULARY PRACTICE

8A The media

1 ▶ 8.1 Match words 1–15 in the box with definitions a–o. Listen and check.

> 1 breaking news   2 the headlines   3 host   4 mass media   5 stream   6 subscription services   7 tabloid
> 8 viewer   9 ad   10 audience   11 broadcast   12 follow   13 network   14 on the air   15 the press

a the main types of communication like television, radio, and newspapers ____
b recently received information about an event or story that is currently occurring or developing ____
c the titles at the top of newspaper articles or the most important items of news on TV or the radio ____
d a person who watches TV or a movie ____
e send or receive audio or video data that can be played continuously over the Internet ____
f a newspaper with a popular style and sensational stories ____
g a person who presents a radio or television program ____
h programs, series, or movies that customers who pay a fee can watch on their television sets ____
i journalists or newspapers viewed collectively ____
j take an active interest in or support someone on social media ____
k transmit or send a radio or television show or program ____
l being shown or heard now on television or radio ____
m a group of TV stations that connect to present the same programs in different locations ____
n an abbreviation or short form of the word *advertisement* ____
o the people who watch or listen to a television or radio program ____

2 Choose the correct options to complete the paragraph.

What are my media habits? An interesting question. Well, first of all, I like to follow ¹*breaking news / mass media* as it develops. And I enjoy watching ²*tabloids / networks* I know because I usually trust them. I also like to watch programs that attract a lot of ³*viewers / the press* so I can discuss them later with people. When a popular show is ⁴*followed / on the air*, I turn it on right away. The only problem is that I really can't stand a lot of ⁵*headlines / ads*, so these days, I prefer to ⁶*stream / broadcast* the programs I like. There's no need to even download them!

3 Complete the reactions to the evening news, choosing the best option.

A *What did you think of the news last night?*
B *I thought it was ...*
1 clearly *fair / biased* against the government. You could tell that the journalist didn't like the president.
2 completely *accurate / sensational*. All of the information was correct.
3 balanced and *objective / inaccurate*. It presented both points of view. I've always felt this channel was fair.
4 emotional and *sensational / biased*, almost like a tabloid. I agreed with its interpretation of events, but it was so exaggerated!
5 really *sensational / fair*. It was based on facts, rather than opinions, and presented the news as it was happening.

VOCABULARY PRACTICE

8C Expressions with *at*, *for*, *in*, and *on*

1 ▶ 8.5 Match the expressions in **bold** in sentences 1–12 with definitions a–l. Listen and check.

1 Everything happened **at once**. I moved, got a job, and got married, all in May! _____
2 Bob was determined to win **at all costs**, and nothing could stop him. _____
3 It would be nice if, just **for once**, you could help me with the dishes! _____
4 We have shortened and adapted the text **for the sake of** simplicity. _____
5 Glenn is so deeply **in debt** and desperate for money that he's selling his car. _____
6 If Mom finds out I only got a D on the test, I'm **in trouble**! _____
7 I suggest we meet **on a regular basis** to discuss your progress. _____
8 The teacher proudly accepted the award **on behalf of** the whole class. _____
9 I was really **in doubt** and couldn't decide which apartment to buy. _____
10 When Bill lost his job, he was **at risk** of becoming homeless. _____
11 We go out for Thai food **once in a while**, but it's a little too spicy for me. _____
12 The police officer was **on duty**, so he was wearing a uniform. _____

a despite the effort needed
b for the purpose or in the interest of
c immediately, at the same time
d often or frequently
e in a situation where you might be punished or blamed
f on only one occasion
g in place of or as a representative of
h working at that moment
i in danger
j occasionally, from time to time
k unsure about something
l the state of owing money

2 Complete the sentences with expressions from exercise 1.

1 Her bike is too close to the cars. She's _____ of being hit!
2 He's _____ because he doesn't know which suit to buy.
3 I can't go and have coffee. I'm _____ right now at work.
4 I'm really _____ – I've just broken a really expensive ornament!
5 I don't see Cindy very often, just _____ .
6 Can't Henry be quiet _____ ! I'm trying to do my homework.
7 I can't pay my rent this month as I'm so badly _____ .
8 They have to stay friends _____ . I hope they start talking to each other soon.

3 ▶ 8.6 Complete the texts with the expressions in the box. Listen and check.

| for a change | on average | for sure | at first | at least | on top of | in control | for no reason |

Last night my girlfriend seemed upset ¹_____ . When I asked her what was wrong, she said, "Nothing." ²_____ , I just thought she was in a bad mood, but when I checked my Facebook page, I realized that it was her birthday yesterday. I'd completely forgotten! And ³_____ that, she told me she'd taken the day off work yesterday so we could celebrate it together. Well, ⁴_____ I won't forget it next year – I've already written it in my work diary and set an alarm on my phone to remind me!

I didn't know ⁵_____ , but I'd always thought that women lived longer than men. So last weekend I went online, and, according to the government website, ⁶_____ , women live between five and seven years longer than men. I thought that my husband and I were rather out of shape, so I suggested to him that we should do more to be ⁷_____ of our health. So yesterday, instead of just watching TV after dinner, we decided to go for a long walk ⁸_____ . I feel so much more energetic today!

◀ Go back to page 70

148

VOCABULARY PRACTICE

9A Collocations with *have* and *take*

1   9.1 Read the quotes and match the **bold** collocations 1–8 with definitions a–h. Listen and check.

1 A person's self-esteem **has nothing to do with** how she looks. (Halle Berry)

2 When you're a celebrity, people think they know you, but they **don't have a clue**. (Willie Aames)

3 When I'm down, I talk to myself a lot. I look crazy because I'm constantly **having an argument with** myself. (Serena Williams)

4 I love cooking and **having friends over** for dinner, so a beautiful table to sit around is a must. (Ella Woodward)

5 Nowadays I'm not even sure if newspapers **take into account** whether a person is a good writer. (Bob Schieffer)

6 I look at life as a one-time opportunity, and you have to **take pleasure in** each moment, even if it is very problematic. (Ori Gersht)

7 Comedy is free therapy. And if it's done well, the audience and the comic **take turns** being the doctor as well as the patient. (Maysoon Zayid)

8 You've got to **take responsibility for** your actions. (Richard DeVos)

a invite someone to your house ____
b consider something when you make a decision ____
c do something alternately with another person ____
d have no idea about something (informal) ____
e have no connection to someone or something ____
f get happiness and enjoyment from something ____
g disagree with someone about something angrily ____
h have a moral obligation or be accountable for something ____

2   9.2 Complete the mind maps with *have* or *take*. Listen and check.

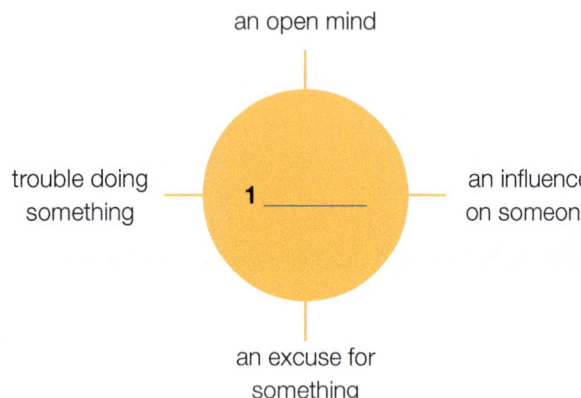
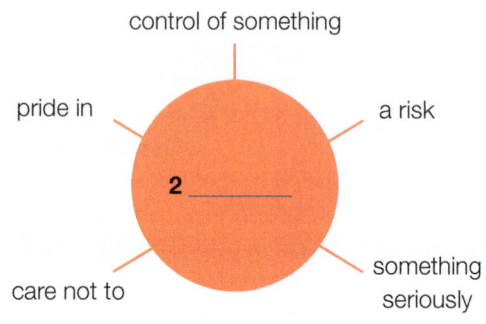

3 Complete the sentences with expressions from exercises 1 and 2. You may need to change the form of the verb.
1 I _____ with my sister, and now she won't even talk to me.
2 This is entirely my decision, and it _____ you, so I'll _____ it if it goes wrong.
3 We're planning a surprise birthday party for Hannah, and she _____ what's going on!
4 I arrived really late, so I entered the room quietly and _____ wake up my roommate.
5 When planning lessons, teachers should _____ students' ages _____ .
6 Sorry I'm late. I _____ finding somewhere to park.
7 I love to bake, and I really _____ making delicious desserts everyone enjoys.
8 At home, my father usually makes dinner, and my mother and I _____ washing the dishes.
9 Don't _____ everything Jane says so _____ . She's just joking!
10 I was sick in bed, so I _____ a perfect _____ not going to the party.

◀ Go back to page 76

9B Colors

1. ▶ 9.5 Match the colors in the box with pictures 1–16. Listen and check.

| ~~blueish-green~~ | bronze | dark blue | ~~gold~~ | lavender | light blue | maroon | multicolored |
| pinkish-orange | ~~reddish~~ | ruby | silver | ~~teal~~ | turquoise | violet | yellowish-brown |

1 gold   2 _____   3 _____   4 _____   5 _____   6 blueish-green   7 _____   8 _____
9 reddish   10 _____   11 _____   12 _____   13 _____   14 teal   15 _____   16 _____

2. Put the colors in the correct category. Which two colors can go in two categories?

metals	gems	single color	shade of a single color	combination of colors
_____	_____	_____	_____	_____
_____	_____	_____	_____	_____
_____	_____	_____	_____	_____
		_____	_____	
		_____		
		_____		

3. Complete the sentences with the correct color.

1. What do you think of this _____ scarf? I'm not sure I like it.
2. Hi, can you help me? I'm looking for a _____ pair of pants.
3. Which ring do you like better, the _____ one or the _____ one?
4. My mother gave me some _____ candlesticks that I use all the time.
5. I have _____ hair, and I'll be wearing a _____ blouse. It will be easy to find me.
6. This sweater is kind of a _____ , but I actually want something darker.
7. I don't like those _____ pants at all. _____ would be better.
8. That dress is too _____ . I'd like something solid, maybe a nice _____ .

◀ Go back to page 78

VOCABULARY PRACTICE

9C Dimensions and weight

1 ▶ 9.9 Study the chart. Then choose the correct options to complete sentences 1–8.

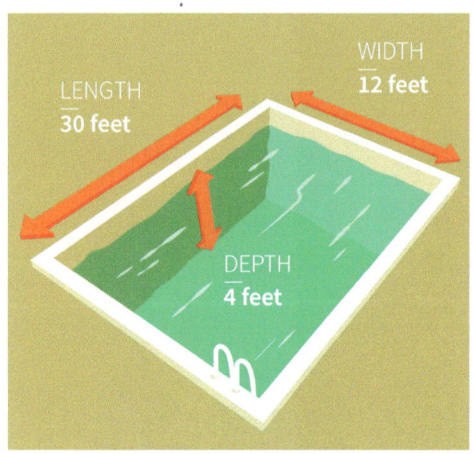
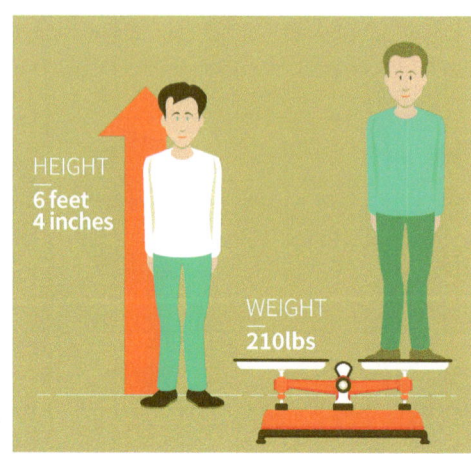

noun	adjective	verb
depth	deep	deepen
length	long	lengthen
width	wide	widen
height	high/tall	heighten
shortness	short	shorten
weight	(heavy)	weigh

1 As of Friday morning, 30% of the state was covered in snow, with an average *deep / depth* of 3.4 inches.

2 The roof of the local police station has collapsed under the *weigh / weight* of heavy snow.

3 If you're driving, be aware that roads can be extremely slippery when wet, which will *length / lengthen* the time it takes to stop.

4 The *short / shortness* of winter is the result of climate change, a trend that will continue.

5 For the first time in decades, the snow in south London and in the suburbs was one foot *deep / deepen*.

6 There is a higher incidence of forest fires in many places around the world, and the *length / long* of the fire season has increased significantly.

7 In this article, meteorologist John Elliot answers a tricky question – just how much does snow *weigh / weight*?

8 After the storm, the city had to spend a fortune on snow removal to clear streets that aren't *wide / width* enough for two cars to pass each other.

2 ▶ 9.10 Study the chart. Then complete sentences 1–5.

linear measure	capacity	weight
1 inch = 2.54 centimeters	1 gallon = 3.8 liters	1 ounce = 28.3 grams
1 foot = 0.3 meters	1 pint = 0.5 liters	1 pound = 0.45 kilograms
1 mile = 1.6 kilometers	1 quart = 0.9 liters	1 ton = 907 kilograms

1 John traveled 500 *miles* and João traveled 700 kilometers, so John traveled further.
2 Ann bought two _____ of milk, and Ana bought two liters of milk, so Ana bought more milk.
3 Paul weighs 170 _____ , and Pablo weighs 90 kilograms, so Pablo weighs more.
4 Alice is 5 feet 2 _____ , and Alicia is 1.75 meters tall, so Alicia is taller.
5 Carl bought half a _____ of cheese, and Carlos bought 250 grams, so Carl bought more cheese.

3 Complete the sentences logically using words from the box.

high   deep   long   tall   wide

1 The pool is only three feet _____ , so you can go in even if you don't know how to swim.
2 I am nearly seven feet _____ , which means everyone in my family is shorter than me.
3 For a wheelchair to go comfortably through a doorway, it must be 32 inches _____ .
4 The Danyang-Kunshan Grand Bridge in China is over 100 miles _____ , so it can take more than an hour to cross.
5 My bed is about three feet _____ , so I have to use a stool to climb into it.

◀ Go back to page 80

VOCABULARY PRACTICE

10A Trends and business

1 ▶ 10.1 Write the words in the box below the correct graphs 1–3. Listen and check.

| decline (n, v)   decrease (n, v)   drop (n, v)   fall (n, v)   grow (v)   growth (n)   increase (n, v)   remain stable (v)   rise (n, v) |

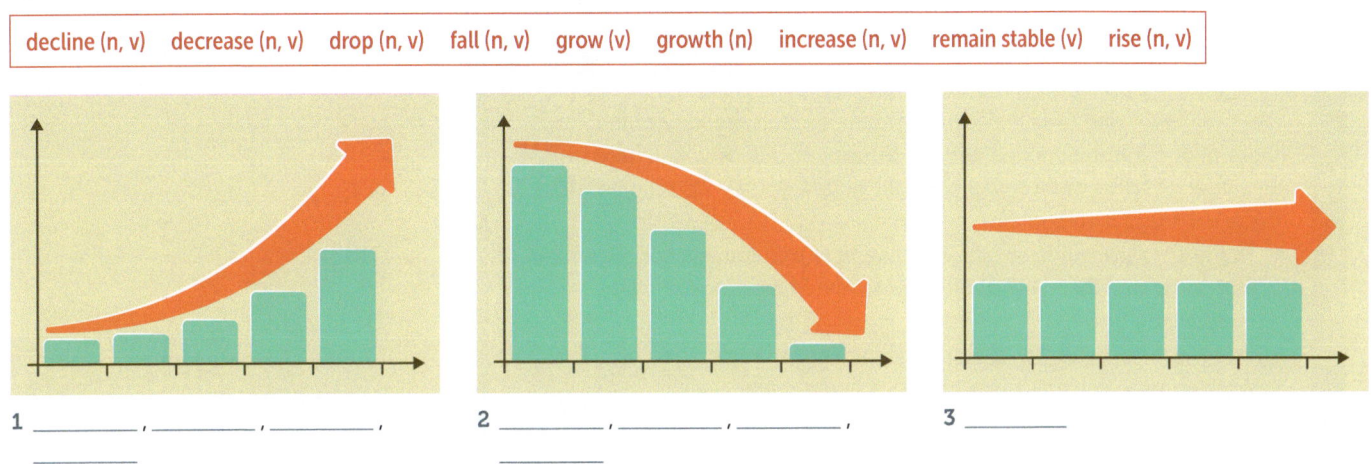

1 _____ , _____ , _____ , _____

2 _____ , _____ , _____ , _____

3 _____

2 Complete the sentences with the correct forms of the words in exercise 1. There may be more than one answer, but try to use each noun or verb only once.

HOME   FORUM   NEWS   SIGN IN

GOOD NEWS FROM AROUND THE WORLD   REPLY SHARE

1 Since the mid-1990s, violent crime in the UK ⬇ _____ by two-thirds.
2 Global average life expectancy ⬆ _____ by five years between 2000 and 2015, the fastest ⬆ _____ since the 1960s.
3 Since 1991, there's been a ⬇ _____ in cancer deaths in the U.S. by 25%.
4 A new report from the European Union said that between 1990 and 2016, the economy ⬆ _____ by 53%.
5 Since 2001, there's been a(n) ⬆ _____ in the number of people with access to electricity to nearly 1.2 billion.
6 A number of studies have shown that bullying in American schools ⬇ _____ slowly, but steadily, year after year.
7 The snow leopard is no longer an endangered species, and populations ⊖ _____ in the past few years.
8 In 2017, there was a ⬇ _____ in UK carbon emissions to the lowest level since the 19th century.

3 ▶ 10.2 Read a company's e-mail to its employees. Complete the sentences with the correct form of the words in the box. Listen and check.

verbs	nouns
launch go out of business manufacture raise provide set up	branch chain main office entrepreneur

Eight reasons why it's been a great year! We have:

- increased sales by 10%, while some of our competitors ¹_____ due to low sales;
- ²_____ a brand new website, which our customers love;
- ³_____ a committee to study ways to attract young ⁴_____ with creative ideas;
- opened a new factory to ⁵_____ our products;
- spent more on training so we can ⁶_____ quality services to our customers;
- acquired a ⁷_____ of stores in multiple locations around the country;
- found innovative ways to ⁸_____ money so we can open a new ⁹_____ ;
- moved our ¹⁰_____ to a more modern and spacious building.

◀ Go back to page 84

152

VOCABULARY PRACTICE

10C Word pairs

1 ▶ 10.5 Read the text. Match the expressions in **bold** 1–5 with definitions a–e. Listen and check.

Working from home: is it right for you?

We hear ¹**over and over** that working from home is the way of the future and that traditional offices will disappear one day. But there are a number of ²**pros and cons** to consider before you set up a home office. These are the advantages:
- There is no commute, so you will save time and money. But remember that ³**now and then** you might have to attend meetings or visit customers.
- There is more flexibility. If you're becoming ⁴**sick and tired** of a 9 to 5 working day, you will enjoy having a home office.
- You can do more work at home. ⁵**By and large**, you can use your time more effectively because you won't have any interruptions.

a in general _____
b occasionally _____
c fed up with _____
d advantages and disadvantages _____
e repeatedly _____

2 ▶ 10.6 Try to guess the meaning of the expressions in the box. Then complete the rest of the text with the correct expressions. Listen and check.

> little by little   once or twice   side by side   sooner or later   peace and quiet   ups and downs   each and every

And these are the disadvantages:
- You have to be organized ¹_____ day of the week, without exception. It's OK to take breaks ²_____ a day, but longer ones shouldn't become a habit.
- It can be lonely. In the beginning, you will enjoy the ³_____ of a noise-free environment, but ⁴_____ the day may come when you'll start missing being with your coworkers.
- It's easier to get to know people when you work in an office. When you work ⁵_____, in the same physical space, day in day out, ⁶_____ you become friends and may start to socialize after work.

So, in sum, think about your personality and what's important to you. For most people, working at home is a positive experience. You may have some ⁷_____, but you'll probably end up enjoying it.

◀ Go back to page 88

VOCABULARY PRACTICE

11A Science

1A ▶ 11.1 Order tips a–d in the most logical way. Listen and check.

> How to **have** a scientific **breakthrough** – the four necessary steps:
> a ☐ **Analyze** the **evidence**. Does it **prove** your **theory**?
> b ☐ **Identify** a **problem** and **make** a **hypothesis**.
> c ☐ Try to **reach** a **conclusion**. Then **publish** the **results**.
> d ☐ **Carry out research** to investigate it.
>   **Do experiments**, if necessary, and **gather** as much **data** as you can.

B ▶ 11.2 Complete the collocations with the words in the box. Listen and check.

> an agreement   information   a hypothesis   a study

You can:
1 **prove** a theory, information, and _____ .
2 **reach** a conclusion, a decision, and _____ .
3 **carry out** research, an experiment, and _____ .
4 **gather** data, evidence, and _____ .

2 Read the text and complete collocations 1–8 with verbs from exercise 1. You may need to change the form of the verb.

> Last year, Dr. Rose Silverstein, from our university, ¹_____ a series of **experiments** to investigate the effect of background music on shopping behavior. She wanted to ²_____ the **hypothesis** she had started to research earlier: that everything from music volume to tempo could influence how consumers spend money. Dr. Silverstein spent six months interviewing customers and ³_____ **data**, and she has ⁴_____ some fascinating **conclusions**. She plans to ⁵_____ the **results** next month. Apparently, loud and upbeat music tends to encourage customers to shop faster and spend less. She needs to ⁶_____ the **evidence** a bit more, but she may ⁷ have _____ a scientific **breakthrough**. At the very least, she has ⁸_____ **a problem** that has concerned many store owners.

3 ▶ 11.3 Complete the chart, using a dictionary if necessary. Listen and check. Then complete sentences 1–5 with words from the chart.

	field	person
	psychology	_____
	_____	economist
	the law	_____
	_____	archeologist
	geology	_____

1 My brother studied _____ in college and now he works for the Treasury Department as an _____ .
2 _____ is a fascinating topic and helps people who are anxious or depressed. But there aren't enough trained _____ .
3 If you don't obey _____ , you might find that you need a good _____ !
4 I went on a tour of an ancient Roman city over the weekend, led by a well-known _____ . It was so fascinating I was sorry I hadn't studied _____ .
5 _____ is an important field that teaches us how to use our natural resources effectively. In fact, our government needs to hire more _____ .

◀ Go back to page 94

VOCABULARY PRACTICE

11B Opposite adjectives

1 ▶ 11.7 Complete the chart with the opposite of the adjectives below. Listen and check.

positive	negative
1 _____	unacceptable
2 believable	_____
3 controversial	_____
4 _____	undesirable
5 imaginable	_____
6 _____	unimpressive
7 legal	_____
8 responsible	_____
9 _____	unsatisfactory

2 Match sentences 1–6 with pictures a–f. Then complete the sentences with an adjective from exercise 1.

1 Sam's behavior in class is completely _____ . He needs to sit down and focus on his work. ____
2 Laurie is a very _____ young woman, and her company is lucky to have such a dedicated worker. ____
3 There's another community meeting tonight about the new housing development. In my view, it's totally _____ . ____
4 I don't think you can park there now. It's only _____ after 5:30 p.m.. ____
5 A lot of what we read in the news these days isn't very _____ . ____
6 I found the lecture _____ and, to be honest, I don't remember much of it. ____

◀ Go back to page 96

11C Sleep

1 ▶ 11.11 Match sentences 1–5 with pictures a–e. Listen and check.
 1 The lesson was so boring that I began to **yawn**. ____
 2 At 11:30 last night, my son **sleepwalked** downstairs and came into the kitchen! ____
 3 My mother **snores** really loudly, and it **keeps** my father **awake** most nights. ____
 4 The dog lay down in front of the fire and **fell asleep**. ____
 5 Alfred texted his boss to apologize when he realized he'd **overslept** again. ____

2 ▶ 11.12 Read the text and match the words in **bold** 1–6 with definitions a–f. Listen and check.

> Feeling ¹**sleepy** at work is a common occurrence. According to a recent study, of the Americans who sleep an average of six hours a night, 45% say they feel very tired at least three times a week. When you're ²**sleep-deprived**, it can be difficult to concentrate and get things done at work. Unfortunately, most people can't ³**take a nap** at the office, so when they feel like they're starting to ⁴**doze off** at work, they drink coffee to help them ⁵**stay awake**. However, most of the people taking part in the survey say they ⁶**sleep in** on Saturday and Sunday mornings.

a not to fall asleep ____
b fall asleep lightly ____
c sleep for a short time during the day ____
d sleep longer than usual on purpose ____
e not getting enough sleep ____
f ready to fall asleep ____

3 Complete the sentences with words from exercises 1 and 2. You may need to change the verb forms.
 1 It was a nice hotel, but the street noise _____ me _____ all night.
 2 Every day my grandmother _____ right after lunch. She says it's the secret to a long life.
 3 Harry opened his mouth and _____ loudly in the middle of the lecture. I thought it was really rude of him.
 4 Unless I drink a large cup of coffee first thing in the morning, I have trouble _____ during the day.
 5 My husband _____ , so I have to sleep with earplugs.
 6 When my grandpa's watching TV, he sometimes _____ for a few minutes and then suddenly wakes up again.
 7 As soon as we set off in the car, the baby stopped crying and _____ .
 8 I was half an hour late for work this morning because I _____ .

◀ Go back to page 98

VOCABULARY PRACTICE

12A Phrasal verbs (2)

1 ▶ 12.1 Complete the list of features below with the correct form of the phrasal verbs in the boxes. Listen and check.

| back up   break down   work out   go through   hang up   note down |
| run into   run out of   set up   sign in   turn down   turn up |

Features of a perfect phone

- a way to automatically ¹_____ if I get an annoying call from a telemarketer;
- an easier way to ²_____ songs and videos so I never lose them – better than the existing "cloud services";
- an alarm if someone tries to unlock my phone and ³_____ my messages when I'm not looking;
- a lifetime warranty so I can get a free replacement if I ⁴_____ a technical problem and the phone ⁵_____ ;
- an app that ⁶_____ important information when you talk to it – and doesn't misunderstand what you say;
- an app that ⁷_____ who is calling you when you don't recognize the number;
- a way for me to increase the volume by simply saying, "⁸_____ the music"… and lower it by saying, "⁹_____ the music" – without touching the screen;
- better password managers so I can ¹⁰_____ to all my accounts more easily;
- a faster way to ¹¹_____ a brand-new phone as soon as I leave the store – without having to go online;
- and last but not least: better battery life! I'm tired of ¹²_____ battery in the middle of the day.

2A Read sentences 1–6 and choose the correct definition for each phrasal verb in **bold**, a or b.

1 Jill lost her job, so she's **going through** a difficult time right now.
   a experience something hard
   b examine something carefully
2 Let's **set up** a meeting for Monday so we can try to come to a final decision.
   a arrange or organize something
   b get something ready for use
3 I **ran into** an old friend at the shopping mall.
   a meet somebody by chance
   b experience a problem
4 Joe, could you **turn down** the air conditioning, please? It's a bit cold.
   a refuse an offer or request
   b reduce the amount of heat, light, or sound
5 The money I thought I'd lost **turned up** under my bed!
   a be found after being lost
   b increase the amount of heat, light, or sound
6 When you write an essay, you should **back up** your main points with facts.
   a support with information
   b make a copy of digital information

B Do any phrasal verbs in exercise 2A have the same meaning as those in exercise 1?

◀ Go back to page 102

12C Collocations with *come*, *do*, *go*, and *make*

1 ▶ 12.4 Complete the sentences with the words in the boxes. Listen and check.

| along   out   to an end   true |

1 The new album is **coming** _____ in July. I can't wait to hear it.
2 I'd always dreamed of appearing in a Broadway show, and last month my dream **came** _____ .
3 An opportunity like this doesn't **come** _____ every day. You should definitely take it!
4 After three long months, the work has finally **come** _____ .

| harm   the minimum   your part   away with |

5 The government should have **done** _____ these useless regulations years ago.
6 A good teacher can help you learn, but you've got to **do** _____ as well.
7 My brother didn't do much work when he was in college. He just **did** _____ to pass his exams.
8 We've **done** a lot of _____ to the environment without realizing how serious the problem is.

| ahead   for   into detail   over |

9 If you really want this job, what are you waiting for? Just **go** _____ it!
10 The government has **gone** _____ with plans to build a new airport.
11 At the end of the lesson, the teacher **went** _____ the main points again to make sure everyone had understood.
12 The newspaper article **went** _____ great _____ about the governor's views.

| a point   sense   an effort   a living |

13 I wish my father would **make** _____ to get along with my boyfriend.
14 My grandfather **made** _____ by selling cars at the local dealership.
15 Jack **made** _____ good _____ during the debate, which really made me stop and think.
16 You're not **making** _____ , Ann. What exactly are you trying to say?

◀ Go back to page 106

COMMUNICATION PRACTICE

7A Student A

1 Complete part of an e-mail from a college student. Try to be creative with the relative clauses.

> School is going pretty well, but I have a lot of work. I have to submit a long report on Monday, which _____ . And I have trouble with lectures containing _____ and classes having _____ . The good news, though, is that I passed _____ , which _____ .
> As for this summer, my parents suggested I get a job working _____ , one that would give me experience in _____ . It's not a bad idea, but I've been thinking of _____ , which _____ !
> Can you give me some advice on these things?

2 Imagine you're the college student in exercise 1. Summarize what you wrote for Student B. He/She will give you advice.

3 Listen to Student B, a recent college graduate. Give him/her advice.

8A Student A

1 Read the text carefully. Then cover it and tell Student B about it in your own words. Try to use the linkers.

Vinyl's back – but who's buying it?

After disappearing from the market for many years, vinyl records (or LPs) have become popular again, and sales have been going up steadily since 2008. As a result, more and more artists are releasing their new albums on vinyl. Interestingly, while most people think only older adults buy LPs, in some locations, vinyl sales are very high with those under 30, too. Perhaps these younger music fans love the sound and feel of a physical object, which, unlike Spotify, is more personal. Also, the renewed interest in LPs is partly due to their availability, as they are becoming easier and easier to find.

2 Now listen to Student B tell you the story behind this photo. Do you personally think Polaroid is a success story?

8C Student A

1 Ask Student B questions 1–5. Listen to each response and then tell him/her your own responses.
   1 Do you still go to the movies?
   2 Do you check your phone as soon as you wake up?
   3 Are you planning to attend a live concert this year?
   4 When you watch a movie in English, do you read the subtitles?
   5 Do you lend books to friends?

2 Listen to Student B's questions. Give a true response, choosing one of the two options.
   1 Yes, I spend some time … / No, I've stopped …
   2 Sure, I wouldn't mind … / No, I'd have a hard time …
   3 Yes, … are fun. / No, I'm not into …
   4 Yes, it's important … / No, there's no point …
   5 Yes, I used to have fun … / No, I was tired of …

COMMUNICATION PRACTICE

8D Student A

1 Comment on these annoying situations to Student B and explain why you feel the way you do. Express doubt if necessary.

 1 companies that make mistakes in your telephone or electricity bill
 2 restaurants that make you wait a long time before taking your order
 3 drivers who park too close to your car
 4 dog owners who don't clean up after their pets

2 Student B will comment on some annoying situations. React to his/her explanations.

9A Student A

1 Listen to Student B describe his/her neighborhood. At the end, write down the eight adverbs you heard. Is each one a comment adverb or an adverb of degree, frequency, or manner?

2 Tell Student B about your plans for next year. Check his/her adverbs, using the key below.

> <u>Personally</u>, I don't plan to go to graduate school. <u>Realistically</u>, I don't think it's a worthwhile expense, and <u>actually</u>, I think you can get a good job without a graduate degree. Also, it's <u>unusually</u> hard to get into some graduate schools, and the entrance exam is <u>really</u> difficult. I think I can do <u>well</u> in the work world without an MA. Things <u>frequently</u> change at companies, and they're <u>always</u> looking for new people.

> **Key:**
> *personally, realistically, actually*: comment adverbs
> *unusually, really*: adverbs of degree
> *frequently, always*: adverbs of frequency
> *well*: adverb of manner

9C Student A

1 Read the text carefully. Then cover it and tell Student B about it in your own words. Include passives and causative *have* structures.

> I have a teacher who makes us work so hard I can rarely go out. We're often assigned homework at the last minute. So far this year, we've been given over 20 unexpected tasks to do. One time, a student was even sent home because she came to class without her homework. My teacher also has us do extra exercises on Friday, so we frequently have to stay late. And since he says we have plenty of free time, he has us do longer projects on the weekend, too!

2 Listen to Student B's problem. What advice can you give to help him/her deal with this situation?

10A Student A

1 Read each trivia question to Student B twice, once with each option. The answers are below.

2 Listen to Student B. How many answers can you guess?

> 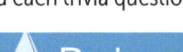 Rainy day quiz
>
> 1 *Not many / Quite a few* people know that Elvis Presley really had blond hair. It was dyed black.
> 2 *Few / Quite a few* people know that the world has 24 time zones, and some are only 30 to 45 minutes apart.
> 3 Bill Gates's teachers had *not many / a lot of* reasons to suspect that he had written a computer program scheduling classes for himself with students he liked.
> 4 *A fair number of / Few* people know Martin Luther King Jr. was a *Star Trek* fan.
> 5 Children's book author Dr. Seuss wrote *Green Eggs and Ham* with *quite a few / not many* words for young children – only 50 in all!
>
> **Answers:** 1 Not many 2 Few 3 not many 4 Few 5 not many

COMMUNICATION PRACTICE

10D Student A

1 Imagine you're upset because you didn't get onto a program you'd applied to. Tell Student B about it.

2 Listen to Student B's problem. React after each sentence and be as supportive as you can.
   1 Show sympathy.
   2 Show the positive side of the problem.
   3 Make a suggestion.
   4 Try to cheer your partner up.

11A Student A

1 Read the mystery slowly to Student B. At the end, give him/her five tries to solve the mystery.

> In two villages in northern Kazakhstan – in Central Asia, south of Russia – people of all ages were suffering from a strange illness. They would fall asleep suddenly, even while they were walking, and would wake up with memory loss, headaches, and a weak feeling. Sometimes they slept for as long as six hours, but when they woke up, they remembered nothing and didn't know they had fallen asleep. Children sometimes claimed that they had seen horses with wings or were sure there were snakes in their beds. Even pets got the strange illness and fell asleep without warning. There were many explanations, and some thought the villagers (and even the pets) probably had psychological problems. Others were sure the problem was nearby mines that had closed years before. *Something* was entering the atmosphere. What could it be?
>
> **Solution**: The old mines were releasing carbon dioxide, and so people weren't getting enough oxygen. They've now moved to different villages.

2 Listen to Student B tell you a mystery. When he/she pauses, ask questions to try to figure out the answer. At the end, Student B will give you five tries to solve the mystery.

I think he must have been someone else the man knew.

12A Student A

1 Imagine you are in each of these situations. Tell Student B at least two things you might wish for, using unreal conditional sentences. He/She has to guess each situation.

a

b

c

I wish they'd answer the phone. And I'd rather ...

2 Listen to Student B, who's having an unpleasant experience. Guess the situation.

COMMUNICATION PRACTICE

7A Student B

1 Listen to Student A, a college student. Give him/her advice.

2 Complete part of an e-mail from a recent college graduate. Try to be creative with the relative clauses.

> Well, I've graduated! But now I want a job offering _____ , and that's not easy to find. There are things I miss, as well. I was really into _____ in college, which _____ . And I used to enjoy _____ , which _____ . The good thing, though, is that I have some friends living across the street who _____ . But my parents say I have to _____ , which _____ ! Can you give me some advice on these things?

3 Imagine you're the college graduate. Summarize what you wrote for Student A. He/She will give you advice.

8A Student B

1 Listen to Student A tell you the story behind this photo. Do you personally think LPs are a success story?

2 Read the text carefully. Then cover it and tell Student A about it in your own words. Try to use the linkers.

Polaroid – the return of an old favorite?

When the first Polaroid camera was invented in 1945, it changed photography completely because of one unique feature: the ability to print photos instantly. However, when digital cameras were launched in the 1990s, all photos became "instant," and, therefore, by the turn of the century, Polaroid cameras had almost disappeared. But today, Polaroid is back, as young people want to experience photography the way their grandparents did, holding a photo in their hands. So whereas other 20th century companies have disappeared, Polaroid may be here to stay.

8C Student B

1 Listen to Student A's questions. Give a true response, choosing one of the two options.
   1 Yes, I enjoy ... / No, I've stopped ...
   2 Yes, it's hard not ... / No, I try not ...
   3 Yes, I'm looking forward to ... / No, I don't expect ...
   4 Yes, I can't help ... / No, I avoid ...
   5 Yes, I don't have a problem ... / No, I refuse ...

2 Ask Student A questions 1–5. Listen to each response and then tell him/her your own responses.
   1 Do you still watch regular TV shows?
   2 Could you spend a whole day without talking to anyone?
   3 Do you like seeing musicals?
   4 Do you limit the amount of time you spend on social media?
   5 Do you miss any friends you've lost touch with?

COMMUNICATION PRACTICE

8D Student B

1 Student A will comment on some annoying situations. React to his/her explanations.

2 Comment on these annoying situations to Student A and explain why you feel the way you do. Express doubt if necessary.
   1 companies that offer to call you back, but never do
   2 restaurants that have run out of most of the specials on the menu
   3 drivers who keep going when a traffic light turns red
   4 dog owners who don't keep their pets on a leash

9A Student B

1 Tell Student A about your neighborhood. Check his/her adverbs, using the key below.

> <u>Fortunately</u>, my neighborhood hasn't gotten more expensive because I'm <u>very</u> happy there. <u>Ideally</u>, the rent won't go up at all during the next few years. It's <u>extremely</u> convenient, and I can get to work really <u>rapidly</u>. I <u>usually</u> go by car, but I take the traffic into account, and I'm careful not to drive in bad weather. I don't drive <u>well</u> in the snow. In fact, you could say, I drive really <u>badly</u>! I'm originally from Florida, so I'm not at all used to the snow up here in Maine.

Key:
fortunately, ideally: comment adverbs
extremely, very: adverbs of degree
usually: adverb of frequency
rapidly, well, badly: adverbs of manner

2 Listen to Student A talk about his/her plans for next year. At the end, write down the eight adverbs you heard. Is each one a comment adverb or an adverb of degree, frequency, or manner?

9C Student B

1 Listen to Student A's problem. What advice can you give to help him/her deal with this situation?

2 Read the text carefully. Then cover it and tell Student A about it in your own words. Include passives and causative *have* structures.

> I have a boss who has us work such long hours that I can never take a vacation. We're frequently given extra work before national holidays. In addition, he often has us take work home on the weekends. A friend of mine was fired for not showing up on Monday with a finished assignment. And my boss has already made me miss three important family events. We're yelled at if we complain, so we can't say anything!

10A Student B

1 Listen to Student A. How many answers can you guess?

2 Read each trivia question to Student A twice, once with each option. The answers are below.

Rainy day quiz

1 U.S. President Theodore Roosevelt read *few / quite a few* books as president, one a day, in fact.
2 Two U.S. capital cities, Austin, Texas and Boston, Massachusetts have names that rhyme. *Both are / Neither is* spelled differently.
3 *Few / A lot of* people are aware that Buzz Aldrin, who walked on the moon, actually wrote a rap song called "The rocket experience" 40 years later.
4 There's *little / a fair amount of* information about the fact that right-handed people supposedly live up to nine years longer than left-handed people!
5 There's *a fair amount / not much* that doesn't interest a four-year-old. They ask around 450 questions a day.

Answers: 1 quite a few   2 Both are   3 Few   4 little   5 not much

168

COMMUNICATION PRACTICE

10D Student B

1. Listen to Student A's problem. React after each sentence and be as supportive as you can.

   1. Show sympathy.
   2. Show the positive side of the problem.
   3. Make a suggestion.
   4. Try to cheer your partner up.

2. Imagine you're upset because there was a mistake with your vacation reservation and the company has canceled it. Tell Student A about it.

11A Student B

1. Listen to Student A tell you a mystery. When he/she pauses, ask questions to try to figure out the answer. At the end, Student A will give you five tries to solve the mystery.

   Well, it might have been something in the water.

2. Read the mystery slowly to Student A. At the end, give him/her five tries to solve the mystery.

   > In a nursing home outside Edinburgh, Scotland, an elderly man had just died. There was nothing unusual about this as he hadn't been in good health. But when a doctor was called to complete the necessary paperwork, she noticed something strange. The man had two dates of birth and three last names. He had no passport or birth certificate to prove his identity, but he had told the staff he once lived in Italy, which seemed strange, too. Eventually, the police discovered that he had been born in Italy and had to leave when he was 21. One of the three names really was his. Another one belonged to a woman he had once shared a house with. But why did he leave Italy? And why did he have so many names? Was he a criminal? Or could there be another reason his identity was a secret?
   >
   > **Solution:** He had escaped from Italy during World War II and already had a fake name when he became a British citizen in 1948. Having learned young that his safety depended on a fake identity, he was most comfortable keeping one (or two) fake names.

12A Student B

1. Listen to Student A, who's having an unpleasant experience. Guess the situation.

2. Imagine you are in each of these situations. Tell Student A two things you might wish for, using unreal conditional sentences. He/She has to guess each situation.

If only they'd tell us ... And it's about time ...

COMMUNICATION PRACTICE

7C Both students

1 Practice the mini-conversations in pairs. Extend each conversation to four or five lines.

1 A Could I borrow your car on the weekend?
   B Yes, as long as …
2 A Can you help me with the gardening on Sunday?
   B Sure. I'll help you even if …
3 A Can I borrow your laptop next week?
   B Yes, OK, provided that …
4 A Could you feed my cat while I'm on vacation?
   B Of course, unless I …
5 A Could you lend me your bicycle tomorrow?
   B That should be fine, as long as …
6 A Can you babysit the children tomorrow evening?
   B Yes, of course, unless …

2 Change roles and practice the conversations again with new outcomes.

10C Both students

1 Discuss the topics below in pairs. Give each other advice and use comparative structures where possible.

1 When speaking in public, …
   a is it better to have lots of detailed notes or just a few prompts?
   b how much should you practice?
   c what are some things you should never do?
2 When meeting someone who's older than you for the first time, …
   a do you need to use more formal language?
   b should you shake hands?
   c is it important to be careful what topics you talk about?
3 The day before an exam, …
   a how important is it to get a good night's sleep?
   b should you do most of your studying on the last day?
   c what can you do to make yourself feel less nervous?
4 On the first day of class, …
   a should you introduce yourself to everyone on the first day?
   b how can you improve your memory and learn everyone's name?
   c is it OK to ask the teacher lots of questions?

2 What's the most useful piece of advice your partner gave you?

> COMMUNICATION PRACTICE

11C Both students

1 Interview your partner about these various sleep experiences.
   1 Have you ever dozed off at school or work, even for a minute?
   2 Does anyone in your family snore?
   3 Do you like to sleep in on the weekends?
   4 Have you ever overslept and arrived late for work/class?
   5 Do you have trouble falling asleep when you're angry or upset?
   6 Do you know anyone who sleepwalks?
   7 Have you ever felt sleep-deprived?
   8 Can you stay awake at night if you need to? How do you manage it?

2 Listen to your partner. Then find a new pair and report your conversation to him/her.
   Carlos admitted that he had dozed off a few times at work.

12C Both students

1 Imagine you regret something you did (or didn't do) in each of the situations below. What would have happened if you had made a different decision? Make notes.
   1 You saw a great apartment that was reasonably priced, but you turned it down because you thought you'd find something even better.
   2 You had a chance to study in New York for a year, but decided it was too expensive and too far away from your family and friends.
   3 You forgot it was your boyfriend's/girlfriend's birthday yesterday. He/She won't answer your calls or reply to your texts.
   4 You decided to work for a year before going to college, but when you finally applied to the college you had chosen, they didn't accept you.
   5 You moved because you accepted a job in a new town, but your new boss turned out to be awful.
   6 You didn't invite a cousin to your wedding because you didn't think he/she would come. Now your cousin isn't talking to you.

2 Share ideas with your partner. Then decide on a solution to each problem together.

12D Both students

Discuss the statements below in pairs. Try to keep the conversation going for a few minutes for each one.
1 Desktop PCs are bound to disappear at some point.
2 It's conceivable that electric cars will replace conventional cars completely.
3 Robots aren't likely to be able to think or feel like humans at any point soon.
4 Whether we'll be able to travel to Mars is anyone's guess.
5 It's conceivable that drones will deliver all of our mail in the future.
6 It's likely that most people will be vegetarian in 100 years.

Phrasal verbs

Phrasal verb	Meaning
back up sb/sth	support sb; save sth
break down	stop working
break out	start suddenly (war, fire, disease)
break up	end a relationship
burn out	become exhausted through overwork
call off sth	cancel
carry out	conduct an experiment (plan)
catch on	become popular
catch up (on sth)	get information; do sth there wasn't time for
cheer up (sb)	make happier
come across	find
come back (to sth)	return (to sth)
come together	join
come up	arise (an issue)
come up with	invent
deal with sth	take action; accept sth
do without sth	manage without
drift apart	separate without actively trying to
figure out sth	understand with careful thought
fit in	be socially compatible (in harmony with)
get on (along) with	have a good relationship
get out of (doing sth)	avoid doing sth
give away sth	give something no longer needed
give in	surrender
go back (a long way)	return; know each other a long time
go through sth	experience sth difficult
grow up	spend one's childhood
hang out	spend time together
hang up	end a phone call
hang sth up	put sth on a hook (hanger)
have sb over	invite sb to your house
hit (it) off	get along very well
hold sb back	prevent sb from moving ahead (succeeding)
let sb down	disappoint

Phrasal verb	Meaning
live up to	fulfill
look after	take care of
look down on sb	think one is better or more important
look forward to sth	anticipate; be happy about
look out for sb	watch (protect)
look up to sb	admire (respect)
make up	become friendly after an argument
mess up sth	spoil (do sth badly)
miss out	lose an opportunity
note down sth	write sth to not forget it
pay sb back	repay a loan
pay off	be worthwhile
put up with sth	accept without complaining
reach out (to sb)	contact; show interest in
run out of sth	not have enough
sell out	sell the last one and have no more of
set up sth	establish; prepare for use
settle down	make a home with sb
show up	appear
stand out	be better; be easy to see
talk sb into	convince (persuade)
take after sb	be similar to a family member
take off	not go to work; succeed
tell sb off	reprimand (scold)
think over sth	consider
think up sth	invent; think of a new idea
throw out	discard (get rid of)
try out sth	use sth to see if you like it
turn up	appear
turn up sth	raise (the volume)
turn down sth	lower (the volume); refuse
turn out	happen (have a certain result)
use up sth	finish (use completely)
work out	exercise; end successfully

Irregular verbs

Base form	Past simple	Past participle
arise	arose	arisen
awake	awoke	awoken
bear	bore	born
beat	beat	beaten
bend	bent	beaten
bet	bet	bet
bleed	bled	bled
blow	blew	blown
broadcast	broadcast	broadcast
burn	burned/burnt	burned/burnt
burst	burst	burst
catch	caught	caught
creep	crept	crept
cut	cut	cut
deal	dealt	dealt
dig	dug	dug
feed	fed	fed
fight	fought	fought
flee	fled	fled
forbid	forbade	forbidden
forecast	forecast	forecast
forgive	forgave	forgiven
freeze	froze	frozen
hang	hung	hung
hit	hit	hit
hurt	hurt	hurt
kneel	knelt/kneeled	knelt/kneeled
lead	led	led
leap	leaped/leapt	leaped/leapt
lend	lent	lent
mean	meant	meant

Base form	Past simple	Past participle
mistake	mistook	mistaken
overhear	overheard	overheard
oversleep	overslept	overslept
seek	sought	sought
set	set	set
shake	shook	shaken
shoot	shot	shot
show	showed	shown
shrink	shrank	shrunk
shut	shut	shut
sink	sank	sunk
sleep	slept	slept
slide	slid	slid
spin	spun	spun
split	split	split
spill	spilled/spilt	spilled/spilt
spread	spread	spread
spring	sprang	sprung
stick	stuck	stuck
sting	stung	stung
strike	struck	struck
swear	swore	sworn
sweep	swept	swept
tread	trod	trodden/trod
undertake	undertook	undertaken
undo	undid	undone
upset	upset	upset
weep	wept	wept
wind	wound	wound
withdraw	withdrew	withdrawn
withstand	withstood	withstood

American English

Personal Best

Workbook

B2
Upper Intermediate

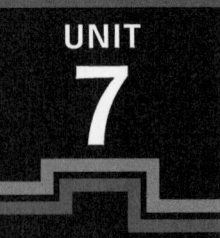

UNIT 7 Lifelong learning

7A LANGUAGE

GRAMMAR: Relative clauses; reduced and comment clauses

1 Choose the correct options to complete the sentences.

1. Is it the play *where / who / that* we saw in New York?
2. In the movie, López plays the guy *that / whose / who* brother is a gangster.
3. Luís, *which / who / whose* I work with, has seen Adele in concert five times.
4. My parents paid for my vacation, *that / what / which* was really generous of them.
5. Anyone *requires / required / requiring* more information should speak to Julia.
6. Applications *submitted / submitting / submit* after this date will not be considered.

2 Use the prompts to write sentences with the simple present that contain relative clauses. Sentences 1–3 should contain reduced clauses, and sentences 4–6 should contain comment clauses.

1. the blond guy / sit / next to / Daniel / be / my boss
   _____
2. he / usually / throw away / any food / leave / at the end of the day
   _____
3. the woman / eat ice cream / be / Sophie
   _____
4. my mother / often / call me / at work, / be irritating
   _____
5. Sara / play / her music / loud, / be really annoying
   _____
6. the train ticket / cost / $100, / I not afford
   _____

VOCABULARY: Collocations with *attend*, *get*, *make*, and *submit*

3 Complete the sentences with the correct form of *attend*, *get*, *make*, or *submit*.

1. I've _____ all my classes this semester!
2. He was asked to _____ a report on the economy.
3. It's extremely important that we _____ this message across to the public.
4. Which college does he _____?
5. She clearly hadn't prepared for the meeting, and she _____ matters worse by being late!
6. She'd never _____ a job application before.

4 Complete the texts with the correct words.

Working from home has its good points and its not-so-good points, as anyone who makes a ¹l_____ as a freelancer will tell you. On the plus side, you get to choose the hours that you work. For example, if it's a beautiful morning, you can make the ²m_____ of it by going out for a walk and starting work a little later. Little things make a big ³d_____, too – like being able to play music and have your dog sit at your feet as you work. But, of course, there are disadvantages, too. You submit a ⁴p_____ to a publisher for a book that you'd like to write, and it's very disappointing when it's rejected. Also, it's sometimes hard to get ⁵h_____ of colleagues that you need to speak to when they're working in an office. You also have to accept that working on your own can be pretty lonely. I attend ⁶c_____ related to my profession twice a year, but apart from that, I don't spend time with other writers. To make ⁷m_____ worse, I live out in the country where there aren't very many people. Not everyone would enjoy that.

PRONUNCIATION: Comment clauses

5 ▶ 7.1 Read the sentences aloud. Pay attention to the pause after the comma and the falling intonation after it. Listen and check.

1. Petra bought me a T-shirt for my birthday, which was kind of her.
2. The train was half an hour late, which meant that I missed my plane.
3. Tom recommended somewhere to stay, which was really helpful.
4. Olga blames Julia for the accident, which I think is a little unfair.
5. There was a store really close to the apartment, which was very convenient.
6. The first course was a spicy fish dish, which she didn't like at all.

SKILLS 7B

LISTENING: Identifying sequence

1 ▶ 7.2 Listen to the interview and choose the correct options.

1 Mariana says that when she was in school
  a she enjoyed math more than any other subject.
  b her least favorite subject was math.
  c she was very good at math.
2 In school, Gabriel
  a learned basic math successfully.
  b was pretty good at math.
  c found it very hard to learn math.
3 Gabriel says
  a his teacher was good at explaining math rules.
  b he couldn't understand what his teacher said.
  c his teacher was bad at explaining math rules.
4 Why does Gabriel think he couldn't learn math in school?
  a His teacher kept telling him he couldn't do it.
  b His sister kept telling him he couldn't do it.
  c He thought he couldn't do it.
5 What do we know about the teacher for Gabriel's evening class?
  a She loves math.
  b She's a brilliant mathematician.
  c She explains things well.
6 What did Gabriel learn in his evening class?
  a It is better to work slowly, from one stage to the next.
  b You should discover the rules by yourself and not ask too many questions.
  c You have to be patient to learn math.

2 ▶ 7.2 Listen again. Focus on the way Gabriel gives tips or advice. Complete the sentences.

1 Basically, _____ a very simple rule, _____ learn a more complex rule.
2 And – and this is *so* important – _____ you have a question, _____!
3 _____ you're totally confused _____ your teacher a question!
4 And, _____, *never* give up!

3 ▶ 7.3 Read the sentences aloud. Pay attention to the underlined schwa /ə/ sound. Listen and repeat.

1 You c<u>a</u>n come, too, if you'd like.
2 What should we eat f<u>or</u> dinner?
3 She worked <u>as</u> a teacher.
4 Someday, I'd like t<u>o</u> go there.
5 <u>At</u> the coffee shop, we had coffee <u>and</u> cake.
6 He w<u>as</u> standing next t<u>o</u> Jamie.

4 Complete the words.

1 Not everyone is c_____ of dealing with such stressful situations.
2 This is very advanced physics. Even I s_____ to understand it, and I'm a scientist.
3 He can't s_____ to understand very basic instructions. I wonder why?
4 Sarah gives great talks. She has a real t_____ for public speaking.
5 I think I was reasonably s_____ at explaining the rules. Most of the children seemed to understand.
6 I'm afraid I completely f_____ to learn Spanish when I was living in Spain.
7 She spoke so quickly. I f_____ it h_____ to follow her.
8 Unfortunately, I couldn't quite m_____ to finish my essay in time.
9 He was giving tips on how to s_____ at learning a musical instrument.
10 He's p_____ good at cooking.

7C LANGUAGE

GRAMMAR: Present and future real conditions

1 Complete the sentences with the words in the box. Use two words twice.

| soon | long | as | even | unless | provided |

1 _____ if not many people come, we can still have fun!
2 The event will take place outside _____ it's raining, in which case, it will be indoors.
3 We'll finish the work before lunch as _____ as enough people show up to help.
4 We'll leave the house as _____ as it stops snowing.
5 It's still enjoyable to sing in a choir _____ if you don't have the best voice!
6 She says she'll come to the concert _____ long as we pay for her.
7 _____ she starts talking to the other children, she's not going to make any friends.
8 They'll start building their new house in June _____ they get permission.

2 Complete the sentences with the verbs in parentheses.

1 Lucía _____ (take care of) the children, provided we _____ (pay) her.
2 You _____ (be) safe as long as you _____ (travel) in a group at all times.
3 Unless we _____ (do) something to stop it, these animals _____ (be) extinct in a few years.
4 We _____ (call) you as soon as the plane _____ (land).
5 I think you _____ (enjoy) yourself even if you _____ (go) on vacation on your own.
6 I _____ (not invite) Carlo to the party unless Jess _____ (insist).
7 Provided there _____ (be) no delays, we _____ (reach) Boston by 2:00.
8 We _____ (have) lunch as soon as Sophia and Gloria _____ (get) here.

VOCABULARY: Mind and memory

3 Complete the sentences with the correct form of the verbs in the box. Use one verb twice.

| cross | change | make up | boost | keep |

1 When you pack for the trip, _____ in mind that it gets very cold at night in the mountains.
2 There are various ways to _____ your memory, such as getting enough sleep and exercise.
3 I can't _____ my mind whether to go to Sophia's party tonight.
4 If you _____ your mind about going to the movies, text me, and I'll buy a ticket for you, too.
5 I've never been to a vegetarian restaurant, but I'll try to _____ an open mind. It might be fantastic!
6 I assumed Jack would come with us. It never even _____ my mind that he might not want to go.

4 Complete the text with the correct words.

My sister's amazing! If you tell her your birthday once, she'll remember it forever.
I'm just the opposite. I have such a bad ¹m_____. Once, in school, a teacher asked us to learn a short poem by ²h_____ for homework. The next day, she asked me to say the poem out loud in front of the class. I stood up, and my mind just went ³b_____. I couldn't ⁴r_____ a single line! It was awful! There are other things, too. My mom is always having to ⁵r_____ me to do things, or I'll just forget. And experiences, too – even special experiences that most people would find ⁶m_____. A few months after they happen, I've forgotten all about them.

PRONUNCIATION: Sentence stress

5 ▶ 7.4 Listen to the sentences. Which are the two stressed words in each underlined phrase?

1 I usually give her a present even if it's only a few flowers.
2 You can use my bike as long as you bring it back.
3 María will go to college next September provided she passes all her exams.
4 Unless you give her some money, she won't be able to go to New York.
5 He can borrow my car as long as he drives it carefully.
6 Provided the weather is nice, you should have a good trip!

SKILLS 7D

WRITING: Writing a set of guidelines

Preparing for an exam

1 You've been learning a subject for months, even years, and yet you're going to be judged on your performance on a single day. No wonder exams are so stressful! Here are some tips to make sure you get the grade you really deserve.

2 _____

Some people like to learn everything at the last minute, but that doesn't work for most of us. I'll never forget the French exam where I decided to study the night before, but had such a bad headache I couldn't. What a disaster! **Besides**, most exams test far more information than you can review in one evening.

3 _____

Have you ever had an experience where you thought you understood something, but when you tried to explain it, you found you really didn't? Explaining what you're learning to your friends or family can really test your understanding. **In addition**, I find that saying it out loud helps me remember.

4 _____

You won't do your best if you don't feel your best. Try to eat well (resist junk food if you can), and drink plenty of water. **Moreover**, it's important to take a break now and then. A tired brain isn't an efficient brain! I know I work much better after a quick walk, when I've gotten some fresh air.

5 Lastly, here's my most important piece of advice for you: take practice tests, more practice tests, and then more practice tests! If you do that, you'll really get to know the exam and what to expect. I didn't do that for my last math exam because I was confident I would do well, but the style of the questions wasn't what I was expecting, and I didn't get a very good grade. Good luck!

1 Read the blog post and choose the correct headings a–e for paragraphs 2–4. There are two extra headings.

a Pretend to be the teacher
b Be good to yourself
c Work with a friend
d Give yourself enough time
e Give yourself a reward for hard work

2 Underline the sentences in paragraphs 2, 3, 4, and 5 that give the reason for each tip. Some paragraphs have more than one reason. Now use your own ideas to give a reason for each of the tips below.

1 When you are choosing a college major, use your heart as well as your head – think about which subjects you really love.
_____
2 If your employer offers you the chance to take a training course, do it!
_____
3 Look for relevant study apps that you can use on your phone.
_____

3 Look at the linkers in **bold** in the blog post. Choose the correct options to complete the sentences.

1 Degrees usually take four years. *Moreover / However*, in some countries, they can be very expensive.
2 It can be difficult to find time for study. *Besides / Nevertheless*, it's usually worth making the effort.
3 It's easy to find books on most subjects. *In addition / Consequently*, you can take an evening class.
4 It's best to study something you enjoy. *Moreover / However*, you need math for some jobs.
5 The college closest to you isn't necessarily the best one. *Besides / Similarly*, going to live in another city can be a great experience.

4 Choose one of the topics below and write a blog post giving a set of guidelines.

1 *Choosing a major in college*
2 *Continuing to learn your whole life*
3 *Making time for study if you have a busy life*

- Write a short introduction explaining the purpose of your post.
- Include 3–4 important tips, organized into paragraphs.
- Give reasons for each tip and include examples or personal experiences.
- Use linkers to add ideas.

41

7 REVIEW and PRACTICE

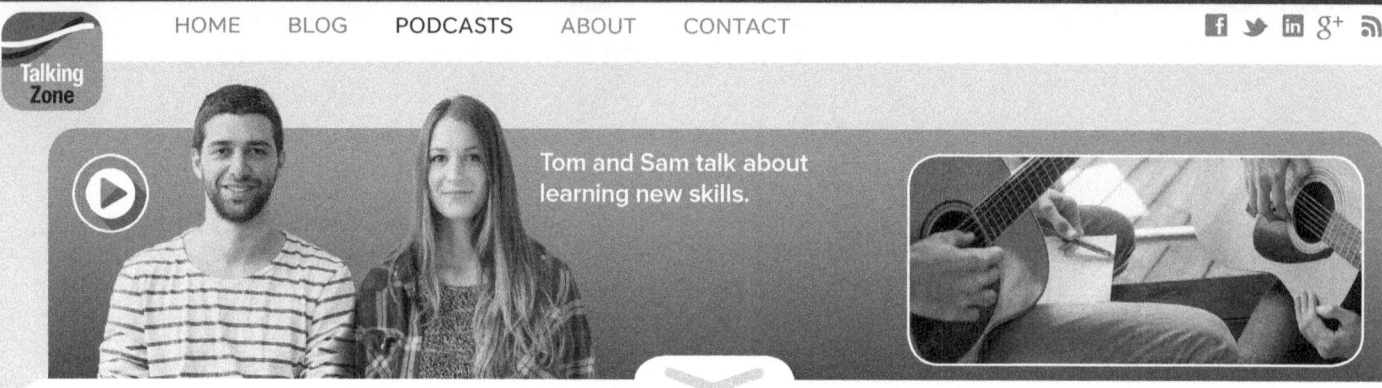

LISTENING

1 ▶ 7.5 Listen to the podcast and number a–e in the order that you hear them (1–5).

a Alice gives the reason for practicing five (and not seven) days a week. _____
b Sam says the name of the guest's blog. _____
c Sam mentions a habit of Barack Obama's. _____
d Alice says that her "learning hour" is in the mornings. _____
e Tom admits he has stopped trying to learn the guitar. _____

2 ▶ 7.5 Listen again and choose the correct options to complete the sentences.

1 Tom is no longer playing the guitar because
  a he has lost interest.
  b he doesn't have time.
  c the lessons are too expensive.
2 Alice wrote a blog about
  a spending an hour a day learning.
  b making the best use of time.
  c playing musical instruments.
3 She recommends studying five days a week
  a so that you don't get tired and make yourself sick.
  b so that your weekends are free.
  c because on some days it's not possible to study.
4 Barack Obama _____ for an hour every day.
  a played an instrument
  b read
  c studied
5 Alice says you should study or practice
  a in the morning.
  b in the evening.
  c at the same time each day.
6 Alice likes studying in the mornings when she
  a is on her own.
  b has lots of energy.
  c can think clearly.

READING

1 Read Hannah's blog on page 43 and choose the best summary.

a Hannah describes all the things that other schools do badly.
b Hannah writes about a typical day at her school.
c Hannah describes what she thinks is special about her school.

2 Are the sentences true (T), false (F), or doesn't say (DS)?

1 Hannah has already met Tom and Sam. _____
2 She thought they were both very funny. _____
3 Hannah believes that only happy, healthy students make progress. _____
4 She thinks that teachers generally disagree with this opinion. _____
5 Hannah says schools do nothing to improve the well-being of their students. _____
6 The English teachers at Hannah's school are in charge of classes on well-being. _____
7 Hannah says that talking to people you know well about emotional problems can be hard. _____
8 New research suggests that children don't speak in class because they are afraid. _____
9 In Hannah's school, speaking is as important as science. _____
10 The first time Hannah gave her talk, she forgot what she was supposed to say. _____

REVIEW and PRACTICE 7

HOME BLOG PODCASTS ABOUT CONTACT

Guest blogger Hannah talks about her school.

A BETTER SCHOOL

As part of Well-being Week last July, Tom and Sam kindly invited me on their show to talk about the amazing school that I attend. They've now given me the opportunity to write a blog on the subject. Thanks, Tom and Sam!

What do we mean by "well-being"? According to the dictionary, well-being is "the satisfactory state of being happy and healthy." I'm starting here because my school firmly believes that well-being is absolutely necessary for success. Unless students are happy and healthy, they won't achieve their goals. In other words, children make the best progress when they're feeling positive and confident in their abilities. Now this may not sound very surprising to you, and I imagine there are few teachers who would disagree with this statement. However, many schools treat the health and happiness of their students as an extra subject to be dealt with once the main subjects have been taught. In our school, well-being is every bit as important as English.

And how is this achieved, you ask? Well, the main thing is that all students have regular well-being sessions run by a teacher who is specially trained in the subject. During these sessions, we're encouraged to talk about anything that's making us feel stressed or anxious. The teacher then talks us through ways of dealing with these feelings. From time to time, all students suffer, but we sometimes can't quite manage to tell the people we're closest to. Sessions like these with someone who's skilled at talking about difficult feelings can make a big difference.

But that's not the only thing that's different (and better!) about our school. A vital life skill (in my opinion) that some schools are giving less attention to these days is speaking. A recent study suggested that, on average, children speak very little in a typical

45-minute class. As a result, a lot of young adults finishing school struggle to express themselves. Our school does things very differently. For us, speaking is a key subject — like science. Discussion is a major part of every lesson, including math. In addition, each term, all students write and learn a five-minute speech by heart on their chosen subject. The first time you give your talk, it's scary. (When I first had to do it, my mind went completely blank!) We help students who feel nervous, though, and they all succeed.

Finally, on every classroom wall is a list of ten school rules, written by the students. Some of these — be polite, do your best, etc. — you might expect; others you may not. "Admit to your mistakes," says number 5, and 6 says, "Keep your promises." I think you'll agree these are good rules for life!

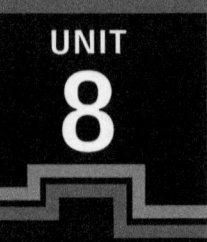

UNIT 8 The changing media

8A LANGUAGE

GRAMMAR: Using linkers (2)

1 Choose the correct options to complete the sentences.

1 _____ you, I actually enjoy driving.
   a While   b Unlike   c Whereas

2 They were badly delayed _____ all the traffic.
   a since   b as   c as a result of

3 Heavy snow is expected this evening. _____, we're closing our store at 3 o'clock.
   a Therefore   b Due to   c Because of

4 María thought he was a lot of fun, _____ I found him pretty annoying.
   a unlike   b since   c whereas

5 _____ I don't jog or go to the gym, I do walk a lot.
   a As a result of   b Unlike   c While

6 I gave away my sneakers _____ I never used them.
   a because of   b since   c due to

7 A number of flights have been canceled _____ the bad weather.
   a as   b since   c due to

8 Some people find his movies really funny, _____ others just think they're silly.
   a as   b therefore   c while

2 Choose appropriate linkers from exercise 1 to complete the sentences. There may be more than one answer.

1 The north of the country has lots of mountains and hills, _____ the south is fairly flat.

2 Unfortunately, the community center had to close _____ financial problems.

3 I stopped going to yoga classes _____ I had a bad back.

4 _____ I don't like all their policies, I do think they've done good things for the environment.

5 _____ Isabel, I don't spend a lot on clothes.

6 Only two people signed up for the class. _____, we've decided to cancel it.

7 Some streets have been closed _____ the recent flooding.

8 I'm actually pretty physically active, _____ the rest of my lazy family!

VOCABULARY: The media

3 Read the statements and (circle) True or False.

1 News that is biased contains facts rather than opinions.   True   False

2 Objective reporting contains opinions rather than facts.   True   False

3 A report that is accurate is true and without errors.   True   False

4 A sensational report is shocking or exciting.   True   False

5 A report that is fair cannot be trusted as it gives only one person's opinion.   True   False

6 Breaking news is information about an event happening now.   True   False

7 A show or person that is on the air is on TV or on the radio.   True   False

8 Tabloids contain mainly serious reports about important events.   True   False

4 Complete the sentences with the correct form of the media words.

1 The newspaper is planning to introduce a s_____ news service for its financial news.

2 He's really funny. I f_____ him on Twitter.

3 The final episode of the series *Friends* attracted an a_____ of over 50 million.

4 I didn't have time to read the paper. I just looked quickly at the h_____.

5 It was reported in the p_____ that over 20,000 people had attended the demonstration.

6 We don't have the movie on DVD, so we're going to pay to s_____ it.

PRONUNCIATION: Emphatic stress

5 ▶ 8.1 Read the sentences and underline the linkers. Listen and notice how they are stressed to emphasize a contrast or a reason.

1 Ollie is very sociable, whereas Lucy is pretty shy.

2 He was in a car accident a few years ago. As a result, he walks really slowly.

3 Nadia works very hard, unlike most of her friends.

4 We had to postpone our trip, due to all the snow.

5 I was in the hospital at the time. Therefore, I was unable to go to their wedding.

SKILLS 8B

READING: Inferring meaning using related words

THE DIGITAL GENERATION GAP

There are a lot of ¹gloomy observations out there about life in the 21st century, the most negative ones, as a rule, made by older people. The digital age, they say, is ruining our brains. The fact is that, at this point in time, no one really knows the effect of the digital age on our brains, and that's because nothing like this has ever happened before.

So what are the over-40s – the so-called *digital immigrants – saying? Well, they quote a recent study suggesting that, generally speaking, we young people can't concentrate. With our laptops and phones always at hand, we're so used to accessing several sources of information ²sequentially, one after another, that we're no longer able to give our attention to just one thing. Is there any truth to this? Sorry, I'll think about this one later – my phone's ringing ... ONLY JOKING!

They also report a piece of research that claims that we read information on a screen more quickly than we read text on paper. But isn't that a good thing? Well, not really, apparently, because we read information on a screen so quickly that we fail to ³retain it, remembering up to 20% less than when we absorb it from a book. Ah, but what if reading more quickly allows us to read *more*? No one mentions that, though!

And what about the claim that we're all sleep-⁴deprived, our bodies lacking the rest that's vital for brain function? We're online half the night, they say, chatting with our friends. Obviously, I can't speak for *everyone*, but if *my* friends are up till the early hours, it's because they're *studying*. Exams these days are tough!

But, hey, it's not all bad news! There's one skill that we have that our parents don't. We're so used to dealing with a mass of online information that we're able to ⁵filter out and ignore what's irrelevant, and get quickly to the facts that we need. So that's something, I guess!

* people who grew up before the Internet, tablets, smartphones, etc. and actually had to learn how to use all this stuff

1 Choose the correct options.

1 What is the author's view of the digital age?
   a He/She is hopeful that it will bring benefits.
   b He/She is worried that it will have negative effects.
   c He/She thinks it is too early to comment.
2 According to older people, why is the younger generation unable to concentrate?
   a They are not in the habit of looking at just one thing.
   b They prefer chatting online with their friends.
   c Their phones never stop ringing.
3 According to the research, what is the problem with reading text on a screen?
   a People generally read it more slowly.
   b People do not usually understand it very well.
   c People do not usually remember it very well.
4 The author admits that young people may lose sleep as a result of
   a being online.
   b chatting with friends.
   c studying.
5 Young people are better than their parents at
   a quickly finding what they need in large amounts of information.
   b remembering very large amounts of information.
   c understanding very large amounts of information.

2 For each of the words below, find a synonym in the same sentence in the text. The synonym may be a word or a phrase.

1 gloomy _____
2 sequentially _____
3 retain _____
4 deprived _____
5 filter out _____

3 Complete the expressions in **bold** in the text below by adding one or two words.

I limit the amount of time I spend looking at a screen. Obviously, when I'm studying for exams, I spend a lot of time in front of a screen, but, ¹_____ **whole**, I spend no more than two or three hours a day on my laptop and phone. ²_____ **speaking**, I think my generation is aware of the problems that screens can cause with sleep and posture. No one wants to have back or neck problems when he or she is only eighteen, so, ³_____ **rule**, we tend to avoid long periods in front of a computer. There's a lot of information out there advising us to take regular breaks and stretch regularly. I think that, **for ⁴_____ part**, this education campaign has been very effective in informing young people about the possible dangers.

8C LANGUAGE

GRAMMAR: -ing forms and infinitives

1 Choose the correct options to complete the sentences.

1. Dan helped me *fill in* / *filling in* the form.
2. He worked all morning without *to stop* / *stopping*.
3. James loves not *having to* / *to have to* shave.
4. She made him *apologize* / *to apologize* to Paul.
5. Some days I just feel like *to stay* / *staying* at home.
6. I ran outside *seeing* / *to see* what had happened.
7. I'd really recommend *taking* / *to take* the train there.
8. Oh no! I forgot *bringing* / *to bring* your book with me!

2 Complete the sentences with the correct form of the verbs in the box.

> try   say   give   get up   go   ask   keep   lose

1. Spending four years in college is expensive so you need _____ that in mind.
2. It's no use _____ to persuade her to change her mind. She's made her decision.
3. I really enjoy _____ early, especially in the summer.
4. Alice offered _____ me a ride to the station.
5. In the end, I called David _____ for his advice.
6. I'm not really into _____ to rock concerts.
7. _____ good-bye to her at the airport was sad.
8. Can I borrow your jacket, please? I promise not _____ it.

VOCABULARY: Common expressions with *at*, *for*, *in*, and *on*

3 Complete the sentences with the expressions in the box.

> at first   for no reason   for once   at once
> in trouble   in doubt   on a regular basis
> on behalf of

1. For over an hour, no one came, and then suddenly, everyone arrived all _____.
2. I'm accepting this award _____ my father who, unfortunately, can't be with us today.
3. _____, I thought she was serious, but soon I realized that she was joking.
4. Luca is _____ with his parents because he hasn't been going to his classes.
5. Greta is almost always late, but _____, she was actually on time this morning.
6. The future of the company is _____ because of falling sales.
7. You should try to exercise _____, not just when you feel like it.
8. My two-year-old son keeps hitting other children _____, and this really upsets me.

4 Complete the crossword puzzle.

Across

2. The nurse on _____ was very inexperienced. (4)
4. He only works part-time, but at _____, that means he has some money coming in. (5)
6. Tom is very difficult. He always wants to be in _____ of things. (7)
8. Today, just for a _____, I decided to ride my bike. (6)
9. Low land like this is at _____ of flooding. (4)
10. I wrote the names in alphabetical order, just for the _____ of simplicity. (4)

Down

1. Once in a _____, I go to an art gallery. (5)
2. Rebecca was pretty badly in _____ at the time. She owed money to three or four friends. (4)
3. She has a full-time job, three young children, and on _____ of that, she has sick parents to care for. (3)
5. On _____, I drink five cups of coffee a day. (7)
7. I think Lara is arriving around noon, but I don't know for _____. (4)
8. A war between our nations must be avoided at all _____. (5)

PRONUNCIATION: Unstressed pronunciation of *to*

5 ▶ 8.2 Listen to the sentences. Notice the unstressed pronunciation of *to*. Listen and repeat.

1. It's so strange to think we'll never see her again.
2. I'd love to visit Quebec in the spring.
3. I'd like to know how much he paid for the car.
4. In the end, we decided to cancel the party.
5. She said she hoped to come back one day.
6. Zara came over to talk to me.

SKILLS 8D

SPEAKING: Expressing annoyance and indifference

1 ▶ 8.3 Listen to the conversation between Julia and Ian and complete the sentences.

1 What's the _____ of visiting someone who just wants to watch TV all the time?
2 I think it's all _____ being lonely.
3 Yeah, that makes _____.
4 Here's what I don't _____.
5 It's hard to _____ why she's being like this, _____ I'm worried that she's a little depressed.
6 Yes, I see what you _____.

2 Complete the sentences with *whatever*, *however*, *wherever*, or *whenever*.

1 Pablo keeps following me _____ I go.
2 _____ hard I study, I'll never pass these exams.
3 "You really need to stop eating so much junk food." "Yeah, _____."
4 _____ I speak to María, she always complains about her job.
5 I'll support her, _____ she decides to do.
6 You should apologize, _____ hard that may be.

3 Match the two parts of the sentences.

1 I see what you mean – _____
2 Yeah, that makes sense, I suppose, _____
3 What's the point of _____
4 I think it's all about _____
5 And, you see, here's what I don't get. _____

a watching shows about other people's problems?
b escaping from your own life.
c it makes that kind of unpleasant behavior seem normal.
d but I'd really like to watch something else now and then!
e My roommate's an intelligent person.

4 ▶ 8.4 Complete the conversation with the sentences in exercise 3. Listen and check.

A My roommate is crazy about soap operas. Whenever I come home, he's watching them.
B Is that a problem?
A Well, I'd prefer to watch something more interesting. ¹_____
A wildlife show or a good movie would be so much better. ²_____
How can he enjoy these ridiculous stories?
B Maybe he just wants something easy at the end of a hard day's work.
A Maybe. But another thing I hate is the way the characters talk to one another. I think it must affect people who watch them too much.
B Ah, yes. ³_____
A Exactly. To be honest, I never understand why these shows are so popular.
B ⁴_____
However stressed you are, you can watch soaps and forget your own problems.
A ⁵_____

5 Write a short conversation between two friends talking about annoying social media posts. Include sentences that clarify how they feel and that show their reactions to each other's comments.

47

8 REVIEW and PRACTICE

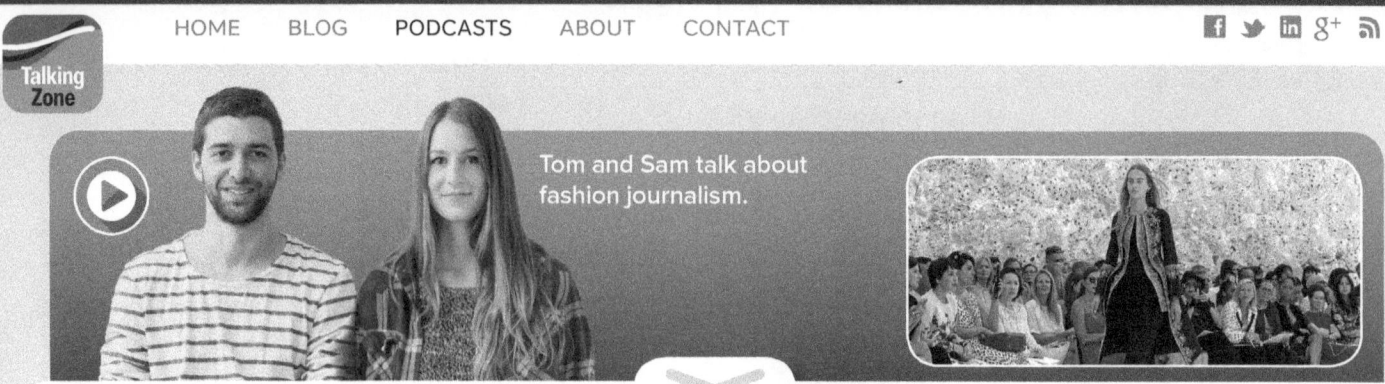

HOME   BLOG   **PODCASTS**   ABOUT   CONTACT

Tom and Sam talk about fashion journalism.

LISTENING

1 ▶ 8.5 Listen to the podcast and check (✓) the things Sam, Tom, and Hannah talk about.

1 the best stores to go to if you want a great pair of jeans _____
2 how Hannah began her career as a fashion journalist _____
3 her experience in fashion before she became a journalist _____
4 why it's a waste of time to go to fashion school _____
5 the high cost of good-quality clothes _____
6 things about fashion journalism that are different from when she started her career _____
7 how journalists can write about fashion shows even if they haven't been to them _____
8 whether or not she thinks that fashion journalism is a good job _____

2 ▶ 8.5 Listen again and complete the sentences with one or two words.

1 Sam makes a joke about Tom's _____.
2 Hannah says that _____ jeans aren't always the best.
3 Hannah has been a fashion journalist for _____ years.
4 She didn't go to _____.
5 When she was starting, she asked lots of fashion magazines for _____.
6 When she was younger, she worked in a _____.
7 The increase in _____ has changed fashion journalism a lot.
8 Fashion shows are often _____, so you can write about them without being there.
9 Hannah enjoys going to the _____.
10 To have a career in fashion journalism, you need to be an _____.

READING

1 Read Marianne's blog on page 49 and choose the best summary.

a Too much news can have a negative effect on both our physical and our mental health, and it is, therefore, better to avoid it.
b It is important to know what is happening in the world, but we need to be careful that we do not become anxious because of what we read or see.
c News reports focus too much on shocking events, and that prevents us from being able to make good decisions.

2 Choose the correct options to complete the sentences.

1 It's so easy to get news that we never think about
  a the quality of news reports.
  b the best places to find accurate reports.
  c the amount of news we watch or read.
2 The media often ignores important issues because
  a they're not dramatic enough.
  b it prefers to report bad news.
  c they're too shocking.
3 Video images of news stories
  a give us a better understanding of what has happened.
  b don't usually affect us emotionally.
  c have a more powerful impact on our emotions.
4 If newspapers and news shows include more happy stories, people
  a suffer fewer negative effects from the news.
  b don't notice them as much as the bad news stories.
  c have a better understanding of how to keep themselves safe.
5 It isn't necessary to know what's in the news because
  a it wastes a lot of time.
  b it doesn't help us with our lives.
  c people feel better when they don't know.

REVIEW and PRACTICE 8

HOME BLOG PODCASTS ABOUT CONTACT

Guest blogger Marianne explains why we should all stop reading the news.

No news is good news!

News is a little like food – the way we consume it has changed enormously in recent years, and, in my opinion, it's really not good for us. Like food (in many societies anyway), there's simply too much of it available, and the fact that we can constantly access small amounts means that we end up having way too much. We no longer know when we're totally full!

Of course, we all want to know what's going on in the world around us, but relying on news reports certainly doesn't provide an objective view because they overemphasize events that are dramatic or shocking, whereas, in reality, other issues are often much more important. So, for instance, the mass media goes crazy if there's a plane crash somewhere, while the huge problems caused by stress and anxiety in our modern society rarely make the headlines.

A recent survey by the American Psychology Association found that 1 in 10 people in the U.S. check the news at least once an hour, and, if you use social media, you can't escape the news there, either. Nowadays, anyone can film images on his/her phone, and this means that news often comes to us in a more visual way, which often makes it seem more sensational and upsetting. To go back to the food comparison for a moment, this diet of shocking facts – just like a diet of junk food – can actually be physically harmful. Some researchers suggest that reading bad news on a regular basis can lead to sleep loss, anxiety, and even heart disease.

People often say to me, "Ah, you just need to read some positive stories, as well as all the awful ones," but I'm afraid our brains don't work that way. We naturally pay more attention to things that frighten us than things we enjoy, which makes sense if you think about it. Our ancestors had to be aware of the dangers around them in order to survive.

Personally, I haven't looked at the news for over three years now, and I can't tell you how much better I feel because of that. I sleep better, my concentration has improved, and I can use all that time I used to waste on the news for things that are really important to me. I know it might sound scary to give it up altogether, but ask yourself this: when was the last time that anything you read in the news helped you make a better decision or improved your life in any way?

If you can't answer that question, it may be time for you to join my news-free world!

UNIT 9

The power of design

9A LANGUAGE

GRAMMAR: Position of adverbs

1 Put these words in the correct order to make sentences.

1 her / really / Alice / forgetting / friends' birthdays / hates
   _____

2 extremely / and / father / was tall / thin / my / mother's
   _____

3 movie / on / got / luckily, / we / time / the / to
   _____

4 often / have / I / wondered / she earns / how / her money
   _____

5 starting / we / to feel / were / bit / a / tired
   _____

6 gave / dollars / generously / us each / my uncle / very / a hundred
   _____

7 to arrive / had to / I / for / the train / wait
   _____

8 I / treat / hope I / children / fairly / my
   _____

2 Cross out the adverbs that are in the wrong position in this text and insert (^) them in the correct position above the line.

> Some of my friends are jealous a little of Sophie because she's so good at everything, but I'm not. I admire her. One of the things I admire really about her is that she's positive amazingly. For example, this year, in addition to studying hard incredibly for her exams, she's working in her parents' store. (Her parents can't afford to hire any more staff.) But Sophie is cheerful always, and she complains never. I hope she'll be able to a little relax when her exams are over and take maybe a vacation somewhere nice.

VOCABULARY: Collocations with *have* and *take*

3 Complete the sentences with the words in the box.

| influence | risk | responsibility | argument |
| pleasure | turns | nothing | control |

1 They had an _____ about who should cook dinner.
2 This conflict has _____ to do with religion.
3 You're taking a _____ buying plane tickets this late.
4 I think Sam is a good _____ on his brother.
5 They took great _____ in their grandchildren.
6 She took _____ of the company when her dad died.
7 Millie and I took _____ carrying the heavy bag.
8 We all have to take _____ for our decisions.

4 Read the conversation. Complete each of the phrases with one word.

A Hey, how did last night go? I hear Paola had you and Jack ¹_____ for dinner?

B Oh, it was OK, I guess. I went on my own, actually. Jack has a really horrible cold, so he had an ²_____ for not going. The evening didn't start so well, though. I was late because I had ³_____ finding Paola's apartment. Then, when I finally got there, I realized it was her birthday. Did you know that?

A No, I didn't have a ⁴_____! She never mentioned it.

B That's right. So, of course, I didn't bring a card or a present, which was a little embarrassing. And, stupidly, I drove there. The weather forecast said that it was going to snow, but I didn't take it ⁵_____. I thought it would be a centimeter at most, not ten centimeters.

A Oh no! And how did the actual evening go?

B Well, it just wasn't very relaxing. Paola lives in this perfect apartment. She obviously takes ⁶_____ in every detail, so I spent the entire evening taking ⁷_____ not to spill or drop anything.

A Oh! That doesn't sound very relaxing.

PRONUNCIATION: Syllable stress with adverbs of degree

5 ▶ 9.1 Listen to the adverbs. Is the emphasis on the first syllable (1) or the second syllable (2)? Listen and repeat.

1 frequently ____   4 incredibly ____   7 truly ____
2 clearly ____   5 carefully ____   8 surprisingly ____
3 amazingly ____   6 obviously ____   9 remarkably ____

| SKILLS | 9B |

LISTENING: Understanding key points

1 ▶ 9.2 Listen to Megan interviewing her guest, Lucas, on the radio. Are the following statements true (T) or false (F)?

1 Lucas advises people on what color to have in their homes. _____
2 Lucas says that the color red is generally very appropriate for homes. _____
3 Megan describes different types of red. _____
4 Lucas recommends orange to people who like warm colors, such as red. _____
5 Megan asks Lucas about the color blue. _____
6 Lucas says blue is always a cold color, even when it is mixed with other colors. _____
7 Lucas mentions two colors that have blue in them. _____
8 Megan says her bedroom is a calming color. _____

2 ▶ 9.3 Listen to some sentences from the interview. Underline the key words that each speaker stresses. (The number of key words is given in parentheses.)

1 Red is warm, and that can be a good thing, especially in the winter. But red also has a lot of energy, and it's a color that gets our attention. (2)
2 It depends on the type of red. (1)
3 I was thinking of a light red – a pinkish-red – rather than a very strong, ruby red. (3)
4 Small amounts can work well in the house. (1)
5 If you like the warmth of red, but want something a little calmer in your home, orange might be the answer. (3)
6 A purplish-blue – violet is also pretty warm. (2)

3 ▶ 9.4 Read the sentences and then listen to the recording. Write ✓ next to the sentence if you can hear the underlined *h* pronounced. Write ✗ if you cannot.

1 Would you like jam on your toast, or <u>h</u>oney? _____
2 The recipe says a teaspoon of salt, but I only use <u>h</u>alf. _____
3 I couldn't <u>h</u>ear what Milo was saying. _____
4 Could you take these boxes? They're pretty <u>h</u>eavy. _____
5 I called Dan, but <u>h</u>e'd already left. _____
6 She doesn't like lettuce, and she <u>h</u>ates cabbage. _____

4 Solve the anagrams to help you find the color words.

1 etal = _____: a dark color that is a mixture of green and blue
2 ovitel = _____: a color that is a mixture of blue and purple
3 ramono = _____: a color that is a mixture of red and brown
4 revalden = _____: a light purple color
5 bury = _____: the dark red color of a jewel
6 qurutosie = _____: a bright color that is a mixture of green and blue
7 vrelis = _____: the light gray color of a metal used in jewelry
8 lodg = _____: the bright yellow color of a metal used in jewelry
9 robzen = _____: the orange-brown color of a metal
10 itlucolemord = _____: having lots of different colors
11 lelywoshi-wronb = _____: the color of chocolate, but with a little yellow in it
12 glith = _____: describes a color that is the opposite of dark

9C LANGUAGE

GRAMMAR: Passives and causative *have*

1 Use the prompts to write sentences using the passive and the tense in parentheses.

1 This wall / build / by my grandfather. (simple past)
___
2 The patients / examine / in this room. (simple present)
___
3 The highway / close / this weekend. (future with *will*)
___
4 He / delay / because of the traffic. (present perfect)
___
5 All the cake / eat. (past perfect)
___
6 The lab / use / by Class 3BZ. (present continuous)
___
7 The results of the election / announce / by tomorrow morning. (future perfect)
___
8 Books / borrow from this library / for up to a month. (*can*, present)
___

2 Rewrite the sentences using causative *have* either in the active or the passive.

1 The hairdresser is coloring my hair this afternoon.
___
2 Our teacher asked us to do extra homework this week.
___
3 Someone cleaned our windows yesterday.
___
4 Someone delivers the shopping to my mom's house.
___
5 Mr. Walker tells us to sing at the start of every school day.
___
6 My pizza is cold. Could you ask someone to reheat it, please?
___
7 Wow, your car looks clean! Did someone clean it professionally?
___
8 At the workshop, they asked us to list our personal problems.
___

VOCABULARY: Dimensions and weight

3 Put these units of measurement in order, from the least (1) to the most (3).

| mile   inch   foot |

1 ___
2 ___
3 ___

| pint   gallon   quart |

1 ___
2 ___
3 ___

| ton   ounce   pound |

1 ___
2 ___
3 ___

4 Complete the sentences with dimensions and weight words.

1 He w___ about 180 pounds.
2 These whales can dive to a d___ of 3,000 meters.
3 This skirt is a little bit short. Can you l___ it?
4 The room measures 18 s___ meters.
5 They've w___ the street to make room for all the extra traffic.
6 He's not short, but he's not especially tall. He's probably about average h___.
7 They've had the river d___ so that larger boats can use it.
8 This structure supports the w___ of the ceiling.
9 These shelves are for large books, so they'll need to be pretty d___.
10 Tell me the length and w___ of the room.

PRONUNCIATION: Stress in passive and causative sentences

5 ▶ 9.5 Listen to the sentences. Which of the words is stressed? Listen and repeat.

1 We were told to come here.
2 Most of the food has already been eaten.
3 I'm having my room repainted.
4 Our flights have been canceled.
5 Has your bike been fixed?
6 He was questioned by the police.

SKILLS 9D

WRITING: Writing a magazine article

LIVING IN small spaces

1 Many of us live in small apartments, sometimes by choice and sometimes not! Although there can be disadvantages to not having much room, it can also be ¹an exciting challenge! Remember, small can be beautiful, and there are lots of things you can do to make your small space work for you.

2 _____
Firstly, you need to think about ²the way you want to live. You might like the idea of lots of stylish, modern kitchen equipment, but if you only cook ³a few times a month, you will probably have to do without it. On the other hand, if your friends come over for coffee most days, you might want to make room for some extra chairs.

3 _____
Many people believe that ⁴small spaces need to be white, but it's surprising how good bright colors can look. If you're not brave enough to paint a wall orange, consider buying a large, colorful painting. Despite what you might think, art isn't only for ⁵the rich – go to local art fairs to find pictures at very reasonable prices.

4 _____
There are several great websites with ideas for small apartments. They show photographs of fantastic interior design solutions from ⁶Tokyo to São Paulo. Many of them show creative ways to use ⁷furniture. For example, beds can be raised high off the ground to make room for a desk underneath, and ⁸the desk can be quite large.

5 If you live in a small apartment, you really need to make the most of every inch. But, with a little imagination, you can create a home you love.

1 Read the article and match headings a–c with paragraphs 2–4.
   a Look online for ideas
   b Decide what is most important to you
   c Be brave with color

2 Look at underlined words 1–8 in the article and match them with rules a–h.
   a Use *a/an* to talk about something/someone for the first time. ____
   b Use *a/an* in expressions of frequency. ____
   c Use *the* before a collective group. ____
   d Use *the* when something has already been mentioned. ____
   e Use *the* for something specific. ____
   f Don't use an article before uncountable nouns in general. ____
   g Don't use an article before plural nouns in general. ____
   h Don't use an article before most proper nouns. ____

3 Complete the paragraph with *a/an*, *the*, or (–).

   Last week, I visited ¹____ exhibit of ²____ kitchen equipment in ³____ New York. ⁴____ exhibit was amazing. I had never seen so many fantastic designs! As a food journalist, I go to ⁵____ exhibits like this several times ⁶____ year, but this was the best one I'd ever seen. They even had a large section of equipment for ⁷____ blind, including things like talking labels for cans. However, ⁸____ thing that impressed me most was ⁹____ fridge that talked.

4 Write an article about something where design is very important. Use one of the ideas in the box, or an idea of your own.

   | websites   cars   fashion   magazines   parks |

   • Give your article an interesting title.
   • Introduce the topic in an opening paragraph that readers can relate to.
   • Develop your ideas in two or three paragraphs and give each one a heading.
   • Summarize your ideas in the final paragraph.
   • Pay attention to your use of definite and indefinite articles.

9 REVIEW and PRACTICE

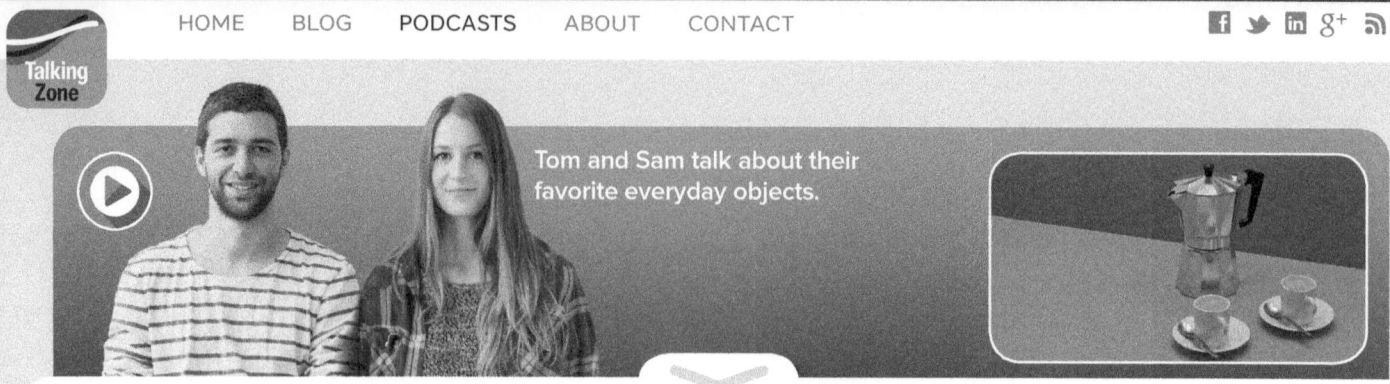

LISTENING

1 ▶ 9.6 Listen to the podcast and check (✓) the statement which is NOT true.

a Sam's chosen everyday object is not new. ____
b Tom's chosen everyday object is very unusual. ____
c Ethan's everyday object was given to him by a family member. ____

2 ▶ 9.6 Listen again. Complete the sentences with one or two words.

1 Sam and Tom are talking about everyday objects that we _____ great pleasure in.
2 Sam says that Tom takes his coffee _____.
3 Sam wants to know what is _____ about Tom's coffee maker.
4 Tom's coffee maker has _____ very little since it was designed.
5 Sam's favorite everyday objects are her _____.
6 She likes it that you can't see a _____ on them.
7 Ethan's favorite everyday object is a _____.
8 Ethan says he takes great _____ in his handwriting.

READING

1 Read Sam's blog on page 55 and choose the best summary.

a She thinks it's stupid to produce tools that are pink.
b She thinks it's wrong that tools designed for women should be pink.
c She's extremely pleased that her new tool box is pink.

2 Does Sam say these things in her blog? Circle Y (Yes) or N (No).

1 She was surprised to receive a tool box for her birthday. Y / N
2 Right now, she has nowhere to put her books. Y / N
3 Her friends have already visited her apartment. Y / N
4 The company that made her tool box says it's especially for women. Y / N
5 Pink used to be a typically male color. Y / N
6 There is no reason to produce tools that are light. Y / N
7 She accepts that men's hands are usually larger than women's. Y / N
8 Women have often had trouble using pens designed for men. Y / N

3 Look at the underlined phrasal verbs in Sam's blog. Complete the sentences below with the correct phrasal verbs.

1 They're planning to _____ _____ a new version of this tablet next month.
2 Can you help me _____ _____ the new curtains I've bought for the living room?
3 My uncle always liked to _____ _____ his latest sports car to his friends.
4 Maggie said she would _____ us _____ for dinner one evening next week.
5 This coat doesn't _____ _____ many sizes – only medium and large.

REVIEW and PRACTICE 9

HOME **BLOG** PODCASTS ABOUT CONTACT

In this week's blog, Sam questions the need for "gendered products," in other words, products designed to be sold only to men or women.

Gifts for her ...

My dad recently bought me a box of tools as a birthday present. Yes, I know, it's not everyone's idea of a nice gift, but I'd actually requested it. You see, I moved last month, and now live in an apartment *with no shelves*. I'd love to <u>have</u> my friends <u>over</u> so I can <u>show off</u> my new home, but they'd have trouble getting past the *mountain* of boxes in the hall containing all my books. Clearly, I need to do something about this!

Anyway, thanks to my generous dad, I now have a *wonderful* tool box to help me <u>put up</u> some bookshelves. The funny thing is, it's *pink*! And so are the tools inside. Yes, I have a *women's* tool box. OK, it's not *exactly* described this way by the manufacturers. Instead, they refer to it as a "light tool box, in a fun color, for small jobs around the house." But I *think* we know what they mean ...

And how do I feel about this? Well, I'm of two minds. On the one hand, I like pink in all its many shades — light pink, bright pink, dark pink. I wear a lot of pink. Last week, I even had the ends of my hair dyed pink. I don't think there's anything wrong with pink. (And, by the way, until pretty recently, there was nothing especially *female* about pink. A hundred or so years ago, it was considered appropriate only for men and boys.) To be honest, I probably prefer pink to black, brown, gray, or whatever other boring color tools usually <u>come in</u>. But why should anyone assume that because people choose *lighter* tools, they want *pink* tools — or the other way around, for that matter? It certainly makes sense to produce light tools, as well as heavy tools, so that people who are not amazingly strong can comfortably use them, but I have a suggestion for the makers of tools and tool boxes. Why not produce both heavy and light tools in a range of colors, including pink?

Do you remember those "pens for women" that they <u>brought out</u> a few years back? The makers said that they were designed to fit the female hand, which is, admittedly, a little smaller than the male hand in general. (Strangely, they seemed not to have noticed that generations of women had for decades been using a pen made for both sexes, without experiencing any problems.) I'm guessing I don't need to tell you what *color* those pens were ...

UNIT 10 The business world

10A LANGUAGE

GRAMMAR: Quantifiers

1 Complete the sentences with the words in the box.

| neither | lots | lot | much | none |
| both | few | awful | quite | good |

1 I'm a vegetarian. I have two sisters and _____ of them are vegetarians, too.
2 I'm afraid there's still a _____ deal of work to be done on the apartment.
3 There are _____ of good restaurants downtown.
4 Acting is a really tough profession. _____ people succeed at it.
5 There are _____ a few Spanish speakers on the course.
6 A _____ of my time is spent writing reports and keeping records up to date.
7 It's surprising she has red hair since _____ of her parents has red hair.
8 There were six of us for dinner last night so there's not _____ food left!
9 Sadly, an _____ lot of this packaging is just thrown away.
10 There are several movies on TV, but _____ of them sound very interesting.

2 Are the underlined quantifiers correct or incorrect? Cross out any mistakes and write the correct quantifiers at the end of the sentences.

1 On such a low salary, there's a little hope that he'll find housing that he can afford. _____
2 There are an awful lot of people here tonight. I've never seen this place so crowded. _____
3 Sadly, not much people offered to help the injured man. _____
4 A few politicians are as popular as Sylva. He's very unusual. _____
5 I work with some really great people. I hope you'll meet few of them tonight. _____
6 There's a fair amount of media interest in the subject. _____
7 We had little time to look around downtown, which we really enjoyed. _____
8 She's taught hundreds of students over the years, and she still sees quite a few them. _____

VOCABULARY: Trends and business

3 Complete the sentences by solving the anagrams in parentheses.

1 Since 2018, prices have risen _____ (tedasily).
2 Sales of plant-based products have gone up _____ (yarlpsh), almost doubling.
3 Global temperatures continue to _____ (nicaeers), and yet our governments do nothing.
4 The chart shows population _____ (togrhw).
5 Urban populations have _____ (irsne), while the number of people living in the country has _____ (nlafle).
6 There has been a sharp _____ (lalf) in the numbers of EU citizens going to the UK.
7 Migration has _____ (cdredaese) by 25%.
8 Many of those interviewed complained that their standard of living had _____ (cedlendi).

4 Complete the words in these two texts.

So, I own a ¹c_____ of electrical appliance stores. Our ²m_____ office is located here in Texas, and we have 28 ³b_____ in the U.S. We sell over two hundred ⁴p_____, most of which are ⁵m_____ in China.

⁶S_____ a small company is hard. Most small companies go out of ⁷b_____ within their first year. So what problems do ⁸e_____ face when they start companies? Let's assume that they've come up with brilliant ideas for products they'd like to ⁹l_____ or services they can ¹⁰p_____. Well, the first challenge is to ¹¹r_____ enough money.

PRONUNCIATION: (a) few and (a) little

5 ▶10.1 Read the sentences aloud. Pay attention to how a few, few, a little, and little are pronounced. Listen and repeat.

1 She's made a few friends since she's been there.
2 I even managed to save a little money last month.
3 Very few people are able to make a living as writers.
4 Life was hard during the war because they had very little money.
5 Few animals survive in these harsh conditions.
6 We stopped and had a little food at a roadside café.

56

SKILLS 10B

READING: Understanding text development

My life as a food courier!

Last month I joined the "gig economy," using my newly purchased bike to deliver fresh pizza, sushi, or ice cream to people in the comfort of their own homes. Depending on your point of view, I'm either:

(a) my own boss, enjoying flexible working hours or

(b) exploited, lacking a contract, vacation pay, and protection against accidents.

Well, so far, my experience has been almost entirely positive, and I'm going with (a)! The job wouldn't appeal to everyone – for obvious reasons, food delivery bicyclists work around meal times when most people see their family or friends. However, my roommates are chefs, and most days they don't get home until midnight. This job means I can do something useful to fill my evenings, making money and getting in shape. What would I do otherwise? Sit on my lonely sofa, staring at a screen? Binge-watch the latest season of some television series?

OK, so it's not the best-paid work. I'm paid about $10 an hour, and while I don't get paid for every food "drop-off," I always get tips. But there are definite benefits. The main advantage is I'm *in shape!* I've never exactly been out of shape – I know my way around a gym – but I've never had legs *this* strong. I'm also three kilos lighter even though I eat chocolate most days! And there's another benefit from all this exercise: having ridden many miles in the course of a day, I sleep like a log! Finally, there's the job satisfaction I get from providing a useful service. (You should see the happy faces when I show up at an address with my box of still-hot pizza!)

Of course, the job's not without disadvantages. For example, there's the rain … on the other hand, it means I do more "drop-offs." (No one wants to go out when it's wet.) Even worse is the wind – every bicyclist's enemy! Also, I sometimes waste time sitting in a restaurant while an order is prepared. That's frustrating, even though some of the friendlier restaurant staff will offer me something to drink.

But, overall, I'd recommend it!

1. Are the following statements true (T) or false (F)?

   1. For the writer, there are more advantages than disadvantages to this type of work. ____
   2. The writer says this type of work would not be right for everyone. ____
   3. If the writer didn't do this job, she would see her roommates in the evenings. ____
   4. The writer thinks the wages for this type of work are excellent. ____
   5. Customers tip the writer when she delivers the food. ____
   6. The writer didn't use to be in shape before she started this job. ____
   7. The writer has lost weight as a result of all the bicycling she does. ____
   8. The writer mentions one advantage of the rain. ____

2. (Circle) the words in the second sentences that are connected to the underlined words in the first. Indicate whether the words in the second sentence are related words [REL], reference words [REF], time words [T], or contrast words [C]. The first one has been done for you.

   1. She started two <u>companies</u>. Both of (them) were successful. <u>REF</u>
   2. But there are definite <u>benefits</u>. The main advantage is I'm in shape! ____
   3. For example, there's the <u>rain</u> … on the other hand, it means I do more "drop-offs." ____
   4. <u>For example</u>, there's the rain … on the other hand, it means I do more "drop-offs." ____
   5. The next few years saw an <u>increase</u> in profits. This rise was caused by two factors. ____
   6. <u>Initially</u>, I found him rather cold and distant. Later, I came to like him and very much enjoy his company. ____

3. Complete the second sentence with two words so that it means the same as the first.

   1. I've never exactly been out of shape.
      I've _____ in pretty good shape.
   2. She had no one to blame but herself.
      She could _____ herself.
   3. Her only problem was her lack of confidence.
      Her only problem was that she _____ any confidence.
   4. Of course, the job is not without disadvantages.
      Of course, the job _____ disadvantages.
   5. Raising the price of gas does little to reduce traffic congestion.
      Raising the price of gas _____ reduce traffic congestion.

10C LANGUAGE

GRAMMAR: Comparison

1 Complete the sentences with the words in the box.

> little   the   slightly   less   most
> one   far   as   by   least

1 _____ more you find out about the case, the more shocking it becomes.
2 Actually, the food wasn't _____ expensive as I thought it would be.
3 It was probably the _____ boring talk I've ever heard. I almost fell asleep.
4 The test was almost impossible. It was _____ more difficult than I'd imagined.
5 I didn't really like the last movie. It was my _____ favorite of the three.
6 The good thing is that the more exams I take, the _____ stressful I find them.
7 That was _____ of the best books I've ever read.
8 She was _____ far the best of the dancers.
9 I was a _____ more nervous before the exam than I thought I would be.
10 They're a similar height, but Lara is _____ taller than her mother.

2 Complete the second sentences so they mean the same as the first sentences.

1 The first and second books in the series were equally good.
   The second book was just _____ the first book.
2 Emily spoke more confidently than any of the other children.
   Emily spoke _____ of all the children.
3 I find that if I start exercising, I want to exercise more.
   I find that the _____, the _____ I want to exercise.
4 Her boyfriend was a little shorter than I was expecting.
   Her boyfriend wasn't quite _____ I was expecting.
5 Klara was more polite than you when she asked for ice cream.
   Klara asked for ice cream _____ than you.
6 The new exam isn't as challenging as the old one.
   The old exam was _____ than the new one.
7 He ran further than anyone else in his group.
   He ran _____ of anyone in his group.
8 I liked the dessert less than the other two courses.
   Of all the courses, I _____.

VOCABULARY: Word pairs

3 Match the two parts of the sentences.

1 I've seen María once ____
2 You'll have to tell him sooner ____
3 He's always making this mistake, and I tell him each ____
4 Every marriage has its ups ____
5 He never helps out, and I'm sick ____
6 She complains about the same things over ____

a or later.
b and every time.
c and tired of it.
d and over.
e or twice here.
f and downs.

4 Complete the word pairs in the text.

> I moved to New York from a small town at the beginning of last year, and, by and ¹_____, it was a very good decision. I enjoy living side by ²_____ with people from all different backgrounds. It makes life so much more interesting. Of course, there are pros and ³_____ to any big change that you make in life. I love all the possibilities that a big city has to offer, but, on the other hand, now and ⁴_____ I miss the ⁵_____ and quiet of the town where I used to live. For example, for the first few weeks I lived here, I couldn't get to sleep because of all the noise outside in the street, but, little by ⁶_____, I got used to it, and now it doesn't bother me at all.

PRONUNCIATION: Sentence stress with *the ... the* comparisons

5 ▶ 10.2 <u>Underline</u> the stressed words in each sentence. Then read the sentence aloud. Listen and check.

1 It seemed like the more I read on the subject, the less I understood!
2 The more she told me about the job, the more terrifying it sounded.
3 The harder I tried to please her, the less she liked me.
4 The more you research this area, the more fascinating it becomes.
5 Certainly, the more projects I manage, the easier it becomes.
6 The less Anna knows about the situation, the better.

SKILLS 10D

SPEAKING: Discussing pros and cons

1 ▶10.3 Listen to the conversation between Ana and Marco. Choose the best endings for the sentences.

1 Marco has to decide whether to
  a take a job in another city or not.
  b move to a bigger company or not.
2 He is attracted to the new job because of
  a the money and the increased responsibility.
  b the chance to work on a bigger team.
3 He is worried about the move because he
  a doesn't know anybody in Quito.
  b enjoys the social life he has in Cuenca.
4 Ana suggests that he could
  a only spend Monday to Friday in Quito.
  b invite his friends to stay with him in Quito.

2 ▶10.3 Complete the phrases Marco uses to discuss the pros and cons of his decision. Listen again and check.

1 I can't _____ whether to take it or not.
2 One of the _____ of being here is that most of our major clients are in Quito.
3 Each option has its _____, so it's really hard to decide.
4 I'm _____ wanting the challenge of a more senior job, not to mention the salary that goes with it, and wanting to carry on as I've been doing.
5 One minute I'm _____ going, and the next minute I think I should stay.

3 Use your own ideas to complete the conversations.

1 A What are you planning to do when you graduate from college?
  B I'm not sure. I can't make up my mind whether to _____.
2 A Have you decided what kind of job you want to apply for?
  B I'm leaning _____.
3 A Are you going to complain about your colleague's behavior?
  B I'm torn between _____.
4 A Have you thought about getting a job in a different department?
  B I'm not sure. One of the drawbacks is _____.

4 Use the phrases in the box and include some ideas of your own to complete the conversation.

| I really sympathize   look on the bright side |
| you could always   don't let it get you down |

A I'm finding it really difficult to work with the boss I have right now. I'm torn between looking for another job and hoping she'll leave soon. She said that she wants to move to Mexico.

B (Express sympathy.)
_____

A I'm leaning towards leaving, but I was happy before I had to work with her. She's not unpleasant. It's just that we have completely different ideas about how to do things.

B (Make a suggestion.)
_____

A That's certainly something to think about. One of the drawbacks of giving up this job is that I'd probably have to move. There aren't many companies around here that do the same kind of work.

B (Show the positive side of the situation.)
_____

A Yes, you're right. I should try to be positive, but it's difficult, and it's so hard to decide what to do. Each option has its pros and cons.

B (Try to cheer A up.)
_____

59

10 REVIEW and PRACTICE

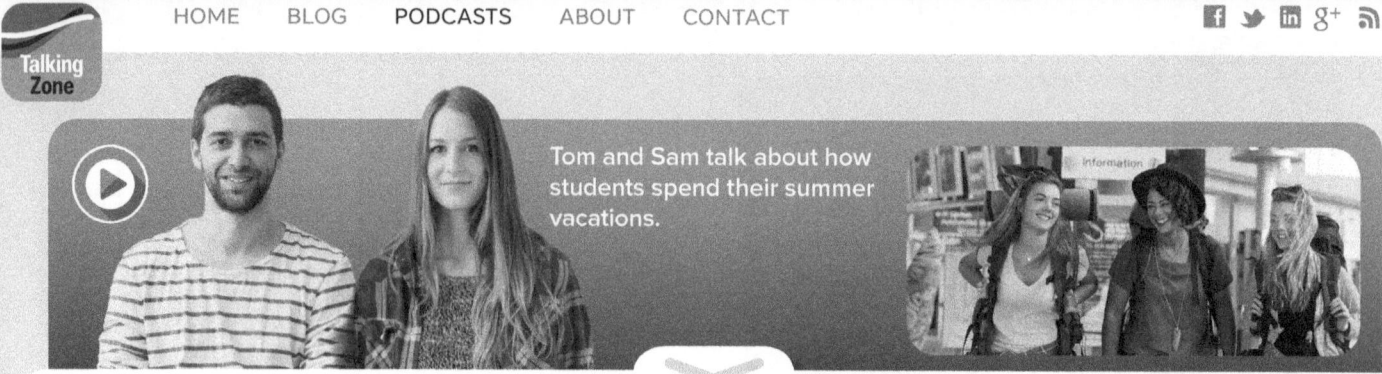

LISTENING

1 ▶ 10.4 Listen to the podcast. Choose the correct options to complete the sentences.

1. Zac feels that getting work experience is *fairly / extremely* important.
2. Melissa has a *similar / very different* view.
3. Melissa *has gotten some / hasn't gotten any* work experience on her vacations.
4. Tom *approves / doesn't approve* of her attitude.
5. Tom agrees with *Zac / Melissa*.
6. Sam agrees with *Zac / Melissa*.

2 ▶ 10.4 Listen again. Who says these things?

	Zac	Melissa	Nobody
1 I worked for two different companies during my vacations.	___	___	___
2 I managed several restaurants.	___	___	___
3 When you apply for a job these days, there are always a lot of other applicants.	___	___	___
4 It's impossible to get a job without work experience.	___	___	___
5 It's a good idea to spend your vacations doing things you enjoy.	___	___	___
6 Employers aren't likely to choose someone who prefers fun to work.	___	___	___
7 Activities other than working can also be valuable.	___	___	___
8 I plan to do some unpaid work.	___	___	___
9 Most students don't have enough money to be able to work without being paid.	___	___	___
10 Young people shouldn't work all the time.	___	___	___

READING

1 Read the blog on page 61. Match paragraphs A–F with sentences 1–8. There are two sentences you do not need.

1. This company uses a clever trick to assess an applicant's attitude towards other people. ___
2. This company pays its staff very well. ___
3. Many employees want to be able to vary their working hours from time to time. ___
4. Tom's friends are not as happy at work as he is. ___
5. This company gives employees time off to do other things. ___
6. This company employs people who have studied creative subjects. ___
7. This company does a lot to make sure its employees are happy. ___
8. People work better when they're in shape. ___

2 According to Tom's blog, are the sentences true (T), false (F), or doesn't say (DS)?

1. Tom has similar problems to the friends he went out with. ___
2. He likes the idea of judging job applicants by how they treat their taxi driver. ___
3. The staff at Google has to work extremely hard. ___
4. Google employees have the freedom to try out their own ideas. ___
5. The facilities provided by Google help improve the home lives of its workers. ___
6. Employees do not achieve as much if they spend time exercising. ___
7. Providing flexible working hours is very difficult for employers. ___
8. Tom's cousin's firm allows employees to take time off whenever they want to. ___

REVIEW and PRACTICE 10

HOME BLOG PODCASTS ABOUT CONTACT

Tom writes about what makes a great workplace.

A happy worker is a good worker

A Last week, I went out with a couple of friends, and both of them spent the whole evening complaining about their jobs. I felt a little left out because I love my work, and it got me thinking about just what makes the difference between a job you force yourself to do because you need the money and one you genuinely enjoy.

B Obviously, colleagues have a lot to do with it, and I'm so lucky with mine. (Are you reading this, Sam?) I once heard about a company that always provides a taxi for people attending job interviews. The applicants don't know it, but the driver is a company employee who reports back on their behavior – the ruder they are, the less likely they are to get a job. That's their way of looking for staff who will treat everyone with respect, and I think it's really cool!

C Apparently, several times, Google has been voted the best place in the world to work. Workers say this is because their work satisfies them: it's creative, they can experiment with new ideas, and employees cooperate well, rather than compete with one another. In addition, the company puts a great deal of effort into creating a pleasant environment, and one that encourages a good work-life balance, for instance, by providing healthy meals, as well as sports, childcare, and even laundry facilities.

D Of course, any job can have its ups and downs, but there's an awful lot of evidence to show that when employees exercise, they are happier and more efficient, and production increases. (Feel like a quick jog before our next podcast, Sam?) Quite a few companies now recognize this by providing exercise classes and gym equipment, or by contributing towards the cost of a gym membership.

E However, while all of these benefits are welcome, employees often say that the most valuable thing for them is the opportunity to work flexibly. In other words, if you need to go home early one day because the electrician is coming, you can work for longer on other days and not have to use up your vacation time.

F Some firms also have programs aimed at employees who have bigger dreams. My cousin's employer, for example, has something they call "Five at Five," which means that when you've worked there for five years, you can take five weeks off to travel, work on your novel, build a new room on your house, or whatever you want to do. I love that idea, because everyone needs a change now and then. Maybe my dissatisfied friends should go and work there!

UNIT 11 Fact and fiction

11A LANGUAGE

GRAMMAR: Present and past modals of deduction

1 Choose the correct options to complete the sentences.

1 You've made so much food, Isabel! You _____ ages cooking yesterday!
   a might have spent b must have spent c 've spent

2 Lucy _____ still be at work, but I'm not sure.
   a might b can c will

3 I don't know the guy that Julia is talking to. He _____ be her brother or maybe just a friend.
   a can b could c could to

4 Joe isn't answering his phone. He might _____ a movie.
   a watch b watching c be watching

5 Daniel _____ told her. That explains it!
   a must have b could c might

6 Ethan wasn't even there last night, so it _____ have been him that you spoke to.
   a may not b might not c can't

2 Rewrite these sentences with modal verbs of deduction. Sometimes more than one option is possible.

1 There's no chance that Paolo has finished all that work already.
   _____

2 It's possible that she's working this evening.
   _____

3 I think I saw her yesterday, but I'm not sure.
   _____

4 I'm almost certain I told you the news! I'm sure I did!
   _____

5 She's definitely his mother. She's way too old to be his sister.
   _____

6 It's not possible that she's his child. Sam doesn't have any children!
   _____

7 I don't know why María was late this morning. Maybe she missed the bus.
   _____

8 You know every dish on this menu, Johnny. You definitely come here a lot!
   _____

VOCABULARY: Science

3 Complete the sentences with science words.

1 The study of the human mind is called p_____.
2 The l_____ is the system of rules in a country.
3 E_____ is the study of the production, distribution, and consumption of goods and services.
4 A_____ is the study of people from a long time ago by looking at their buildings, tools, etc.
5 G_____ is the scientific study of the Earth's structure and how it was formed.

4 Complete the crossword puzzle.

Across
3 Once you have your data, you need to _____ it. (7)
5 The children did an _____ in the lab. (10)
6 They were unable to _____ a conclusion. (5)
8 There's been a _____ in cancer research. (12)
9 She's going to _____ the results in a journal. (7)
10 That research allowed him to prove his _____. (6)

Down
1 Darwin _____ data about the natural world. (8)
2 He made a fascinating _____. (10)
4 She's _____ a problem she wants to research. (10)
7 He wants to _____ research on dyslexia. (5, 3)

PRONUNCIATION: Reduction of past modals

5 ▶ 11.1 Read the sentences aloud. Pay attention to the way that *have* is pronounced /əv/. Listen and repeat.

1 I suppose it could have been Sophie.
2 I'm sure he must have seen your reply.
3 He might already have told her.
4 You must have heard of him!
5 They can't have arrived already!

62

SKILLS 11B

LISTENING: Identifying conclusions

1 ▶11.2 Listen to Scott and Paloma's conversation and choose the correct options.

1 Who believes there will be a lot of snow next week?
  a Paloma
  b Scott
  c Paloma and Scott's friend, Sarah

2 Paloma says
  a it never snows where they live.
  b it only snows a little where they live.
  c it often snows where they live.

3 Sarah told Scott that
  a an actress sometimes pretends to be the president's wife.
  b the president is married to an actress.
  c the president does not have a wife.

4 Paloma thinks that the story about the president's wife is
  a surprising, but possible.
  b very likely.
  c extremely unlikely.

5 Paloma says that news stories about food
  a change all the time.
  b are usually accurate.
  c are never accurate.

6 Paloma says that people should not repeat stories
  a they have read online.
  b relating to food.
  c without making sure they are true.

2 ▶11.2 Listen again. Complete the phrases that the speakers use to show that they are reaching a conclusion.

1 I mean, _____ items in the news are true.
2 It's _____ which of these "facts" is true.
3 But before you go repeating it to all your friends, _____, as far as you can tell, it's true.
4 Yeah, I guess _____ part of the problem.
5 And _____ false stories about people can really hurt them.

3 ▶11.3 Listen to these sentences and phrases from the conversation. Link the two words where a /t/ is pronounced as a flap /ɾ/. The first one is done for you.

1 And she thought‿it was true.
2 Sarah says it's not actually the president's wife.
3 Yeah, I guess if you don't do that, then you're just part of the problem.
4 I know we're laughing about Sarah, but it *is* a serious problem.

4 Choose the correct adjective and add the prefix *un-*, *il-*, or *ir-* to give it the opposite meaning.

1 For most people, being separated from your children for several months would be completely ____*imaginable*. / ____*controversial*.

2 The service in the hotel was rather slow and ____*satisfactory*. / ____*responsible*.

3 The problem with the book was that the main characters were ____*acceptable*. / ____*believable*. They didn't behave like anyone I'd ever met.

4 By law, they can't refuse to hire you because you're female. It's ____*legal*. / ____*responsible*.

5 These medicines can have ____*impressive* / ____*desirable* effects on some patients, such as problems with sleeping.

6 Most parents would agree with the statement that raising children is difficult at times. That's fairly ____*controversial*. / ____*satisfactory*.

7 This small, gray building looks rather ____*believable* / ____*impressive* from the outside.

8 No one should be so rude to their colleagues. It's completely ____*acceptable* / ____*legal* to behave so badly at work.

9 It seems rather ____*responsible* / ____*believable* to leave such a young child alone in the house.

11C LANGUAGE

GRAMMAR: Reported speech patterns

1 Choose the correct options to complete the reported speech sentences.

1 "I annoyed Rebecca with my comments."
She *told / said* that she *has / had* annoyed Rebecca with her comments.

2 "I've been very busy with my coursework."
Sam explained *me / to me* that he *had been / was* very busy with his coursework.

3 "I could meet you and Sara a little later."
He said he *could / had been able to* meet us a little later.

4 "I've been seeing a little more of Tom recently."
He *said / told* me that he *had seen / had been seeing* a little more of Tom recently.

5 "By next summer, I will have saved up enough to go traveling."
Milo *said / said us* that by next summer, he *would save / would have saved* up enough to go traveling.

6 "Don't forget to take your passport!"
My mom reminded me *to take / take* my passport.

7 "When did you take the exam?"
James asked *me / to me* when *did I take / I took* the exam.

8 "Elephants are the only animals that can't jump."
Freddie claimed that elephants are the only animals that *can't / can't have* jump.

2 Read what Sophia said. Then complete the reported speech sentences with the correct information.

> "Have you heard the news about David and me?"
> "I can't afford to go on vacation this year."
> "I've been going to yoga classes recently."
> "I'm feeling a little stressed about my exams."
> "You really have to try Café Blanco!"
> "You absolutely can't mention the party to James."

1 A Did she mention David at all?
B Well, she just asked _____ David and her.

2 A Is she going away this summer?
B No, she said _____ this year.

3 A Is she doing any kind of exercise these days?
B Yes, she mentioned _____ yoga classes recently.

4 A Is she calm about her exams?
B Not really. She said _____ them.

5 A Did she recommend anywhere to eat?
B Yes, she urged _____ Café Blanco.

6 A Did she say anything about her party?
B Yes, she's forbidden _____ to James.

VOCABULARY: Sleep

3 Read the sentences and circle True or False.

1 People often oversleep on the weekend when they don't have work. — True / False
2 If you snore, you breathe noisily while you're asleep. — True / False
3 People never intend to sleep in. It happens by accident. — True / False
4 People who sleepwalk don't know that they're doing it. — True / False
5 You often yawn when you're tired or bored. — True / False
6 Someone who's sleepy is fast asleep. — True / False

4 Complete the sleep phrases in the text.

> Ever since I moved downtown, I've been having real problems sleeping. I just can't get used to the noise in the street. Most nights, it ¹_____ me awake until two or three o'clock in the morning. I'm getting three or four hours of sleep a night, which just isn't enough. In fact, I'm so sleep-²_____, I find it hard to ³_____ awake during the daytime when I'm at work. Just this afternoon, I almost dozed ⁴_____ in a meeting. It's so embarrassing! A colleague of mine recommended that I take a ⁵_____ when I get home – just half an hour or so while it's still quiet enough outside. The problem is that if I sleep when I get home, I find I can't ⁶_____ asleep at bedtime. Arghh!

PRONUNCIATION: /t/ and /d/

5 ▶ 11.4 Listen to the sentences. Underline when /t/ and /d/ are fully pronounced. Listen and repeat.

1 He asked me to wait.
2 They told us it had rained a lot the day before.
3 I urged her to reconsider.
4 When I reminded her, she promised to call him.
5 Tom mentioned that he really wanted to go traveling.
6 She asked us to lend her some money.

SKILLS 11D

WRITING: Writing a personal recommendation

Dear Ms. O'Reilly,

Alex Chambers has asked me to recommend him for a summer job at your riding school, and it is with pleasure that I do so. Alex is a friend of my own son, and I first met him when they started school together – around 15 years ago. I run a large farm in southern Wisconsin, and Alex has often worked for me on weekends and during school (now college) vacations.

Alex is an extremely [1]_____ man. His [2]_____ manner has helped him develop a good relationship with all the animals on our farm. However, it is clear that he has a particular love for our three horses, and he spends a lot of time with them, even when he is not working. Alex is one of the most [3]_____ people I have ever met. He once sat up all night with a sick cow even though he had classes the next day.

Alex also has [4]_____ skills. He gets along well with everyone he meets and is always polite and cheerful. Last month, a group of schoolchildren visited our farm, and I asked Alex to help with them. I was impressed with the way he took care of the children and answered all their questions, and I am confident he would work well with the young people who come to your school.

Over the last few years, Alex has been a [5]_____ member of the farm's team, and I would not hesitate to recommend him to work for you. If you have any other questions, please feel free to contact me at the number below.

Sincerely yours,

Jack Bussell

608-555-8269

---

1 Read Jack Bussell's personal recommendation and fill in the blanks with the pairs of adjectives below.

  a excellent personal
  b calm, patient
  c energetic, reliable
  d pleasant young
  e hardworking, dedicated

2 Read Jack Bussell's personal recommendation again and answer the questions.

  1 How long has Jack known Alex? _____
  2 How did they meet? _____
  3 What example does Jack give of Alex's hard work? _____
  4 What adjectives does he use to describe Alex's excellent personal skills? _____
  5 How should Ms. O'Reilly contact Jack if she needs to? _____

3 Is the order of adjectives and the use of commas correct or incorrect in these sentences? Cross out any errors and write the corrections below. Check (✓) the correct sentences.

  1 His easygoing positive personality would be perfect for this job. _____

  2 She is able to understand financial complicated information. _____

  3 She worked for a Japanese small company that designs websites. _____

  4 He acts in a confident, professional way at all times. _____

  5 She knows a lot about the fascinating, historic city. _____

  6 He would enjoy working in a rural peaceful environment. _____

  7 She is an expert in modern German literature. _____

  8 He is a thoughtful intelligent person. _____

4 Think of a vacation job and someone you know who would do it well. Write a personal recommendation.

  • Explain how you know the person.
  • Describe the person's qualities and give examples.
  • Offer to provide more information.
  • Include at least three pairs of adjectives of opinion and fact, and make sure they are in the correct order.

11 REVIEW and PRACTICE

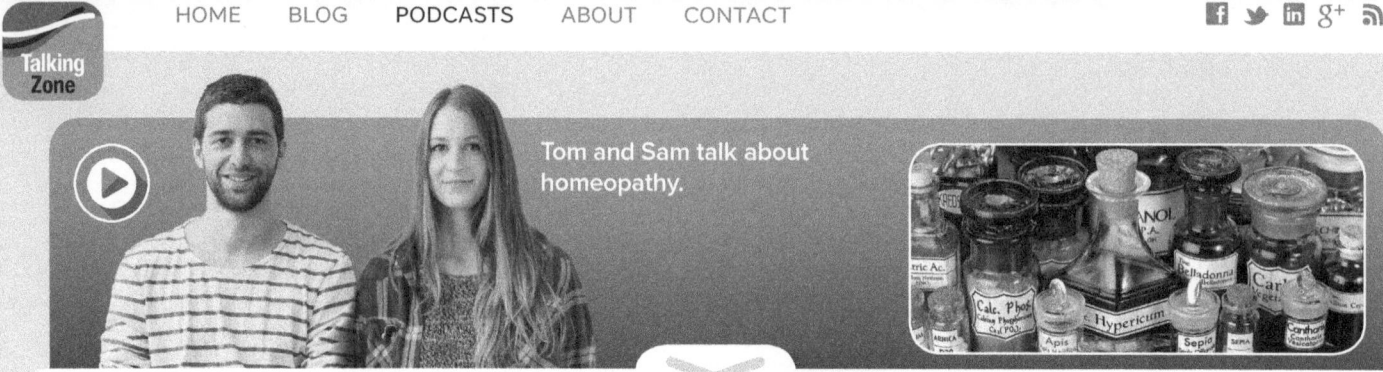

HOME   BLOG   **PODCASTS**   ABOUT   CONTACT

Talking Zone

Tom and Sam talk about homeopathy.

LISTENING

1 ▶ 11.5 Listen to the podcast and number a–e in the order that you hear them (1–5).

a Sam's friend's snoring problem _____
b Tom's opinion of homeopathy _____
c Scientific experiments _____
d Sam's sister's sleeping problem _____
e a definition of homeopathy _____

2 ▶ 11.5 Listen again and choose the best options to complete the sentences.

1 Tom says he and Sam had been having
  a a chat.
  b a discussion.
  c an argument.

2 Sam says she and Tom had been having
  a a chat.
  b a discussion.
  c an argument.

3 Tom thinks that homeopathy
  a can make you sick.
  b works for some illnesses.
  c is useless.

4 Sam's sister found that she was
  a falling asleep during the day.
  b awake during the night.
  c unable to get to sleep.

5 Sam describes a time when she couldn't sleep because
  a of her lifestyle.
  b she didn't have enough pillows.
  c her friend was snoring so loudly.

6 Tom thinks that people sometimes get better when they
  a believe that a medicine will help them.
  b have someone to talk to.
  c can choose their medicine.

READING

1 Read Sam's blog on page 67. What is her opinion of virtual reality?

a She approves of it and thinks it will have many uses.
b She thinks it is too soon to judge whether it is a good thing.
c She does not approve, especially in relation to its effect on the brain.

2 According to Sam's blog, are the sentences true (T), false (F), or doesn't say (DS)?

1 Some people are worried about virtual reality. _____
2 People wearing virtual reality headsets sometimes have accidents. _____
3 Our brains understand that a virtual reality experience is different from a real experience. _____
4 A virtual reality experience may have a physical effect on the body. _____
5 Sam hasn't been to many art exhibits. _____
6 Sam is often bored at art exhibits. _____
7 Modigliani lived to an old age. _____
8 The studio was Modigliani's home, as well as his place of work. _____

3 Look at the underlined words in Sam's blog. Complete the sentences below with the correct words.

1 When I was in London, I saw an amazing _____ of Roman sculptures at the British Museum.
2 When he realized that the dog wasn't tied up, his heart started to _____.
3 The Uffizi Gallery in Florence is full of wonderful _____ of _____ from the fifteenth and sixteenth centuries.
4 When people feel tired or bored, they often _____.
5 At that time, he was a _____ artist. He wasn't well-known, and he had very little money to live on.

REVIEW and PRACTICE 11

HOME **BLOG** PODCASTS ABOUT CONTACT

This week, Sam finds that virtual reality helps her appreciate art as never before ...

Reality, but not as you know it!

There's a degree of public concern these days about the use of virtual reality — that is, artificial places and experiences produced by computers that feel *like* reality to the person experiencing them. Of course, there's the obvious danger of VR users being blind to the real world around them when they're wearing a headset. (People using VR headsets can knock into, and fall over, physical objects if they're not watched and carefully guided by others!)

Then there's the more worrying question of what effect VR has on the brain. After all, psychologists tell us that the brain experiences virtual reality as *actual* reality. Our body responds to a VR experience exactly as if we were really having a *real-life* experience, for example, fear causing our breathing to become quicker or our heart to pound. Surely, this can't be good for the brain? It must be confusing, to say the least. Well, like all very recent inventions and developments, we don't yet know what the long-term effects will be. Only time will tell ...

In the meantime, VR is out there, and I can tell you from personal experience that it can be put to *amazing* use. My friend, Sarah — a big fan of the painter Modigliani — took me to see an exhibit of his work when I was in London. Now, don't judge me, but I'm not a huge fan of art exhibits and quite often find myself yawning as I look at picture after picture. This, however, was an exhibit with a difference — I wasn't bored for one second. There was, of course, an extensive display of the artist's paintings, but there was also a VR recreation of Modigliani's Paris studio — an unimpressive, narrow room, "reimagined" in unbelievable detail. Wearing a VR headset, we "stepped into" that studio and looked around the room where he painted in the final months of his short life.

Leaning against the walls were beautiful works of art, some completed, some not. The artist's brushes and tubes of half-used paint lay where he'd left them. I almost felt as if I could *smell* the paint drying. The room was dark, an open window letting in a little light, and a mattress lay on the floor. Clearly, the struggling Modigliani must have lived here, as well as worked here. Talk about confusing VR with real-life experiences — I got such a strong sense of actually *being* in the studio that I felt that Modigliani might at any point walk into the room and ask me what on earth I was doing there! Having "visited" the place where the works of art were created, I then found myself unexpectedly fascinated by the exhibit of his paintings. If only every art exhibit had a VR element!

67

UNIT 12

New discoveries

12A LANGUAGE

GRAMMAR: Present and future unreal conditions

1 Complete the sentences with the words in the box.

| could | time | only | rather |
| would | wish | if | were |

1 If I earned more money, I _____ afford to buy a car.
2 I love the ocean. If _____ I lived near the water.
3 If I _____ you, I'd tell him how you feel.
4 I _____ I could sing as well as you.
5 I _____ look for a new job if I were you.
6 He's thirteen now. It's about _____ he started helping out around the house!
7 It's a private issue. I'd _____ you didn't tell anyone else about it.
8 _____ only I had enough money to give up work.

2 Complete the sentences with the correct form of the verbs in the box. Use one verb twice.

| not live | spend | buy | be able |
| be | have | speak |

1 I'd love to go surfing more. If only I _____ more free time.
2 If you didn't spend so much money going out all the time, you _____ to save up for your vacation.
3 I'm so sad. I wish you _____ here with me.
4 I don't understand. I wish I _____ Spanish.
5 I'm sure Joe would happily spend all day on his laptop, but I'd rather he _____ time with his friends.
6 Why are his parents still buying his clothes? At 31, it's about time he _____ his own clothes!
7 She's bored. She wishes she _____ in a small town.
8 Sarah _____ more money if she were willing to work a few more hours!

VOCABULARY: Phrasal verbs (2)

3 Match the two parts of the sentences.

1 Yesterday Alan's car broke _____
2 I've forgotten my password, so I can't sign _____
3 I can't figure _____
4 I can't make you a sandwich because we've run _____
5 It's important to note _____
6 You should just hang _____

  a out of bread.
  b up if he calls you again.
  c down on his way to work.
  d out what's wrong with my phone.
  e in to my social media account.
  f down these points.

4 Complete each pair of sentences with the correct forms of the same phrasal verb.

1 a I've looked everywhere for that book but I can't find it. I'm hoping it will just _____ _____.
  b I love this song. Could you _____ it _____, please?
2 a When you make a statement in an essay, you need to _____ it _____ with evidence.
  b You really don't want to lose your work so make sure it's _____ _____ on a USB drive.
3 a She's been _____ _____ a hard time recently with health problems and difficulties at work.
  b I've just _____ _____ my desk drawers, but I can't find that letter anywhere.
4 a We've _____ _____ a meeting to discuss the problem.
  b I need ten minutes to _____ _____ the laptop.
5 a The salary's higher, so he won't _____ _____ the job.
  b Could you _____ your music _____, please?
6 a Hey, guess who I _____ _____ in town?
  b The project started well, but then we _____ _____ a few difficulties.

PRONUNCIATION: Consonant-vowel linking

5 ▶12.1 Read the sentences aloud. Underline any consonant-vowel linking in each sentence. Listen and check.

1 Can I borrow this pen, please?
2 He asked Alice to get a plate from the kitchen.
3 Did Andrea buy a ticket for the show?
4 Could Oliver come with us this evening?
5 When Isabel was a little girl, she had a dog.
6 Is it OK if I take this chair?

SKILLS 12B

READING: Predicting

More plastic than fish?

The oceans on our planet are full of plastic, and we have no one to blame, but ourselves. Shockingly, we dump the equivalent of a truck-load of plastic in our oceans every minute of every day. If this keeps on, by 2050, there will be more pieces of plastic in our oceans than fish. This is, of course, a disaster for all of us – wildlife and humans alike. Indeed, it is claimed by some environmentalists that plastic pollution in our oceans is as serious a problem as climate change. Clearly, we urgently need to do something about it.

Fortunately, there are some brilliant people out there using new technologies to develop tools that will help tackle this very serious problem. Two Australian surfers have invented a device called the SeaBin, a floating garbage can that sucks garbage off the water's surface. (The same device also removes oil.) Another potentially brilliant invention by a young Dutch engineer, Boyan Slat, hopes to collect half of the plastic garbage in the Great Pacific Garbage Patch within five years. (The Great Pacific Garbage Patch is a huge pile of floating garbage – twice the size of France – in the Pacific Ocean.)

Other brilliant innovations include an instrument that can be attached to a ship that measures plastic pollution as the ship moves along. Theoretically, the data gathered by this instrument will allow us to figure out how the plastic is moving and exactly where it is ending up. This, in turn, will help us deal with the problem.

Obviously, inventions like this won't completely solve the problem of plastic pollution in our oceans. As a matter of urgency, we humans need to change our behavior. We must use far less plastic, finding alternatives to the plastic bottles and bags that find their way into our rivers and oceans by the millions. And we must find cost-effective ways to recycle what we do use. In the meantime, we should all be extremely grateful to these inventors and support their efforts in any way we can.

1 Read the first paragraph only of the text and predict (✓) which of these summaries best describes the whole of the article.

   a Which is more damaging – climate change or plastic pollution? ___
   b The drastic fall in the number of fish in our oceans. ___
   c The serious problem of plastic pollution and new ways to solve it. ___
   d How climate change is affecting our oceans. ___

2 Check (✓) the statements that are true.

   1 We use trucks to put plastic in our oceans. ___
   2 There are now more pieces of plastic in our oceans than fish. ___
   3 Some people are as worried by plastic pollution as they are by climate change. ___
   4 A device has been invented that takes garbage and oil out of the water. ___
   5 Another device has removed half of the plastic garbage in the Great Pacific Garbage Patch. ___
   6 The plastic in our oceans does not stay in the same place. ___
   7 Fortunately, we are starting to use less plastic in our daily lives. ___
   8 We should do everything possible to encourage people who create devices to deal with the problem of plastic pollution. ___

3 Circle the comment adverb that makes the most sense in each sentence.

   1 *Shockingly / Understandably*, no one apologized for the terrible way in which she had been treated.
   2 This situation is *fortunately / theoretically* possible, although, in practice, it is highly unlikely.
   3 He was *understandably / luckily* upset by the sad news.
   4 For a short guy, he's *surprisingly / obviously* good at basketball.
   5 My train was canceled. *Understandably / Fortunately*, Steve was able to give me a ride home.
   6 It started raining, but, *luckily / apparently*, I had my umbrella with me.
   7 Lucy and I got together yesterday. *Apparently / Theoretically*, Laura has a new job.
   8 It was a complete accident, so *surprisingly / obviously* no one is to blame.

12C LANGUAGE

GRAMMAR: Past unreal conditions

1 Read the sentences and write T for third conditional sentences and M for mixed conditional sentences.

1 If I hadn't eaten that dessert, I wouldn't feel so full now! ____
2 If she'd worked a little harder, she might have gotten into college. ____
3 I would have bought extra food if I'd known you were coming. ____
4 If she hadn't taken so many risks, she would probably still be alive today. ____
5 The steak would have been better if they hadn't cooked it so long. ____
6 He'd look better if he hadn't dyed his hair. ____
7 If you hadn't upset her, she would be here now. ____
8 If we'd left earlier, we might have reached London by now! ____

2 Complete the sentences with the verbs in parentheses in the correct order. Where it says T, write third conditional sentences, and where it says M, write mixed conditional sentences.

1 If you _____ me about the problem, I _____ you. (help / tell) **T**
2 If we _____ the train, we _____ there by now. (be / not miss) **M**
3 It's strange to think that if I _____ a different job, I _____ you! (not meet / take) **T**
4 I'm sure I _____ her face if I _____ her. (remember / meet) **T**
5 If I _____ it was a party, I _____ something more attractive. (wear / know) **T**
6 If he _____ himself, he _____ so sick now. (not be / look after) **M**
7 You _____ how to use the machine if you _____ the instructions! (read / know) **M**
8 I _____ to the party if I _____ you needed a ride. (know / drive) **T**

VOCABULARY: Collocations with *come*, *do*, *go*, and *make*

3 Complete the phrases in the sentences with the correct forms of *come*, *do*, *go*, or *make*.

1 She has a new movie that's _____ out later this year.
2 Thankfully, they've _____ away with the old registration system, and now it's much easier to sign in.
3 William's never been a hard worker. He just _____ the minimum to pass his exams.
4 As far as I know, she's still _____ ahead with her plans to open a restaurant downtown.
5 I have no idea what she means in that last paragraph. It doesn't seem to _____ any sense.
6 You've got to _____ an effort to get to know people if you want to make new friends.
7 Alice _____ the point that they'll close the community center unless more people use it.
8 I won't go into detail about the plans, but I'll quickly _____ over the main points.

4 Complete the phrases in this e-mail with the correct forms of *come*, *do*, *go*, or *make*.

To: Mom

RE: Greetings!

Hi Mom,

When I came out here six months ago, it felt like a lifetime in front of me. I can't believe my stay in Africa is [1]_____ to an end. I'd always wanted to work with elephants, so when I came here, it felt like my dream had [2]_____ true. I'll always be grateful to you, Mom, for encouraging me to come here. I wasn't 100% sure I wanted to do it, but you told me to [3]_____ for it and pointed out that opportunities like this don't [4]_____ along every day. You were so right. I've absolutely loved working with the elephants – feeling that I'm [5]_____ my part to help them survive. It's so sad that people have [6]_____ such harm to their habitat over the years. They really need all the help they can get. I'm even beginning to think that one day I might [7]_____ a living from this kind of work. I've been talking to one of the team leaders about how it might happen. I'll [8]_____ into detail when I see you …

Love, Klara xxx

PRONUNCIATION: Stress in past unreal conditional sentences

5 ▶ 12.2 (Circle) the stressed word in the underlined part of each sentence, and then read the sentence aloud. Listen and check.

1 I wish Sarah had seen the movie. <u>She would have loved it.</u>
2 <u>He might have come</u> if you'd asked him.
3 If I'd been worried, <u>you would have known about it</u>.
4 <u>You wouldn't have made</u> so many mistakes if you hadn't rushed the essay!
5 If I hadn't been sick that night, <u>I would have joined you</u>.
6 If I lived closer, <u>I could have gone</u> to her party.

SKILLS 12D

SPEAKING: Talking about future trends

1 ▶ 12.3 Listen to Laura and Adam discussing new technology. Number these phrases in the order that you hear them. Listen again and check.

- a Speaking of … _____
- b … I don't know how many … _____
- c It's a little like … _____
- d That reminds me … _____
- e … or whatever … _____
- f The thing that looks like … _____
- g You mean …? _____
- h What exactly do you do with it? _____

2 According to Laura and Adam, what:

1 is bound to happen?
_____

2 is conceivable?
_____

3 is anyone's guess?
_____

4 is unlikely to happen soon?
_____

3 Use your own ideas to complete these sentences.

1 One day, someone is bound to invent _____
_____ .

2 In the future, it is conceivable that everyone will be able to _____ .

3 _____ is a fad that isn't likely to last.

4 Whether _____
will be possible in the future is anyone's guess.

4 ▶ 12.4 Use phrases from exercise 1 to complete the conversations. Listen and check.

A Have you seen this phone charger?
¹_____ a credit card.
B ²_____ this thing? You can really charge a phone with something this small? That's amazing! I really need one of them. My phone runs out of battery ³_____ times a week.
A Yes, it's very useful and so easy to carry around.
⁴_____ very small things, I read that there's now a computer that's the same size as a grain of salt.

A What's that on your table?
B ⁵_____ a small music speaker? It's to help keep my apartment safe when I'm not here.
A ⁶_____?
B You just turn it on in the evenings,
⁷_____ time you want, and it makes noise to make people think you're at home.
A That's a good idea.
B Yes, it is. ⁸_____ – I should turn it on now if we're going out.

5 Think of a modern invention and write a short conversation about it.

A (Introduce the topic of the invention.)
_____

B (Ask for clarification.)
_____

A (Describe the invention.)
_____

B (Make a prediction about the invention.)
_____

A (Introduce a new topic in a general way.)
_____

71

12 REVIEW and PRACTICE

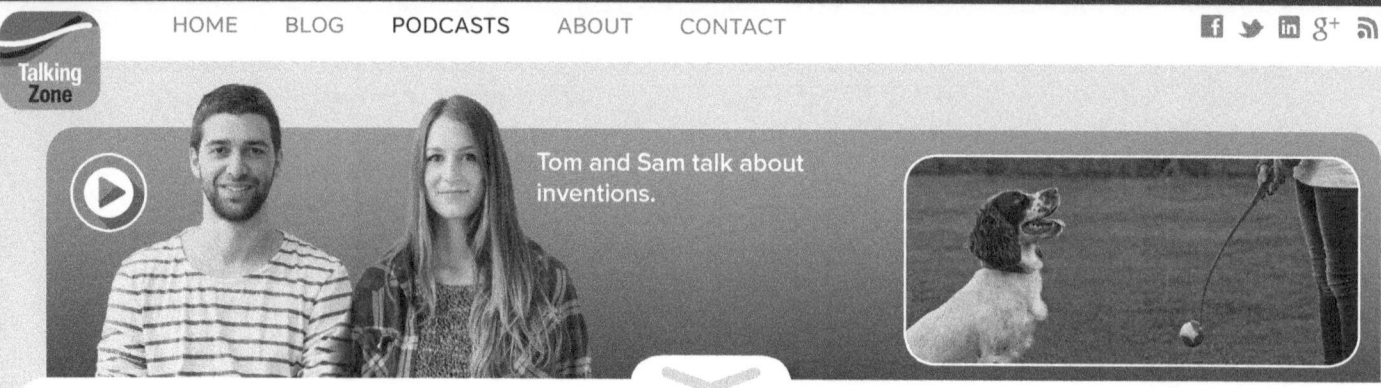

Tom and Sam talk about inventions.

LISTENING

1 ▶ 12.5 Listen to the podcast. Check (✓) the inventions that Tom, Sam, and Lorna mention. Then check (✓) the inventions that already exist.

	mentioned	already exist
1 dog ball throwers	___	___
2 a house on legs	___	___
3 an electronic insect	___	___
4 windows that make energy from the sun	___	___
5 phones that don't need batteries	___	___
6 phones that can see around corners	___	___
7 artificial skin that can feel things	___	___
8 invisible objects	___	___

2 ▶ 12.5 Listen again and complete the sentences.

1 Tom doesn't like bending down to _____ _____ his dog's ball.
2 He says plastic throwers are a _____, _____ solution to the problem.
3 Lorna's favorite invention is the _____ _____.
4 It can move as fast as a _____.
5 Solar windows in a Dutch bank generate enough electricity for employees to _____ their _____.
6 Smart gloves could be printed using _____ _____.
7 Tom wants to have a _____ that would make him _____.
8 According to Lorna, a _____ of _____ is working on making invisible objects.

READING

1 Read Lara's blog on page 73 and choose the best summary.

a Lara finds it annoying when her parents can't use their phones, but she tries to be patient and help them because she understands that using phones is difficult for older people.
b Lara's parents enjoy making her angry with the way they use their phones because she made them angry when she was a teenager. Lara tries to be patient with them, but finds it very difficult.
c Lara finds her parents' struggle to use their phones extremely annoying. She wonders if they are doing it on purpose because she caused them problems when she was younger.

2 Check (✓) the statements that are true.

1 Lara thinks her parents are too young to find phones difficult. ___
2 Lara's mom knew that her bus was likely to be late. ___
3 Lara thought it should have been obvious to her mom that she needed to have her phone on. ___
4 Lara doesn't think her dad should need help doing things on his phone. ___
5 He usually remembers what to do if she explains carefully. ___
6 Lara's own phone isn't as good as her parents' phones. ___
7 Lara's parents aren't aware of many of the things that their smartphones can do. ___
8 Lara doesn't really believe that her parents are pretending to have problems with their phones. ___
9 She's always nice to them when they ask her for help. ___
10 They're good at texting quickly. ___

HOME   BLOG   PODCASTS   ABOUT   CONTACT

Guest blogger Lara writes about helping her parents use technology.

Mom, Dad, and the modern world ...

If only my mom and dad weren't so hopeless with their phones! They're not even that old, so they can't use that as an excuse. I'm beginning to suspect that they do it on purpose to annoy me. Maybe it's their way of punishing me for the dreadful time I gave them as a teenager. Whatever the reason, it drives me crazy!

For example, a couple of weeks ago, I arranged to meet my mom for lunch in town, but my bus got stuck in a traffic jam. I tried and tried to call her, but her phone went straight to voicemail. Then she was really annoyed that I was late, and when I protested that I'd tried to call her, she just said, "Oh, my phone's not turned on." So, there she was, wondering what had happened to me and getting angrier and angrier, but it didn't even cross her mind to turn her phone on! Honestly, I give up!

In some ways, my dad's even worse. He's always asking me how to do stuff like attaching a photo to an e-mail or turning up the volume. Now, I don't think I've ever, in my whole life, needed anyone to tell me these things because they're COMPLETELY OBVIOUS! Still, I try (not always successfully!) to explain patiently, and he nods his head and thanks me. But the next time he wants to do them, he's completely forgotten, and I have to go over it all again. And again. And again ...

Another thing that makes me furious is that they both have the latest smartphones – far nicer than anything I can afford – but they could do so much more with them if only they understood them better. For example, my dad was telling me a story about driving around and around Boston and being completely unable to figure out how to get to where he wanted to go. When I asked him why he hadn't used his phone, he said, "My phone has a map on it?" in total astonishment!

Maybe if I hadn't been such an awful teenager, my parents would make more of an effort not to annoy me by being so hopeless with their phones. But, sadly, I think their problems are genuine. One part of me (the nice part!) wishes I could be kinder to them about it, but the not so nice part thinks it's about time they moved into the twenty-first century and learned how to use their phones like normal people! And don't get me started on watching them text with one finger ...

WRITING PRACTICE

WRITING: Writing a set of guidelines

How to write a great blog

Your best friend writes a car-racing blog, and your neighbor posts 2,000 words on tropical fish twice a week. But how many of these articles do you read? Probably not many, and yet some bloggers are so successful they have thousands of followers. How do they do it?

Have something unique to say

It's fine to write about the same subject as other people, but you need something original to attract readers to your blog. For instance, there are thousands of fashion blogs, but I always read a particular one about really unusual sportswear. I'm never going to wear those clothes, but I find the posts interesting. ¹_____, the author has a really nice writing style and a great sense of humor.

A picture is worth a thousand words

Yes, a blog is about writing, but everyone likes a picture. It makes the page look attractive. ²_____, it can give an instant clue to what the post is about. My friend writes a blog about jogging and he says that posts with pictures always get more likes and comments.

If a thing's worth doing, it's worth doing well

Always check your work carefully. I was reading a post about money-saving tips recently. ³_____, it had so many spelling mistakes, I didn't really trust the author's advice. ⁴_____, if you want readers to spend time reading your blog, you should respect them by making sure it's correct.

Know your readers

I'll end with my most important piece of advice: familiarize yourself with the people that read your blog. You need a clear idea of who they are. Communicate with them – answer their comments, and notice which posts they like best. The best way to get people to come back to your blog is to give them what they want!

1 Read the blog post. Choose the best linker for each blank.

1 However / Moreover / Similarly
2 In addition / Nevertheless / However
3 Besides / Moreover / However
4 Similarly / Besides / However

2 <u>Underline</u> the sentences in the blog post in which the author includes an example or a personal experience.

3 Match guidelines 1–5 with reasons a–e.

1 Always make sure you know who can see your social media pages. _____
2 Ignore people who post unpleasant comments. _____
3 Never put your address on a social media site. _____
4 Don't include too much information. _____
5 Never tell anyone your passwords. _____

a Only people you trust and know well should know where you live.
b Readers only need to know the basics at first.
c They could post on your pages as a joke or to get you into trouble.
d You might not want future employers looking at photos of you at parties!
e If you react, it just encourages them to do it again.

4 Choose one of the topics below and write a blog post giving a set of guidelines.

Staying safe online.
How to get the best from social media.
Helping your grandparents use the Internet.

- Write a short introduction explaining the purpose of your post.
- Include three or four important tips, organized into paragraphs.
- Give reasons for each tip, and include examples or personal experience.
- Use linkers to add ideas.

WRITING: Writing a magazine article

How to get a promotion

1 You may have been in your job for a couple of years, or maybe for only a few months, but you know you have more to offer your company and you want to aim higher. How do you persuade your boss to give you a promotion?

2 _____

First, look around you. Is there an obvious next step? You won't be promoted if there's no job to promote you to, so if the job doesn't exist, think about whether you can create it. Do you have experience or knowledge that's not being used? Could your department be organized in a different way?

3 _____

The people in your company need to know how good you are. If you finish a piece of work early, tell your boss. If a client praises you, tell your boss. Remember that even the hardworking among us don't get what they deserve if nobody notices what they've achieved. Just make sure you don't annoy your colleagues. After all, they may be working for you soon!

4 _____

Someone needs to visit a client in Baltimore on the weekend. Someone needs to update the company website once a week. Why not offer? If your company realizes you are willing to work hard and do the things other people don't want to do, it won't want to lose you, and that will put you in a strong position when you ask for that promotion.

5 There's nothing wrong with wanting to have a good career. People who stay at the same level often get bored with their jobs and don't do them very well. It's good to have a challenge, so if you feel you're ready for a promotion, go for it!

---

1 Read the article and choose the best headings for paragraphs 2–4.

Paragraph 2:
a Get a new skill   b Find the job you want   c Read the job ads

Paragraph 3:
a Get yourself noticed   b Be better than your colleagues   c You are better than your boss

Paragraph 4:
a Do something different   b Fight for what you want   c Make yourself useful

2 Look at the underlined uses of *a/an*, *the*, or (–) in the article. Now fill in the blanks in the sentences below with *a/an*, *the*, or (–).

1 Try not to plan _____ meetings for the end of the day.
2 _____ California has a lot of high-tech companies.
3 Don't check your e-mails more than twice _____ day.
4 Make sure you have _____ clear reason for having a meeting.
5 Try to leave _____ office early on Fridays.
6 Only _____ lonely enjoy working on the weekends.
7 People like their colleagues to show _____ enthusiasm.
8 If you work in _____ open-plan office, don't talk on the phone loudly.

3 Write an article about one of the topics below.

What makes a good colleague?   *How to have effective meetings*   *Keeping a good work-life balance*

- Give your article an interesting title.
- Introduce the topic in an opening paragraph that readers can relate to.
- Develop your ideas in two or three paragraphs and give each one a heading.
- Summarize your ideas in the final paragraph.
- Pay attention to your use of definite and indefinite articles.

WRITING PRACTICE

WRITING: Writing a personal recommendation

Dear Mr. Swain,

This letter is to recommend Lara Manning as a house sitter while you are working abroad for two months. I first met Lara when she came to me for piano lessons in 2012. I taught her for four years, and we have kept in touch since she left to go to music school where, as you may know, she is studying modern classical music.

Lara was a quiet, serious student, and one of the most talented musicians I have ever taught. At the age of 15, she started to babysit for my own children on Saturdays while I was teaching. She was a reliable, friendly babysitter, and despite being a little shy, she was also a lot of fun: she loved running and playing games with the children. They enjoyed being with her, and I was confident that they were safe and were being well taken care of.

Lara has told me that you have a large vegetable garden. I know that Lara enjoys gardening, and she has helped her parents a lot with a garden they have. In addition, I am certain that she is an honest person, something that is essential for a house sitter. She has fed our cat on several occasions while we have been on vacation, and I have been very happy to let her have the keys to our house.

Lara is a charming young woman, who I'm sure will treat your home with respect. I would not hesitate to recommend her, but if you have any questions, please feel free to call or e-mail me.

Sincerely yours,

Jeannie Evans

1 Read Jeannie Evans's personal recommendation. Underline the places where she:

1. says what kind of person Lara is.
2. says how Mr. Swain can get in touch with her.
3. gives specific examples of Lara's personal qualities.
4. explains how she knows Lara.

2 Find four pairs of adjectives in the personal recommendation above. Then match the two parts of the sentences below, and add commas after the first adjectives where necessary.

1. He knows how to take care of valuable _____
2. She is a positive _____
3. He decided to move because of the difficult _____
4. My father has always had stressful _____
5. He has excellent _____

a. confident person.
b. demanding jobs.
c. interpersonal skills.
d. antique furniture.
e. political situation.

3 Imagine you are writing a personal recommendation. Use your own ideas to write about a quality that fits the example that follows.

1. _____
He traveled through Africa alone when he was only 18.

2. _____
He sat with the elderly patients all afternoon and made sure they had everything they needed.

3. _____
He spent all day checking the document and discovered several errors in it. He then explained the errors very politely to the author.

4. _____
He designed our student magazine and took all the photographs for it.

4 Think of someone you know who would be a good house sitter. Write a personal recommendation.

- Explain how you know the person.
- Describe his/her personal qualities and give examples.
- Offer to provide more information.
- Include at least three pairs of adjectives of opinion and fact, and make sure they are in the correct order.

Richmond

58 St Aldates
Oxford
OX1 1ST
United Kingdom

ISBN: 978-84-668-2631-0
© Richmond / Santillana Global S.L. 2019

Publishing Director: Deborah Tricker
Publisher: Simone Foster
Media Publisher: Sue Ashcroft
Workbook Publisher: Luke Baxter
Content Developer: Deborah Goldblatt
Editors: Peter Anderson, Jamie Bowman, Lauren Cubbage, Debra Emmett, Sarah Foster, Shannon O'Neill, Emma Wilkinson
Americanization: Shira Evans, Debbie Goldblatt
Design Manager: Lorna Heaslip
Cover Design: This Ain't Rock'n'Roll, London
Design & Layout: Lorna Heaslip, emc Design Ltd
Photo Researcher: Magdalena Mayo
Talking Zone video: Bagley Wood Productions
Audio Production: Tom, Dick and Debbie Productions
App Development: The Distance

We would also like to thank the following people for their valuable contribution to writing and developing the material:
James Styring, Jake Hughes, Brigit Viney, Diarmuid Carter (video script writer), Belen Fernandez (App Project Manager), Rob Sved (App Content Creator)

We would like to thank all those who have given their kind permission to reproduce material for this book:

Illustrators: Beach-o-matic Ltd; Victor Beuran c/o Astound Inc.; Roger Harris c/o NB Illustration; Guillaume Gennet c/o Lemonade; Julia Scheele

Photos:
D. Lezama; V. Atmán; 123RF; AGILEBITS INC.; ALAMY/Moviestore collection Ltd, Photofusion Picture Library, seewhatmitchsee, Everette Collection Inc, RosalreneBetancourt 6, ZUMA Press, Inc., Steve Moss, RosalreneBetancourt 9, Martin Parker, Moviestore Collection Ltd, Jeff Greenberg, Mr Pics, Hemis, RosalreneBetancourt 7, Collection Christophel, Magdalena Mayo, Radharc Images, Game Shots, urbanbuzz, NetPhotos, Image Source, CandyAppleRed Images, Art Directors & TRIP, RosalreneBetancourt 3, Chris Willson, Education & Exploration 2; COLIN BEAVAN; EVERNOTE; FERDI RIZKIYANTO; GETTY IMAGES SALES SPAIN/Flashpop, WALTER ZERLA, BSIP/UIG, hoozone, ImagesBazaar, Dmitry Ageev, Tolimir, By LTCE, Newton Daly, sturti, alxpin, AndreyPopov, Tainar, pinkomelet, jaochainoi, CasarsaGuru, izusek, Paul Morigi, Astarot, chepkoelena, DenBoma, Svtist, YangYin, MachineHeadz, ilbusca, bymuratdeniz, FS-Stock, CarmenMurillo, JGalione, Rouzes, Thinkstock, Tom Merton, RUSS ROHDE, Peter Cade, CoisaX, Maskot, AnaBGD, Adam Berry, thall, mrgao, istock/Thinkstock, Roberto Westbrook, omgimages, kali9, jacoblund, isitsharp, pixdeluxe, roundhill, tommaso79, Jose Luis Pelaez Inc, Chema Alba, Detailfoto, M.M. Sweet, acilo, Placebo365, flashfilm, SensorSpot, Richard l'Anson, Nikada, gradyreese, gregobagel, Westend61, MileA, Stockbyte, AngiePhotos, Jon Hicks, Felix Wirth, Hero Images, Matt Dutile, dszc, JangoBeat, PetrePlesea, Sam Edwards, franckreporter, hanapon1002, mediaphotos, Dan MacMedan, Walter Bibikow, Goodshoot,

All rights reserved. No part of this book may be reproduced, stored in a retrieval system or transmitted in any form by any means, electronic, mechanical, photocopying, recording or otherwise, without the prior permission in writing of the Publisher.

Jaunty Junto, Kieran Stone, CHBD, PeopleImages, Prasit photo, Ben Gabbe, A330Pilot, ferrantraite, Bernhard Lang, FOX, Caspar Benson, Daniel Ingold, Dougal Waters, ronnybas, Barcroft Media, Anadolu Agency, richiesd, SIphotography, Peathegee Inc, quavondo, Patrick Orton, Michael Blann, funstock, Florin Prunoiu, Jemal Countess, PhonlamaiPhoto, Sigrid Gombert, Thomas Barwick, Thomas Bullock, Mark Mainz/BC, James Devaney, jackscoldsweat, Comstock Images, Emir Memedovski, Gabriela Tulian, LWA/Dann Tardif, Photos.com Plus, cirano83, BahadirTanriover, Deborah Harrison, Dennis Macdonald, TravisPhotoWorks, blackestockphoto, David Paul Morris, Fancy/Veer/Corbis, GraphicaArtis, Fredrik Skold, Fred Stein Archive, Hannelore Foerster, MacFormat Magazine, Oleksiy Maksymenko, BG008/Bauer-Griffin, Fitria Ramli / EyeEm, RichLegg, Kantapat Phutthamkul, Gareth Cattermole/TAS, Maximilian Stock Ltd., Michael Ochs Archives, Photos.com/Thinkstock, Science Photo Library, Patchareeporn Sakoolchai; GREENPEACE; I. PREYSLER; ISTOCKPHOTO/Getty Images Sales Spain, monkeybusinessimages, Joel Carillet, cindygoff; PIRIFORM; SHUTTERSTOCK/Linda Bestwick, Mike Kuhlman, Giovanni G, Dima Moroz, kibri_ho; SOUTHWEST NEWSSWNS; WWF INTERNATIONAL; Chris Griffiths; Iwan Baan; ARCHIVO SANTILLANA; 123RF; ALAMY/Arco Images GmbH, Oliver Knight, Elizabeth Whiting & Associates, Moviestore collection Ltd; GETTY IMAGES SALES SPAIN/Sturti, Bloomberg, Serts, Alex Wong, Filadendron, Yuri_Arcurs, DGLimages, LEON NEAL, PhotoAlto, Erierika, Thinkstock, Ronniechua, Diane39, Piotr Marcinski/ EyeEm, Hero Images, Sam Edwards, Scott Olson, Emir Memedovski, Boston Globe, Ethan Miller, Image Source, bymuratdeniz, Inti St Clair, Martinedoucet, Antnio Guillem, PhotoQuest, ClarkandCompany, Rindoff/Dufour, Photos.com Plus, Dreet Production, TheCrimsonMonkey, valentinrussanov, Caiaimage/Sam Edwards, Sdominick, Tetra Images-Rob Lewine, Highwaystarz-Photography, Future Publishing/Olly Curtis, Alvarez; ISTOCKPHOTO/Getty Images Sales Spain; SPACEX

Cover Photo: GETTY IMAGES SALES SPAIN/Martin Dimitrov

Texts:
p87 Text adapted from article 'Why starting a business at 19 was one of the best decisions I've ever made' by Chris Griffiths, 17 September 2013, published in The Globe and Mail, reprinted by permission of the author.

We would like to thank the following reviewers for their valuable feedback which has made Personal Best possible. We extend our thanks to the many teachers and students not mentioned here.
Brad Bawtinheimer, Manuel Hidalgo, Paulo Dantas, Diana Bermúdez, Laura Gutiérrez, Hardy Griffin, Angi Conti, Christopher Morabito, Hande Kokce, Jorge Lobato, Leonardo Mercato, Mercilinda Ortiz, Wendy López

The Publisher has made every effort to trace the owner of copyright material; however, the Publisher will correct any involuntary omission at the earliest opportunity.

Printed in Brazil
Lote: 792973
Código: 290526310